FINAL
DESTINATION

FINAL DESTINATION

Riding Britain's Trains to the End of the Line

NIGE TASSELL

MUDLARK

Mudlark
HarperCollins*Publishers*
1 London Bridge Street
London SE1 9GF

www.harpercollins.co.uk

HarperCollins*Publishers*
Macken House, 39/40 Mayor Street Upper
Dublin 1, D01 C9W8, Ireland

First published by Mudlark 2025

10 9 8 7 6 5 4 3 2 1

© Nige Tassell 2025

Map by Liane Payne © HarperCollins*Publishers*

Nige Tassell asserts the moral right to be identified as the author of this work

For Jess

CONTENTS

CONTENTS

The Sixteen Final Destinations

Direction of travel:

Start ●————■ End

1 — Wick / Inverness

2 — Mallaig / Glasgow

3 — Glasgow / Stranraer

4 — Newcastle Airport / South Shields

5 — Middlesbrough / Whitby

6 — Morecambe / Leeds

7 — Manchester / Buxton

8 — Pwllheli / Birmingham

9 — Ebbw Vale / Cardiff

10 — Severn Beach / Bristol

11 — Sheringham / Norwich

12 — Fenchurch Street / Shoeburyness

13 — Chesham / Aldgate / Paddington

14 — Hythe / Dungeness

15 — Ryde Pier Head / Shanklin

16 — Penzance

INTRODUCTION

DEPARTURES

Perhaps you meant to be here. Or perhaps your just-woken-up presence was unplanned.

But here you are, at the end of the line, the point at which your train can travel no further. A dead end, a cul-de-sac. You could choose to stay on board and head off in the opposite direction back up the line, or you could hang around a while, have a poke around to see what's here, have a good snoop.

I'm going to do just that. In fact, I'm going to have a good snoop in 16 different places, 16 dead ends, seeking out the histories and heritage of each place, uncovering their purpose and their people. Who lives there? Who travels there? Where did they come from? And will they ever leave?

In order to get to the end of the line, of course, you've got to travel along it, so I'll also be undertaking 16 different train journeys, wildly different ones, from full-day affairs that traverse human-free wildernesses to comparatively short and speedy hops across and under metropolitan areas. Each time, though, I'll be staying on board until the buffers, until there's nowhere else to go. The last man sitting.

The intention is to zigzag my way down the British Isles, north to south, going with gravity. Spoiler alert: I don't start in John o'

Groats or finish in Land's End. Neither of them is served by trains, after all. But I do visit the stations closest to them – and more than a dozen fascinating destinations in between, both coastal and inland. I'm off to hear their secrets, to experience their essence, to loiter with the locals.

In doing so, I'll also effectively be taking the temperature of Britain, of a country that's experienced a tumultuous few years, on the mend from a pandemic but still ailing from the effects of Brexit. I'm keen to see what has changed and what's stayed the same, and to measure how a town survives if its glory days are over: how it reinvents itself; how it develops a new character. And what does all this reinvention mean for the notion of national identity? What does Wick have in common with Morecambe, or South Shields with Chesham, or Ebbw Vale with Penzance?

Such a quest needn't be a solo expedition, though. This double seat has plenty of room and I've bagged us a table. And I've packed more than enough sandwiches for two. So, come join the trip, why don't you? But hurry. I can hear that whistle blowing…

— 1 —

RETURN TICKET TO
TIMBUKTU

Inverness–Wick

It's February half term and, on the concourse of Inverness railway station, the talk between the teens of the Highlands' only city is all about next year's academic options.

'You can't do woodwork as a Higher. Just metalwork.'

'Fuck off.'

'I'm not shitting you. It's true. Ask Aaron.'

'Fuck off.'

A beat.

'I need woodwork for my apprenticeship. That's that fucked then.'

The rest of those here on the concourse – the two dozen of us waiting for the 2 p.m. service to Wick – aren't experiencing such potty-mouthed, existential anger. At least, we aren't *now*.

It was a different matter an hour ago. The Far North Line – the curling, snaking track that this afternoon will take us up into the wilds of Sutherland and Caithness, finally depositing its remaining human cargo at Wick, nearly four and a half hours after we set off – has been shut for several days. Halfway up the line, between Brora and Helmsdale, the coast has taken a battering from a tag team of spring tides and fearsome storms, resulting in a landslip at the point at which track meets tideline.

3

Over the intervening days and nights, 350 tonnes of rock and stones have been deposited there, shoring up the sea wall. The line only reopened less than an hour ago, having passed the forensic scrutiny of Network Rail. Our train will be the first northbound service over the repaired track. Wish us luck.

At the stroke of two, our train – normally one of four daily services, with just a single one on Sundays – rumbles into action, inching out of the station and arcing around the back of town. We're leaving the angsty teens of Inverness behind. Ahead of us aren't difficult decisions about our future education. Ahead of us is an afternoon of adventure as we push north. Ahead of us, at the far end of the Far North Line, Scotland's Timbuktu is waiting.

Once the service has carefully negotiated the swing bridge across the Caledonian Canal, it's full diesel ahead along the marshy banks of Beauly Firth. Bodies of water will be a frequent view out of the window for the next four hours. There'll be up to 24 station-stops too.

The first of those stops is at the village of Beauly, a station remarkable for one thing in particular. Its platform is the shortest in Britain, measuring just 15 metres, shorter than the length of one of this train's two carriages. Deirdre, the train manager, issues a warning over the crackling PA. 'Only one door will open. That's the rear door of the front carriage. I repeat, that's the rear door of the front carriage.'

As she wanders through the train checking and scanning tickets, Deirdre is also jotting down each passenger's destination on a mini-clipboard. She has to keep a tally, just in case someone wants to leave the train at one of the line's eight request stops. Although it's a Friday afternoon, with the potential for passengers heading north for a weekend away, she tells me there are currently only 28 of us on board, plus her and the driver. 'I think everyone's decided to steer clear because of the work on the line. This train was showing as cancelled just an hour or so ago.'

By the time we roll into Dingwall, more passengers swell our number, be they workers slipping off home early for the weekend or shoppers shuffling on with lumpy bags of groceries. These regulars seem surprised at how quiet the train is today. Deirdre repeats her explanation.

A couple of stops later, a man who looks simultaneously like both Michael Gambon and Richard Harris, but sounds nothing like either, settles down across the aisle from me. He too remarks – in a surprisingly high-pitched voice – about how roomy the carriage is this afternoon. Deirdre's theory gets another airing.

Industry makes its presence felt at Invergordon. There are several oil rigs out in the firth and dozens of refinery tanks between the railway line and the shore. Houses in this part of town, presumably once white-washed and shining, stand shaded by the grey and black grime of industrial discharge.

After the station at Fearn, where cute wooden steps on the low platform carry passengers up to the carriage doors, the train draws an arc to the left and heads inland towards Tain. Another coastline – that of Dornoch Firth – soon reveals itself. Beyond Tain, the track squeezes itself between the shore and the buildings of the Glenmorangie distillery.

Mountains begin to loom in the distance, slow-turning wind turbines on their crests. Their presence provokes a heated – well, mildly lukewarm – debate about wind farms to break out further down the carriage. The two sides are entrenched and unmoving, but peace is restored when talk shifts to the unifying subject of Rishi Sunak and his government's two by-election defeats last night.

At Ardgay, the Far North Line's single track becomes a double, a rare point at which trains heading in opposite directions can pass one another. The corresponding train to ours, running south from Wick, is behind schedule, causing us to sit and await its arrival. One late train means others become late trains.

Further along, the announcement for the request stop at Culrain segues, without any pause, into the announcement for the request stop at Invershin, the other side of a high viaduct over the Kyle of Sutherland. There's a reason for this. It's the shortest distance between two stations anywhere on the entire national network, separated by fewer than 700 metres. To travel between the two takes 60 seconds. And costs £1.80.

A couple of miles further down the line, in the lower paddock of a croft, a barking border collie charges towards us at absolute full pelt. It's a routine he/she presumably re-enacts several times a day whenever he/she can detect the sound of an oncoming diesel engine. It's not the only wildlife spot from the window. While there's neither hide nor hair of a stag's magnificent profile this afternoon, in Kildonan a gang of turkeys waddle across a back-yard. An old man stands on the step of his tumbledown cottage and waves at the train. And, no matter how remote, there are always sheep. Heaps of sheeps.

By the time we get to Golspie, the train has curled back round to the coast. It's late afternoon now, with a powder-blue sky and some rare golden sun warming the sea. The water is calm today, but it can be vicious given the right provocation. After all, once we're past Brora, we reach the point at which nature caused the trains to stop running earlier this week. Understandably, our two carriages pass through this section gingerly, cautiously. All that rock that has rebuilt this sea wall may not be bedded in just yet.

But we make it through this stretch, the waves gently lapping just a few feet away. Then it's on to Helmsdale, home of former Orange Juice frontman Edwyn Collins. He's nowhere to be seen at the station – sadly, he's not heading Wick-wards for his Friday night – but I can at least appreciate why this beautiful stretch of coastline would be the perfect place in which to recover from the two cerebral haemorrhages he suffered in 2005. It's the ideal peaceful location in which to both sketch the local birdlife and write the occasional pop song.

While the adjacent A9 continues to hug the shore, the Far North Line moves inland again, unable to cope with the rugged geography of the coastline. The train now accompanies the wide River Helmsdale, which is rushing in the opposite direction, foaming over just-under-the-surface rocks. The sun has slipped the other side of the hills and the silvery water is returning to grey, the sharpness of daylight dulling into dusk. Nature's shapes and lines are softening, converging towards dark, towards black. Only the odd shock of white – a distant farmhouse, a patch of summit snow – offers definition or scale.

We're now approaching the Flow Country, an enormous expanse of blanket bog that will, in a few months' time, receive World Heritage Site status. On days unlike today, on days when fog and drizzle and sheet rain come visiting, it must rank as one of the bleakest, most desolate places in Britain. It's a place of dark secrets lost underneath its peaty ways – a place of stones and bones and bodies. I'm reminded of the words of the writer Malachy Tallack who, writing more specifically about Shetland, talks of the geography 'being scarred by the remnants of the past, by history made solid by landscape'. Those remnants litter the land beyond the train window. It's a land of crumbling walls and abandoned cottages – the stumps of past lives.

The further north we travel, the greater the distance between villages, between stops. The terrain is hillier now too – open, rolling moorland, coated in soft heather and crackly bracken.

But still the stations come, often in places where no station should rightfully be, in locations where barely a single dwelling is visible in any direction. Most are now request stops and the train just ploughs on without stopping. One of these is Altnabreac, a halt that's both 11 miles from the nearest village and 7 miles from the nearest paved road. The station can only be accessed via a five-mile private dirt road. In theory, at least. It turns out that trains on the Far North Line don't currently stop here, even if a passenger requests them to. There's an ongoing dispute over access to the station, with Network Rail Scotland being denied, by members of the sparse local population, the right to maintain it. There have been reports of access roads being deliberately blocked. (Indeed, two weeks after my trip, a local couple appear in court, charged with trespassing on Network Rail property. One of them also faced a charge of 'culpably and recklessly standing on the tracks in the path of the oncoming train'. Blimey.)

After the last request stop, Scotscalder, there are only two stations between us and Wick. But there's still nearly an hour of travel. That's pretty much how long it takes to get from Paddington to Swindon, or from Manchester to Leeds. So why so?

The answer soon comes. At Georgemas Junction, the last station before Wick, trains go into reverse to take the branch line that justifies the Far North Line moniker. The line carries passengers up to Thurso – Britain's northernmost station – rather than south-east to Wick. This detour must frustrate Weekers (as Wick's residents are known) no end, as they come within a comparative whisker of their hometown before they're carried off in the opposite direction. It's scheduled and it happens with every service, whether travelling towards or from Inverness.

The change in the direction of travel is disorientating too. With the landscape outside the window now swallowed by the dark of night, and without a single light or reference point visible, you can't tell whether you're rattling forwards or rattling backwards. I'm reminded of that scene from the film *Willy Wonka and the Chocolate Factory* where, such is the discombobulating motion of the boat in the factory's Tunnel of Terror, its dazed and confused passengers have no idea in which direction the boat is moving.

There have been only three other people in my carriage since Helmsdale – the mildly argumentative types halfway back – and they leave at Thurso, presumably bound for onward travel to the Orkneys. The train heads back to Georgemas Junction. Forwards again. And I'm travelling solo.

Then, just as we career on towards Wick – and to add to the whole ghost-train feel – the lights in the carriage go out. No emergency lighting comes on, either. Pitch-black. Inky black.

Deirdre the train manager fumbles her way through the carriage to the driver's cab. His lights have gone out too. A quick reboot and things return to normal.

'That's a new one on him,' she says. 'Never happened before.'

Deirdre also informs me that I'm not the only passenger left on board. There's a woman in the other carriage. I ask Deirdre whether the train is always this quiet at this stage in its journey.

'It used to be that the train split at Georgemas Junction. One half went to Thurso, one half to Wick. On the return journey, they'd join up again at Georgemas. But now that it's just one train, the Wick passengers resent having to travel via Thurso every time, so most of them choose to drive down the A9 to Helmsdale and pick up the train from there.

'It's a Wick/Thurso thing!' Her laughter echoes around the empty carriage.

And then the lights go out again.

Located a handful of miles south of John o' Groats, Wick is Britain's Timbuktu because it's shorthand for somewhere far away, distant and difficult to reach. The town is 140 miles closer to Bergen in Norway than it is to London ('Wick' derives from 'vik', the Norse word for 'bay'). In the Half Man Half Biscuit song 'RSVP', it's the faraway destination, the bolthole of choice, of an escaping wedding-party poisoner.

It's also very quiet. Or, at least, it is on this particular wind-whipped Friday night. A few youths linger in the square, as they do in every town square across the land on a Friday night, but other than them, the only other human presence is the occasional customer pulling up outside a takeaway to pick up their dinner.

The pubs are largely empty, too. In Wick's heyday, when it was one of the great fishing capitals of the nation, there were 45 pubs here. An estimated 5,000 bottles of whisky were drunk in the town on a weekly basis. But, in 1920, a referendum was held, the upshot of which was the prohibition of alcohol for quarter of a century, from 1922 until 1947. Unsurprisingly, Wick's great thirst didn't dry up overnight, and a number of speakeasies could be found secreted along its dark streets.

Perhaps that's where everyone is tonight. Robert Louis Stevenson encountered busier times when he regularly visited Wick in his younger years with his engineer father. 'The streets are full of the Highland fishers,' he wrote, 'lubberly, stupid, inconceivably lazy and heavy to move. You bruise against them, tumble over them, elbow them against the wall – all to no purpose; they will not budge: and you are forced to leave the pavement every step.'

(Stevenson seemed particularly down on Wick. In a letter to his mother, he declared that it 'possesses no beauty: bare, grey shores, grim grey houses, grim grey sea; not even the gleam of red tiles; not even the greenest of a tree'.)

One hundred and fifty years on, while grey remains the primary colour of the town's architecture, I've not been forced to leave the pavement at all. No bruising, no tumbling, no elbowing. Were it that there were.

I wander towards the darkness on the edge of town, away from the bright lights of the takeaway outlets and late-closing betting shops. In lieu of some human interaction, I'm in search of some celestial excitement. This corner of Caithness can provide some stunning lightshows from a vivid and bright aurora borealis. Not tonight it can't. Cloud has descended, cover that a half-moon has trouble penetrating. After a quick pint in the sparsely populated market-square pub, The Alexander Bain, I head to my hotel. A quiet night in.

The following morning, the overall sense of desertion is echoed by the front-page headline of the latest edition of the *John O'Groat Journal*: 'THE BEGINNING OF THE END FOR THE HIGHLANDS'. After centuries of clan warfare, and after Wick attracted the extended attentions of the Luftwaffe during World War II, it appears that the erection of new electricity pylons, as high as 'a twenty-two-storey building', will cause the 'industrialisation of the landscape'. Apparently, it is 'the beginning of the end'.

This appears to be the new battle of the clans: the people vs the corporations. 'We're the small people,' says a protestor. 'We don't kid ourselves. We know exactly what we are. Historically, we've always been marginalised. We're a minority up here. We've always been discriminated against.'

Elsewhere in the paper, in less dystopian news, a local couple celebrating their diamond wedding anniversary make it onto page three, and there's a call-out for any local Caithness households needing to declutter to apply to be featured on the BBC One show *Sort Your Life Out*. Impressively, bearing in mind the paper came out yesterday afternoon, there's even the story of the Far North Line reopening, even though that was only confirmed at lunchtime. An impressive work ethic in the *Journal's* newsroom, there.

I head out to learn more about Wick's boomtown years. Across the River Wick from the town centre is the area known as Pulteneytown, home of the Wick Heritage Museum, where the town's history can be revealed in admirable depth. Only it can't. Not today, at least. It doesn't reopen until April. These aren't the only doors closed to the historically curious. Nucleus, the futuristic building on the northern edge of town near the modest airport, which houses the nation's nuclear archives as well as the Caithness county records, doesn't open on weekends. And Wick's Carnegie Library, paid for by the famous Scottish-American philanthropist, is now a foodbank.

I've got to fend for myself. Fortunately, the town also boasts the Telford Trail, a self-guided, all-weather walking tour of Pulteneytown, endowed with information boards by the dozen. The trail is named after the great Thomas Telford who, in the early nineteenth century, was the British Fisheries Society's chief engineer. The Society had earmarked Wick as suitable for the location of a deep-water harbour, which Telford promptly set about designing, along with a settlement in which to house the fishing industry workers.

This settlement was Pulteneytown, this grid of streets rising up the hill. Its houses were swiftly occupied. Before Telford's work commenced, just six people lived on this side of the river. By 1816, the Pulteney population was into four figures. And it would continue to grow as Wick established itself as the herring capital of the world, the capital of the 'silver darlings'.

The numbers are simply astonishing. On one particular day in 1864, 3,000 gutters and packers processed no fewer than 24 million herring. *Twenty-four million* in a single day. The heroes of the hour were the 'gutting girls', extraordinarily speedy and prolific workers able to gut 40 herring a minute.

On the pebbledash wall of one building, there's a permanent outdoor photography exhibition of sorts, lined as it is with the work of Alexander Johnston, who founded his local photography business in 1863, at the height of Wick's boomtown years. His photographs show scenes from this heyday, whether these be huge fleets of fishing boats returning with their catches or the teams of gutters on the quayside, working their way through immense piles of herring.

One of Johnston's most arresting portraits is of two deep-sea divers sitting for his camera, their helmets removed and laid at their feet. Other than facially looking decidedly nineteenth century, they could pass for being the earliest astronauts.

Wick's herring industry went into sharp decline during the early decades of the twentieth century, at which point the town reinvented itself as a centre for whitefish, a trade that didn't last, thanks to the Cod Wars between the UK and Iceland. What fishing does occur out of Wick harbour these days is largely in pursuit of crab, lobster and clam. A wall of lobster pots sits in front of the restored Wick Herring Mart, 'the first purpose-built building in Scotland which provided shelter and offices for fish salesmen'. The quayside has seen no frantic, frenetic commerce for a generation or two.

At the top of the hill in Pulteneytown, up above the lower streets where the recent spring tides have deposited a coating of sand and seaweed, stands a memorial, on top of which stands a statue of Neptune. The memorial tells of Black Saturday when, in 1848, the fiercest of storms ran a succession of returning fishing boats onto the rocks before they could make safe harbour. The lives of 37 Wick fishermen were lost.

There are twentieth-century ghosts here, too. Another memorial commemorates two bombing raids on the town in 1940. One of those, believed to be the first daylight air raid on mainland Britain, saw a pair of bombs land here on Bank Row, a direct hit on a row of homes and shops. Fifteen people were killed, eight of them children. Three of those – Eric Blackstock, Betha Miller and John Wares – were just five years old.

The ghosts seem to patrol these haunted streets. Entire rows of houses look boarded up and vacant, but then a resident will open their front door and deliver a stare that says 'Yes, I do live here. What are you looking at?'

There are a few odd shops dotted around Pulteneytown. Really dotted around. A street might have residential rows on both sides, but halfway along, away from any other shops, there might be a random butcher or a hairdresser or an autoparts dealer, trading in splendid, if slightly bemusing, isolation. There's even a lingerie shop, Secrets, complete with a reassuring slogan: 'Not a second's judgement about size or preference'.

Despite the ghostly, occasionally moribund feel of Pulteneytown, one of its streets does appear in the *Guinness Book of Records*. I'm back at the start of the Telford Trail now, on Ebenezer Place. Or am I? It's hard to tell. For Ebenezer Place is officially the world's shortest street. Its length measures just two metres and six centimetres – or six foot nine in old money. (Only one building has Ebenezer Place as an address: Mackays Hotel, the original base of Wick's temperance movement, which now boasts a bar serving more than 500 different whiskies.)

It's a ridiculously short street, the length of which makes the diminutive platform at Beauly station look like a marathon course. Indeed, if an average-height NBA player were to lie down in the road in front of Mackays Hotel, his head, torso and feet would be in three different thoroughfares.

Heading back across the bridge from Pulteneytown, a short caravan of campervans wobble past on the pockmarked, pot-holed main road. They've been drawn here by what *Condé Nast Traveller* magazine has anointed 'the best road trip in the world'.

In the mid-2010s, a giant 516-mile circuit of road from Inverness, looping into and around the Highlands' northernmost reaches, was given a marketing sheen by the local tourist board. This collection of A-roads would now be known as the North Coast 500 – or, more popularly, the NC500.

In the 10 years since, the circuit has brought visitors in their hundreds of thousands to these upper highlands, many of whom discovered the route when Jeremy Clarkson and his two buddies drove along part of it on their show *The Grand Tour*. It has quickly established an international reputation, a fixture on the bucket lists of innumerable owners of campervans and high-performance sports cars. But the tourism it brings has also prompted discord.

The local writer Gail Anthea Brown has written extensively about both the environmental and the cultural impact on the area. Railing against 'the perception of a landscape designed for leisure', she explains that 'the North Highlands existed well before 2015 and the NC500. Suggestions that the whole region would collapse without it have something of a condescending air.' To

Brown's eyes, the area has become a playground for outsiders. She cites 'numerous examples of uncontrolled camping and inconsiderate motorhome parking, with a minority of travellers causing anguish through littering, parking up at unsuitable locations and – worst of all perhaps – the unconcealed dumping of human waste'.

Obviously, not all the drivers on the NC500 behave that way.

In a car park next to the river, a couple in their thirties are corralling a pair of cockerpoos – Ben and Jerry – back into a rented campervan, having given them a constitutional along the riverbank. Simon and Jen are from Edinburgh and are 'doing the NC500', electing to go in an anticlockwise direction.

They're taking advantage of the quieter roads of February, but not necessarily by design. 'We're against the clock,' says Jen, revealing the bump underneath her coat. 'I'm due in April, so it was now or never to do the NC500. Well, perhaps not never. But not for a good few years.'

'We were considering getting some winter sun instead,' says Simon. 'Tenerife or somewhere.' He pulls his scarf tighter up his neck. 'Maybe we should have…'

I ask them what they think of Wick and whether they, too, intend to wander along the Telford Trail. They swap awkward glances.

'We only got here 20 minutes ago and we're away now.'

Once they've grabbed supplies and filled up the campervan at the giant Tesco superstore on the northern outskirts, that will be the last the couple will see of Wick. As with much of that summer traffic, the town is a pitstop rather than the finish line. It's rarely even a destination for the night. The sparse number of guests at the breakfast buffet in my hotel this morning, and the number of empty spaces in the car park overnight, is evidence of this.

Indeed, the brown NC500 traffic signs on the A99, pointing drivers out of town in both directions – known respectively, in non-nonsense, utilitarian fashion, as the north road and the south road – are effectively saying, 'Push on. Keep going. No need to stop *here*.'

Tesco will feel the benefit of Simon and Jen's money, not the struggling smaller concerns in the town centre. The couple could have refuelled at the Bridge Street Café, where the husband-and-wife proprietors know the names, the orders and the business of their clientele. They ask kids how their gymnastics class went. They ask new mums how their babies are getting on. And they know which customers appreciate a large jug of gravy to accompany their egg and chips.

You don't get that at Tesco. There, Simon and Jen will almost certainly use the self-service checkouts. Other than mine, the pre-recorded announcement instructing them to place their items in the bagging area will be the only voice they'll hear during their time in Wick.

There are some visitors to Wick today who are going to hang around longer than Simon and Jen. For the whole afternoon, in fact.

At 1.40 p.m., 80 minutes before kick-off, a coach containing the players of Lossiemouth FC pulls up outside Harmsworth Park, home of today's opponents, Wick Academy. Wick Academy are, by some distance, Britain's most northerly semi-professional football club. This means that, once a season, the 17 other clubs in the Highland League have to venture all the way up here, play a match and travel all the way back, in a day.

Brora Rangers are Wick's local rivals. Brora is more than an hour down the A9 – or two hours if their supporters have opted to take the Far North Line as it detours across the wilderness of the Flow Country. 'Local' is doing some very heavy lifting here.

Lossiemouth's players wearily climb off the coach and start to unfold their limbs, which will be required to perform at their peak in little more than an hour.

'How long was the drive?' I ask one of their players as he heads for the dressing room.

'About three and a half hours.'

So, ideal preparation for a match?

'Oh, aye.'

'And was there no chance that the club could have forked out for a hotel last night for you guys? It's only once a season you have to come up here, after all.'

A hollow laugh. 'We'd be lucky to even get a tent...'

Opposition teams have been travelling up to Harmsworth Park for away games for more than 130 years now. You'd have thought that 13 decades of existence would have been ample time in which Wick could have flattened the pitch a bit. It rises up in the far-left corner, from which slopes run both across the pitch and down its nearside length.

The Wick players start arriving. To a man, they are locals; no one travels this far north to merely further their footballing careers. A few of them might have done time at professional outfit Ross County down in Dingwall during their years in youth football but, having been released without a sniff of a contract, gravity has brought them back, returned them to their meridian, ready to serve their hometown club for many seasons to come.

With possibly misplaced confidence, they gamely park their cars behind one of the goals. The referee and one of his linesmen are here too and are inspecting the pitch, slope and all. The refer-ee's tracksuit top is sponsored by Specsavers.

The match will be played in bitterly cold conditions, which even the local fans, who've grown up in such bone-shaking tempera-tures, are complaining about. Robert Louis Stevenson once moaned about the 'black wind' that would impose itself on the town. Today's isn't quite that, but it is at least dark-grey in hue.

I glance up at the dark clouds approaching from the south and steel myself. Any concern about not having brought a brolly dissolves when I notice a sign detailing the club's rules and regulations. 'Fans can bring collapsible umbrellas into the stadium and retain them, but cannot use them during the game.' So, if you brought along a small umbrella simply to keep it in your coat pocket while the rain lashed down on you, you're in luck. (Another sign also tickles me slightly: 'No alcohol permitted in the ground.' This instruction is just below the words 'Shirt sponsor – Old Pulteney Whisky'.)

This afternoon's match is a lumpy affair on a soft pitch between two teams loitering in the lower half of the Highland League table. Wick play down the slope in the first half and take the lead after 15 minutes with an excellently planted header from their left-winger. (Not that it will be the most impressive header of the afternoon. That'll be one by a Wick defender which not only clears the stand but also the wall of the cemetery beyond.) The home side's advan-tage is doubled on the half-hour mark when Lossiemouth's centre-back haplessly passes the ball into his own net.

At half-time, the sensible spectators are those who swerve the lengthening queue for Scotch pies and tea at the refreshment hut and head into the warmth of the branch of Lidl over the road to defrost. The teenagers and sub-teens in the ground find their own way to stay warm when a mass 15-vs-15 game breaks out on the grass behind the far goal.

Despite playing up the slope in the second half, Wick add a third when their right-winger embarks on a Maradona-in-'86 dribble to put the result beyond doubt. This third goal prompts one of the more senior members of the Wick crowd to break into song. He's got a fine tenor voice, helped by the acoustics of the steel stand.

'We are the army,' he starts to sing. 'The barmy army / We are mental / And we are mad.'

The song then moves into a call-and-response passage – only it's all call and no response.

'Barmy army!'

Silence.

'Barmy army!'

More silence.

He changes tack and launches into a different song, one that doesn't require the participation of his reluctant fellow Wick fans.

'We're black / We're white / We're really dynamite...'

The hits are coming thick and fast now.

'Can you hear the Lossie sing? / I can't hear a bloody thing.'

The Lossie can't be heard singing because a) they're three–nil down and have nothing to sing about, and b) I've yet to identify a single away supporter in the entire ground who's made the trip north today.

I ask John, the Wick fan I'm stood next to, whether it takes an extra level of devotion to support Academy, bearing in mind the demanding distances involved.

'If you go to away games, yeah. I go to a few, but most people here never go. It's understandable, with the price of petrol and everything. It can be a full tank of fuel for some of those games. Plus, all the other grounds are in the same direction. You're travelling down the same road every time. That gets boring.'

'Brechin away next Saturday, John?' asks the fan on the other side of him. It's a question that we know the answer to. Brechin City, who played at the second level of Scottish football just six years ago but who now find themselves down here in the fifth tier, are by far the most southerly club in the Highland League. Just half an hour from Dundee, in fact. It would be a 430-mile round trip for John; two and a half hours to Inverness, and the best part of three more across the Cairngorms. And, of course, the same again to get back home. Almost certainly a little longer in the dark, in fact, if he didn't further shell out for a hotel.

Plus, Brechin are the current league leaders. The chances of Wick getting much from the game would be slim. A right thumping could be the outcome.

'I think I might sit that one out, Jim,' says John.

It's not just distance that's key here in the Highland League. There's also the weather. Unsurprisingly, postponements abound during the winter months, creating fixture backlogs and forcing some teams to play catch-up with their rivals. As things stand this afternoon, Brora Rangers have played *10* fewer games than Rothes, the team directly below them in the table.

The final whistle goes and the Wick fans shuffle out of Harmsworth Park, cold but happy. About 40 minutes later, the Lossiemouth players emerge from their dressing room, silent and sheepish. Once they're all aboard the coach, the doors shoosh shut and it's off down the south road, past the lights of Lidl and into the dark night.

They made this journey in reverse just a few hours ago, but now – after a three–nil defeat in which they mustered just a single attempt on target – Wick feels even further from home.

Goodbye to Timbuktu for another season.

2

THE WILD WEST

Glasgow Queen Street–Mallaig

'**M**y favourite British line is the West Highland Line.'
It's rare that I agree with Michael Portillo. There's the politics, for starters. And then there's the fashion choices.

But his declaration of love for this particular stretch of railway – this long and snaking stretch of railway that reaches upwards from Glasgow to its northern terminus 164 miles later, at the small port of Mallaig – is right on the money. For its near-continuous picture-postcard views, it just can't be beaten.

I first rode this line 14 years ago, en route to a compact and bijou music festival on the equally compact and bijou Inner Hebridean island of Eigg. Not even the most horrific seasickness imaginable on my sea crossing could sour what had just been the most glorious five-and-a-half-hour train journey of my life.

Portillo and I are not the only ones to feel this way. Far from it. According to readers of various travel magazines – British travel magazines, admittedly – no other railway in the world can compare to the West Highland. The Trans-Siberian? The Bernina Express between Tirano and St Moritz? The Bullet Train connecting Tokyo with Osaka? Argentina's Tren a las Nubes, taking passengers into both the Andes and the clouds?

Apparently not.

I'm going to double-check my workings, re-riding the West Highland just to make sure. I'm bound for Mallaig.

It's midday at Glasgow Queen Street station, the sun pouring through the vast sloping grid of windows onto the concourse. Trains head north, east and west from here – but mainly north. Most people are waiting for the next service to Edinburgh. Sure, it's a fine city and everyone has their reasons to go there today, but they're missing the romance, the sense of escape and the drop-dead-gorgeous backdrop that the train about to leave Platform 4 will be serving up.

There's no surge or rush to get on board, unlike those fidgety, Edinburgh-bound travellers. Those strolling towards the Mallaig train are a combination of retired folk taking advantage of both spare time and subsidised public transport to explore places they've always wanted to explore, and hirsute students lugging impossibly heavy rucksacks while simultaneously munching their way through supersized packets of expensive hand-fried crisps. There are no sprinters here.

Each passenger holds hopes and expectations of an adventurous weekend to come. It's just that some adventures will be more sedate than others.

For the time being, though, it's going to be sedate for us all. Sit back. Relax. Be gobsmacked by the view. And the next one. And the one after that.

The train heads underneath Glasgow's streets before re-emerging above ground and curving around its outskirts, through unremarkable suburbs and dormitory towns. This isn't the portion of the journey that's won the West Highland Line all those accolades and all that swooning praise. That's to come.

Until then – until the views open up when, after passing the Faslane naval base, repository of Britain's nuclear arsenal, we reach the banks of Loch Lomond – the three hirsute students sat at the table across the aisle have set up a card school. They've even brought poker chips with them. They each play with headphones clamped around their ears, a silent game orchestrated by hand gestures and nods.

The tip-tap of poker chips being stacked up forms a duet with the unpopping of a Tupperware lid further down the carriage. We're all in it for the long haul.

At five and a half hours, the journey to Mallaig is even longer than that to Wick but, with a half-full carriage, it's nowhere near as solitary. The Tupperware openers, a retired couple called Jim and Janet, are on their second excursion of the day along the West Highland. They rode these very rails earlier, albeit in the opposite direction, leaving Fort William at quarter to eight this morning on the first train towards Glasgow. In the 40 or so minutes between that train arriving at Queen Street and ours leaving, the couple took refreshments ('a nice Italian coffee') at a George Square café before retracing their steps and getting back on board, this time on the opposite side of the carriage.

'Didn't you want to see more of Glasgow?' I ask, not unreasonably. 'Have lunch? Look around the shops? Visit a gallery?'

'No,' says Janet, the chattier half of the pair. 'Everything we want to see is outside these windows. It's all about the train ride for us, those glorious views.

'We do this trip twice a year, spring and autumn. And until the clocks change, it has to be a quick turnaround in Glasgow to make sure we have daylight there and back. There's no point riding this train in the dark.'

Jim sinks his teeth into a sausage roll and gestures out of the window, where Loch Lomond has appeared below us. 'I mean, what can Glasgow do that's better than that?' he says, pastry tumbling from his lips.

Spring is positively springing outside. Loch Lomond sparkles. The landscape is re-greening. The lambs gambol, the students gamble.

From Loch Lomond onwards, this is a journey that demands your full attention, that requires your senses to be on high alert. The train trundles past endless sun-blessed mountains, thick pine forests and calm, dark lochs. *Look at me, look at me.*

Books remain unread, and the playing cards return to their pack – the card school ending amicably, without recrimination. Honours even. Settle back and enjoy the rest of the ride.

At Ardlui at the top of Loch Lomond, pleasure boats, corralled for the winter, impatiently strain at their moorings, aware of spring's arrival, crying for freedom. Waterfalls gush hundreds of feet down steep escarpments from mountain peaks. Buzzards circle overhead. It's more dramatic than the Far North Line to Wick, the landscape here on the western side of the Highlands rippled – by seismic shifts, by geological squabbles – into sharper peaks and narrower valleys.

When we reach Crianlarich, a couple of hours into the journey, the train divides into two. The front half will head due west to Oban, while our two carriages will continue to plough north-wards. 'Please check you are seated correctly' warns the scrolling digital display.

Some proper-job walkers get on at Crianlarich, complete with the kind of gear you'd think more suited to an assault on the Himalayas. Then I notice Ben More, the 1,174-metre peak which looms over the village. It certainly looks Himalayan, thanks to a generous covering of snow. Perhaps these walkers bagged another Munro for their collection before lunch.

Once the Oban service has peeled off west, we continue straight on. At Upper Tyndrum, a stick-thin cyclist and his mountain bike get on board, as do two straight-laced men in their late fifties – grey-haired and bespectacled – who take their seats behind me. They begin a discussion about which band they've seen the most number of times. I'm expecting Coldplay or Elbow. For both, though, it's thrash-metal outfit Slayer. The man in the window seat has seen them on 16 occasions.

The train reaches the desolation of Rannoch Moor and I reach for my phone. There's an episode of the Radio 4 series *The Patch* that I've been saving for the occasion. Using a random postcode generator, the presenter, Polly Weston, sends herself to a specific part of the country to unearth a story yet to be told. For this episode, the postcode generator brought Polly to this barren moor – a place which, you'd think, had very little need for a postcode. I listen to the episode, an unravelling story involving a reclusive estate owner and three sudden deaths on his land.

Polly was told that, here on the edge of the Blackmoor Forest, she was 'as likely to meet rutting deer as people'. This local advice is pretty much spot-on for me, too. Other than the small handful of passengers waiting on lonesome platforms, I've seen no human activity out of the window for at least an hour now. But I have just seen a regal-looking stag and two younger males – the king and his princes – barely 50 yards from the railway line. No rutting, mind.

By the time we've crossed the moor and reached Corrour, we're still only just past the halfway mark of our journey. As with Altnabreac on the Far North Line, Corrour station is a byword for remoteness. It's a 10-mile walk to the nearest tarmac-coated road. Fortunately, there are no known disagreements with the locals here, though. None of the beef of Altnabreac. Still, Corrour does have two claims to fame.

The first is that it is the highest mainline station in the UK, standing at 410 metres above sea level.

The second is that it was featured in the film adaptation of Irvine Welsh's *Trainspotting*, the remote station to which Renton, Spud, Sick Boy and Tommy travel in a bid to remove themselves from the pharmaceutical temptations of Scotland's Central Belt. The widescreen views which open up as their train pulls away from the platform don't impress them much. 'Now what?' demands a disgruntled Sick Boy.

There's one person waiting on the platform at Corrour today, a walker who stands in a curious manner, with his hiking poles stuck out behind him like those of a downhill skier. His cheeks are rosy. It looks as though he's been striding hard to catch this service, to not be left waiting six hours for the next, and last, train of the day.

A couple in their thirties get off here with no luggage. As they take pictures of both the train and the station sign, I assume they're *Trainspotting* fans who are grabbing a quick souvenir. But they don't get back on board. The woman gives a little wave to the guard as the train leaves both the station and them. The couple only have the smallest of backpacks between them and the sun will be setting in little more than an hour. Where on earth are they going? Should we be concerned?

The stick-thin cyclist has also got off here. He powers away down a gravel track. That's one person who knows where he's off to.

After stopping at the neatly kept station at Tulloch, the train bears due west towards Fort William. This is where the three card-playing students are heading and so, as we drift into town, with snow-capped Ben Nevis glowing in the late-afternoon sun, they deposit multiple empty crisp packets into the nearest bin and drag their rucksacks down from the overhead racks. A weekend of adventure in the Ben Nevis foothills awaits.

Most of the other occupants of the carriage get off here too. Jim and Janet are among them, their day-long odyssey now over. The carriage falls much quieter, especially as, for the last hour, Janet has been amusing herself (and no one else) by impersonating the train's two-note horn every time it sounds as we approach an unmanned crossing. This is when she hasn't been loudly playing videos of her grandkids to herself and Jim. Perhaps gazing upon the Scottish Highlands at their finest can't completely hold the attention for an entire day.

Indeed, there is the distinct possibility that, after a few hours of glorious vista after glorious vista, some sense of anaesthesia kicks in, that even the most eager passenger could get numb and nonchalant about the shifting scenery outside the window, with Munro peaks coming at the train from each and every direction. Some could get numb and nonchalant. Not me, though.

We reverse out of Fort William. We're low now, down from the altitude of Corrour and close to the waters of Loch Eil. The sun is lower too, edging closer to the point at which it will disappear behind the big peaks to the west. Shadows are being cast; silhouettes are forming.

There's an unscheduled stop along the banks of the loch, the reason for which is contained in the riddle 'Why did the chicken cross the railway track?' Then we're climbing again, up through the granite in order to make it across the best-known feature of the West Highland Line, its poster boy. The train's PA crackles into action. 'Ladies and gentlemen,' comes the voice of the guard. 'Please get your cameras ready. We are about to go over the world-famous Glenfinnan Viaduct.'

The Glenfinnan Viaduct is to the region what the Clifton Suspension Bridge is to Bristol or Tower Bridge is to London: the engineering wonder that launched a thousand postcards. It has become world-famous because of its appearance in several *Harry Potter* films, with the Hogwarts Express powering around its curve and over its 21 high-standing arches as it takes carriages of young wizards back to their seat of learning. The viaduct's use in the films has been significant to the local economy for 20-odd years, driving tens of thousands of visitors to the region every year, often on specially chartered steam trains. The chambers of commerce of this particular corner of the Western Highlands owe the franchise's location scouts a sizeable favour.

After his announcement, the guard presses 'play' on a tinny version of what I'm guessing to be the Harry Potter theme tune. I suspect he's holding his phone up to his handset. It sounds less than epic.

This last hour of the journey, this last leg into Mallaig, is the most dramatic stretch of the whole line. The hills and mountains are more intensely packed together, and the train battles the topography to find a serpentine trail between them. We wind, we twist, we snake.

The train hits the coast at Arisaig, the white-sand beaches of which (and those of the next station stop, Morar) were used in Bill Forsyth's wonderful film *Local Hero*. Grassy knolls and hillocks speed by, and the islands of Eigg and Muck become visible. Skye too.

The train audibly decelerates and we glide into Mallaig, the end of the line. The dozen or so passengers left on board disembark. The driver climbs down from his cab.

'Are you the envy of train drivers across the land?' I ask.

'Oh, I don't know about that,' he says, zipping up his hi-vis jacket. 'I've just been lucky growing up round here. If I'd been born in London, I'd probably be a Tube driver with no view at all. But, yes, it's definitely a privilege. There's no doubt about that. You never get bored. There's always something you've never noticed before, no matter how many times you've been in the cab. A hill or a waterfall or whatever.'

There are many, many great train journeys in the world, but they do not – *they cannot* – compare to the West Highland Line.

Whisper it, but Michael Portillo is dead right.

In the song 'Considering a Move to Memphis', the latter-day jug band the Colorblind James Experience weigh up the benefits of moving to a certain city in Tennessee. One of Memphis's virtues is that it only takes the narrator, the aforementioned Colorblind James, 'an hour and a half to walk completely around it'.

It takes considerably less time to walk around Mallaig. Mallaig is not a big place. But I could consider a move there too.

As dusk descends, the islands of the Inner Hebrides disappear in the milky light. There are plenty of campervans gazing across to them, parked up in the long-stay car park, staying there overnight before tomorrow morning's ferry crossings.

Mallaig purrs with an ever-present, low-level hum, the sound of an open-all-hours fishing harbour. The port's lights are never extinguished either. But aside from the odd fork-lift truck circumnavigating the village's single roundabout, its streets are otherwise quiet, hushed. Once checked into the warm and cosy West Highland Hotel, but eager to stretch my legs after being sat down all afternoon, I head back out to wander up lanes, down passageways and across quays for an hour or two. I double-back on myself, looping around the place several times. But, aside from a couple of teens in the Co-op buying sugary snacks to accompany an evening of Netflix ('I'm not watching a bloody romcom,' cautions one of them), it's rather a silent night in Mallaig.

I look through darkened shop windows. Only one shop is taking advantage of the Harry Potter connection, boasting a fair selection of nick-nacks that feature the image of the boy-wizard, complete with the specs and the forehead scar. Round the corner, though, is an establishment aimed at the more hardcore enthusiast of supernaturalism. Housed in a converted Portakabin, The Raven, The Cat & The Witches Hat offers 'witchcraft supplies' – wands, runes, pendulums, charms, spells and 'ritual tools'.

I walk back up the hill to my hotel but choose to give the peaceful-sounding Chlachain Inn a look-in on the way. It's an establishment that must have some impressive soundproofing as, on opening the door, I'm met by a torrent of noise and ebullience from a very busy pub. Thursday night is quiz night here, clearly something of a red-letter day for many of the local residents who range from hoary old men of the sea propping up the bar to gangs of sixth-formers pooling their knowledge at the corner tables.

The older participants are at an advantage when asked to identify a picture of Gary Numan, but the younger set are quids in when required to name a particular villain from the animated kids TV show *Ben 10*. I appear to straddle both camps, getting both answers right. Thankfully, all 13 teams are able to answer 'France' when asked in which country the Eiffel Tower can be found. It's a lively, unpretentious quiz, devoid of the pettiness and rancour that can often be found at such events. The bonhomie of the quizmaster sets the tone, even if his pronunciation of Salman Rushdie's name is decidedly suspect.

A couple of hours later, I take, as I did in Wick, a near-midnight ramble in search of those elusive Northern Lights. No joy again. Instead, the only lightshow is provided by the twin beams of an oncoming train – the third and final service of the day from Glasgow Queen Street. It's 20 minutes to midnight. Not a single soul gets off. The driver heads to bed.

On my way back up the hill, the Chlachain Inn is still boisterous. Someone opens the door to leave and out escapes the sound of the bar's hardy perennials belting out John Denver's 'Take Me Home, Country Roads'. It's a song that will be reprised in an hour or two's time when the guest in the room next to mine decides, in a state of advanced refreshment, that the rest of the hotel needs to hear his version. I also strongly believe him to be the prime suspect behind the fire alarm that will go off at 6.20 in the morning. It's not just the loudest fire alarm I've ever heard, it's the loudest *noise* I've ever heard. The decibel reading would be that of those 16 Slayer concerts combined.

Come morning time, which has arrived somewhat quicker to us hotel guests than was hoped thanks to that alarm, the relentless hum from the harbour is now accompanied by a frequent, closer rumble – the sound of suitcases being wheeled along Mallaig's pavements towards the ferry port.

Perfectly placed between the village's biggest hotel, its railway station and the ferry terminal (which is little more than a transparent bus shelter), the Jac-o-Bites Café is the natural stopping-off point for those seeking the refreshment denied them on the train. The café serves a mean egg roll. A positively transcendental egg roll, actually. Suitably refuelled, its customers leave when they can see their ferry heading into port outside the window.

The first ferry of the day to what are known as the Small Isles – Rum, Muck, Eigg, Canna – glides into the harbour and gracefully swings around to reverse into the slipway, its pre-recorded passenger announcement bouncing off the harbour wall. The ferry workers and dockers spring into action, repeating the moves of their time-worn ballet – those of guiding the ferry's ramp into place before ushering cars off the boat.

Eight vehicles drive off, followed by a quintet of foot passengers, the latter ready to kill time in the Jac-o-Bites Café (and in the extensive and delightfully disordered charity bookshop next door) until the lunchtime train. Twice as many foot passengers board the ferry, ready for a day, a weekend or a week of peace and isolation on one of the islands. One passenger has an impressive array of photographic equipment poking out of his rucksack. Another wheels a bicycle aboard, its panniers swollen with his worldly goods.

A waiting motorcade of Transit vans and small trucks reverse their way with ease down the slipway and across the narrow ramp. They've all done this plenty of times before. The one single car carrying tourists does so much more gingerly, tracing a nervous line backwards, its driver frequently dabbing the brakes to avoid an embarrassing shunt – possibly a watery one. Once the manoeuvre is complete, one of the ferry men applauds, almost certainly sarcastically.

The ballet finishes, the ramp is raised and the safety announcements ring out. The ferry is quickly on its way. The passengers to Eigg will land in an hour and 20 minutes' time. Those heading to Canna, the last stop, have a voyage of more than four hours ahead of them. The sunlight hits the ferry as it reaches the Minch, the body of water between the mainland and Eigg, the body of water which forced that violent bout of seasickness on me all those years ago. The Minch looks a gentler soul today.

The port reverts to that gentle hum. Like Wick, it wasn't always this quiet. I head towards the Mallaig Heritage Centre, a small building next to the railway line, to find out all about those days of glory. The gate is open but the lights are out and the door is locked and bolted. The stationmaster tells me it doesn't reopen until the other side of Easter. Apparently, history lessons are only available in the summer season. It's Wick all over again.

There was one particular photograph I wanted to see on the walls of the Heritage Centre. It's nothing special – just a snap from 1980 of a second-year class at the nearest secondary school, Morar High. But it launched a fascinating social history project.

One of the pupils in the class became a photographer in adult life. Donald MacLellan lives in the Cotswolds now and has enjoyed a successful career; portraits he's taken of the great and good are on display at the Scottish National Portrait Gallery. One day, on a visit back home to Mallaig, he saw the school photograph and it set him wondering: whatever happened to his classmates? Where are they now?

Donald decided to track them all down, to make them the subject of his next photography project as they all approached their fiftieth birthdays. Some had moved to Inverness or Fort William or Selkirk or Ireland. They were now financial advisers or teachers or farmers or care assistants.

Some had stayed in Mallaig. And I'm now off in search of one of them, a fishing-boat skipper by the name of Robert Summers. He'll be able to give me the history lesson about the port that the closed Heritage Centre was unable to. And I also want to understand just why he never left his tiny hometown of Mallaig, why he's always succumbed to its gravitational pull.

Within a minute of meeting him, I discover that Robert is now a *former* fishing-boat skipper, having sold his boat two months ago.

'Not being able to get crew was my main reason for selling it,' he explains. 'If you work within twelve miles in UK waters like we did, you're not allowed to have foreign crew. All the younger generations now are moving away, going to university and getting good jobs. When I was young, fishing was the best job to go to. Nobody earned more money than fishermen. At eighteen, nineteen, I was on one of the better boats in Mallaig and earning twenty thousand a year. My friend was earning about thirteen thousand driving a train. He retired two or three years ago and he was on sixty thousand a year by then. That would be a big year for a fisherman now. There wouldn't be many guys in Mallaig earning that.'

Last year was actually, in Robert's 35 years as a skipper, the most profitable in all his time since first going to sea. In summer, prawns and langoustines were what he caught; sprats in winter. But it's that absence of crew, rather than any paucity of catch, that sounded the death-knell for him. It's a hard, difficult working life, after all.

'A typical week would be going to sea at one or two o'clock on Monday morning, landing back on Thursday night, then straight back out. Land again on Sunday night, but straight back out again until Thursday. And then four days off.' Fishing no longer outstrips other industries when it comes to rewarding such hardship. There are easier ways to make a living these days. 'There are only five local boats left now in Mallaig. There were more than a hundred when I left school.'

Robert's future, now he's in the second half of his fifties, is likely to mean attending college to update his skills so that he can freelance on standby boats. Going back to school seems harsh for someone of his age with so many decades of experience on the high seas. 'The new way is the best way, apparently...'

But what of the future of Mallaig?

'It was a busy place all year round, and when it's busy now, it's in the summer and because of tourism. The talk is that the steam train is already booked up for this summer, that there's a two-year waiting-list to ride on it. That's four hundred people coming here every day. Plus, coach parties too. Most people are glad because they can make money out of them. But in the winter, it's dead.

'Properties are being bought up for the tourist trade, for holiday lets and Airbnb. I speak to people in Devon and Cornwall, and they've got the same problems down there. Mallaig needs more houses to attract young locals to stay. And we're struggling to get teachers here because they can't get accommodation. The village has a bad case of depopulation, and I don't know how you build the population back up.'

Robert hasn't lived anywhere but Mallaig his whole life, this village at the end of the line. And he has no intentions to ever leave. My theory is that, because he was at sea so much, claustrophobia and cabin fever never had time to take root. He nods his agreement.

'We could be anywhere from the Clyde right round to North Shields. We were only home for a few days.' There's a sense of sadness in his voice. 'I've never had any regrets about staying in Mallaig, but I didn't see my kids growing up because I was away all the time. When I was younger, they resented me for it.'

He smiles a painful smile. 'I was never there.'

Robert's portrait of boomtown Mallaig has whetted my appetite for local history. I head over to the library which, unlike the Heritage Centre, finds no reason to shut for winter. There I spend a warming hour pouring over books of photographs of Mallaig over the years, tracing its evolution from a windswept hillside of a handful of crofts to the bustling fishing port it would become. There are several volumes dedicated to the history of the West Highland Line, in which I learn of the initial local dissent against the railway being extended north from Fort William to Mallaig.

The port of Oban voiced its opposition, aiming to protect its own thriving fishing industry and not help promote and develop a competing port. Elsewhere, local landowners weren't keen on the railway making an incursion onto, or even near, their property. One such owner had multiple concerns, among them that the blasting of the rock required for the line's construction would interfere with the spawning of the local salmon. Another objection she held was due to her intention to establish a deer forest. 'But', as the annals of Parliament down in Westminster noted, 'that deer forest did not exist, except in the lady's imagination.'

I also spot plenty of pictures of my hotel, the West Highland, standing in imposing fashion above the train tracks, back when it was known as the Station Hotel. It's time to walk back up that hill. Before I check out, I have an appointment with its co-owner, Sine MacKellaig Davis.

Sine (pronounced 'Sheena') was, like Robert, born and brought up round here, but she left the west coast for university, later settling in Cumbria with her Mancunian husband and enjoying a career as a teacher. Fourteen years ago, though, she returned to Mallaig, now with husband and four kids in tow. It was an unscheduled homecoming, as she tells me as we take the comfy seats in the hotel reception.

'I never, ever planned to buy a hotel in my life. It was just one of those things that evolved, due to a very good salesperson! I remember as a child, thinking *Oh, isn't that a big grand place? Isn't it wonderful?*'

Sitting on the hill above the railway line, the hotel has been a prominent fixture of the childhoods of all Mallaig's sons and daughters. Its history runs parallel to that of the village.

'Mallaig came to life when the train came here. The place was mainly crofting. Fishing was growing and growing, but Arisaig was going to be the port. The then Lord Lovat convinced people to come off the croft – my grandfather was one of them – and into the village to service the fishing industry.

'The hotel was built then. People would come here to take the sea air and to travel on to the Outer Hebrides. You'd get a certain element of the hunting and shooting lot. It was a very grand hotel at the time – all linen tablecloths. It was very elegant in quite a rough fishing village. A strange juxtaposition.'

But then the original Station Hotel burned down in 1927. We're joined by Sine's colleague Fiona, whose connections with the place go far back. Her grandfather's sister and husband ran the hotel when the fire struck; the place was rebuilt and renamed the same year. Sine and Fiona attempt to untangle the twisted roots and branches of the hotel, of its complicated history, of the various families who've owned and run it over the generations.

Its own history plays a central role in that of Mallaig. The pair remember the village still enjoying its boom years when they were kids, high times brought about by the buoyancy of the fishing trade. 'Everybody was rich,' says Sine. 'They seemed to have a new car every month. And the three pubs were always full.'

'It was busy,' agrees Fiona. 'Real busy. Not so much goes on now. When we were young, there were three discos a week. And ceilidhs. And fish market dances.'

Life in twenty-first-century Mallaig has seen tourism usurp fishing as its main reason to be, but this is seasonal, ebbing and flowing.

'It's very busy in summer,' says Sine. 'Wall to wall. But in winter, all the holiday lets are empty, all the second homes are empty. It becomes very, very quiet. But it's getting busier. We've had more people this February than we've ever had in previous

Februarys. I think that's a change in how people take their holidays now. COVID has changed people's attitudes to going away, to maybe not having a big holiday abroad but perhaps having more smaller holidays in the UK.'

Who is the hotel's average visitor? Someone just here for a single-night stopover before catching a morning ferry or someone using it as a base while exploring the wider area?

They chime in unison. 'Both.'

'One of our big challenges,' Sine expands, 'is to get people to stay longer. This is a fantastic base. Yes, go to the islands, but come back again. Go to the beaches but come back again. You can day-visit everywhere from here. And it's usually a lot cheaper than staying on the islands. As soon as you go there, you can pretty much add fifty per cent onto the price of everything.'

'Before COVID,' says Fiona, 'people didn't realise how beautiful their country was. We've got Loch Morar, the deepest loch in Europe. We've got all these stunning beaches. And the wildlife! Orcas, sperm whales, minkes, dolphins, basking sharks, sea eagles...'

'Sometimes you can see the orcas from the hotel window,' says Sine, with no small amount of pride. 'People travel halfway across the world to see a sight like that.'

Alongside the *Harry Potter* effect, other films and TV shows have introduced the local scenery to international eyes: *Breaking the Waves*, *Rob Roy* and *Killing Eve* ('They stayed here! But neither of the two stars unfortunately. It was a scenic shot and they had stand-ins') were all filmed nearby. *Game of Thrones* was partly shot on Skye, just across the water.

'It's more than fifty per cent foreign guests now in the summer. Mostly European, although the market is stretching. Last year we had more from the US and the Far East.' Coach parties of German tourists were mainstays of the hotel for a number of years but, on taking it over, Sine wanted a more individual client base.

'And the thing about coach parties,' says Fiona, 'is that they just come to the hotel and then they move on. They're not bringing anything to the village.'

If the hotel's summer bookings take care of themselves, that elusive round-the-calendar clientele needs persuading and nurturing, with events such as the book festival held at the West Highland every November. It's called A Write Highland Hoolie. 'My favourite weekend,' beams Fiona. 'It's fantastic.'

'A few more visitors at this time of year would really invigorate the community,' says Sine, who used to be the director of the local chamber of commerce. 'People say "Oh, there's no restaurants open", but they would be open if there was a reason to open. There's just not enough people.'

The economics of running a boutique hotel at the end of the line aren't exclusively tied to visitor numbers. Sine confides that Liz Truss's meddling with the British economy in her 49 days as prime minister resulted in the hotel's mortgage rising by £1,000 a month. 'That's twelve grand a year. That's a member of staff. Well, a part-time one…'

Down the hill, I can hear the engine of my train starting up. It's due to leave in 10 minutes.

But Sine is in full flow, a passionate advocate for both the local region's economic well-being and its unique character. She explains about the creation of Morag the Monster, who apparently lives in the deep, dark depths of nearby Loch Morar and who is supposedly a relative of the Loch Ness monster.

'Do I want the area to become Loch Ness? As a hotelier, I should, but I don't. Do I want this place to become a theme park, or to stay what it is – charming and rural and remote? With my local's head on, I don't want it to get any busier. And with my business head on, I don't want it to get any busier either.

'What I would like is for people to appreciate it at this time of year. Come now! Why are you waiting for the summer? You're not going to get a suntan here anyway, so it doesn't matter if it's February or July when you come.

'Just put a coat on...'

3

THE QUIET CORNER

Glasgow Central–Stranraer

T here are superheroes at Glasgow Central.

It's Saturday morning and members of the Fantastic Four, Avengers and Guardians of the Galaxy are congregating on the station concourse. During the week, underneath the make-up and outfits, these are call-centre operatives and bar workers and civil servants and teachers. But it's the weekend, and cosplay is publicly permitted, especially when the ACME Comic Con is in town. At the SEC Centre further along the banks of the River Clyde, a line-up consisting of a former Doctor Who, actors from the Terry Pratchett-connected TV series *Good Omens*, comic-book artists and screenwriters await to be worshipped by these cosplaying acolytes.

Some have merely opted for the kind of off-the-peg superhero onesie favoured by rooftop Fathers 4 Justice protestors. Others have clearly been up since the wee small hours putting the finishing touches to their costumes and applying highly elaborate make-up. There are plenty of bright blue and bright pink wigs on show too. The plain-clothed Glaswegians on the concourse gaze on in puzzlement.

But if they looked in the opposite direction, they'd spot the act of genuine superheroism going on right now by Platform 2. A woman has offered to get the coffees in for her and her two companions. All three are heading for Euston. She joins the queue at the Starbucks concession. There are five people waiting to place their orders ahead of her. And there are seven minutes until the London train leaves.

'Just get them once we're on board,' suggests one of her pals.

'It's only Nescafé on there. I'm not drinking that shite.'

The queue is slow. The clock ticks. Her friends elect to get on the train, wheeling all three suitcases between them. The coffee order has been placed, but it's still a waiting game while they're made. She paces nervously. She involuntarily stamps her foot with impatience. A glance at the departures board. The Euston train will be leaving on time. It will leave in two minutes. If she misses it, it'll be £125 to catch the next one. She will, though, at least have plenty to drink on board, drowning her sorrows with three caramel macchiatos. That's one seriously expensive round.

Her name is finally called and a cardboard tray of coffees is handed over. She's off on her heels, charging around the corner and down the platform, showing the kind of raw speed that brought success to the likes of Liz McColgan and Laura Muir at major athletics championships. She reaches the door of the carriage as the guard blows his whistle. Two ScotRail staff cheer. She's off to London. And not a drop has been split. Give that woman a medal.

The cos players are away as well, off for a day of travelling to a different dimension.

I might be too. I'm going to Stranraer.

———

'Stranraer?!' yells Brian Potter in the opening episode of *Peter Kay's Phoenix Nights* when he learns that the Phoenix Club's lorry-driving keyboard player is missing in action just ahead of the venue's launch night. His last-known location is some way from Bolton. 'Stranraer?! In Scotland...?'

It's mainly lorry drivers who can quickly point to Stranraer on a map – and, even then, these are lorry drivers of a certain vintage. Located around 80 miles from Glasgow in Scotland's south-west corner, at the far end of Loch Ryan, for around 150 years the port was the primary point of departure from mainland Britain for Northern Ireland by sea, it being a comparatively short hop from there across the water to the port of Larne.

In 2011, though, Stena Line moved their ships out of town, relocating a few miles to the north at Cairnryan, where P&O Ferries already had its own port and was offering a shorter cross-ing time across to Larne. With Stena's retreat, the port of Stran-raer fell silent, the sound of ships' horns no longer hanging on the air, the growl of endless juggernauts rolling into town heard no more.

I'm off to see what effect that withdrawal has had on the place.

The seven-carriage train rolls out of Glasgow Central, over the Clyde and above the rooftops of the city's south side. These early views are of rubble-strewn, derelict brownfield sites and of an endless parade of anonymous warehouses containing goods of an unknown nature.

Beyond Paisley, the landscape widens into open – and often flooded – farmland. Furrows are filled with water, long stripes of silver. Unlike the West Highland Line, the topography allows us to travel arrow-straight and speedily, powered along by overhead cables all the way to the coast.

Again unlike the West Highland, this isn't a line for dreamers. This is no destination in itself. It's a functional service that simply takes people where they need to go to fulfil the duties of their daily lives. A busy commuter line during the week, on weekends its patrons are fewer and farther between. There is still, though, a half-hourly service.

At Kilwinning, a handful of guests for a wedding are waiting on the platform. Curiously, perhaps superstitiously, the suited-and-booted men – several of whom are wearing suits a size too small – climb aboard one carriage, while the women, in elaborate hats and sporting generously proportioned corsages, climb aboard another.

By the time we near the coast at Irvine, the view out of the window has changed. There haven't been too many landmarks to look out for en route, although the football-minded will have spotted the home ground of St Mirren on the edge of Paisley. Another sport is more conspicuous now. Golf courses begin to proliferate on both sides of the tracks, wide sandy fairways and neatly cut greens among the pasture and gorse.

This is Ayrshire's Golf Coast.

As we head south, diligently following the coastline, it's golf course after golf course after golf course. None are better kept, nor more prestigious, than Royal Troon which this summer will host the British Open for the tenth time in its illustrious history. Come July, these long, lingering fairways will bear the footprints of tens of thousands of spectators. Things are a bit less frantic this lunchtime, just keen amateur players scratching their way around its 18 holes.

Next along is Prestwick Golf Club, the course at which the first Open was played back in 1860. History seeps out of every bunker, every divot. Plane passengers taking off from, or landing at, adjacent Prestwick Airport must get a terrific view.

In a change to the usual schedule, though, our train will terminate at Prestwick Town. It won't be going all the way to Stranraer.

It won't even be going to Ayr, just a couple of short stops further on. Instead, we all leave our seven-carriage train and wait for a two-carriage affair to take us across the River Ayr.

There's a reason for this downsizing.

Nearly six months ago, on an early Monday evening in September, 15 fire engines were called to Ayr station where the once-grand Station Hotel was ablaze. The fire was raging, the fire brigade struggling to contain it, hampered by cuts made to the service; there was a sizeable delay in high-reach equipment arriving from significantly further afield.

The fire devastated the building, gutting its interior and leaving its remains unsafe. With the railway line being immediately adjacent to the hotel, the station was instantly put out of action. Almost half a year on, its single usable platform can only safely handle services that are no longer than two-carriage trains, hence the decanting of passengers back in Prestwick Town onto a much shorter service.

The disablement of Ayr station has also meant that no trains have run south of here since last September. The line down to Stranraer has been silent all that time.

Instead, ever since, a bus replacement service has been doing the five-times-a-day shuttle 50 miles down the coast, stopping at all stations en route, regardless of whether any cheesed-off passenger wants it to. This, coupled with the shuffle between the two-carriage and seven-carriage trains – performed on a half-hourly basis in both directions, and of course requiring extra trains and extra personnel – has created one giant logistical headache. A costly one, too. Three teenagers have been arrested in connection with the fire.

Outside Ayr station, our chariot – a 30-seater bus – awaits. We're down to a handful of passengers now, a small group reluctantly swapping the smoothness and the speed of the rail line for the lurch and bump of gear-jamming road travel.

Although it does make those visits to the intermediate stations of Maybole and Girvan, the bus doesn't trace the same route as the train line. Challenging topography forces trains to head inland at certain junctures, but the bus largely stays on the coast road.

This means passing another championship golf course, that of Turnberry – or, rather, Trump Turnberry as it was rebadged following its purchase by you-know-who in 2014. I saw the news today and so know that the current owner is otherwise engaged, busy entertaining Hungarian president Viktor Orbán down at Mar-a-Lago. Reassuringly, this means there's no danger of the bus's windscreen being smashed by an errant tee shot from the amateur golfer once labelled 'the commander-in-cheat'.

Turnberry is known for its views across the Firth of Clyde towards Ailsa Craig, the steep dome of granite rising from the sea eight miles out from shore. The view of the island accompanies us for some time as we hurtle, in boneshaking fashion, further down the A77. The coastline becomes more dramatic, explaining why the train line opted to head inland. We're up above the beaches, gazing down on wide-winged gannets patrolling the sands. The road twists and turns, bordered by rocky outcrops. Imagine those fishermen's shacks to be Malibu beach huts, and turn those grey skies to blue, and we could be hurtling down California's Pacific Coast Highway. Almost.

We zoom past Cairnryan's ferry ports: Stena Line's first, then P&O's. Scores of container trucks are patiently lined up waiting for the next service. It might be a comparatively short crossing, but the waters between here and Larne, known as the North Channel, aren't always welcoming. Rough seas have made trucks topple over on the ferry deck, flattening any cars in the way. In 1953, one ferry, the MV *Princess Victoria*, sank in a storm with the loss of 135 lives. One of those victims was David Broadfoot, the ship's radio officer, who gallantly stayed at his post as the *Princess Victoria* went down, sending messages and directions to the coastguard to aid with any rescue effort. He was posthumously awarded the George Cross.

Stranraer is visible now, stretching out along the bottom curve of the loch. As we arrive in town, we're reunited with the railway line after its inland incursion. But the location of the station confirms the town's previous priorities. The line heads for the town centre before selling it a dummy, giving it the slip. Instead, it diverts out onto a wide, derelict concrete pier, one previously used by ferry companies to give easy passage to foot passengers using their services. A simple hop, skip and a jump from train to ship. Our bus heads out on this pier too.

South-west Scotland is home to the most handsome railway station in the whole country, a curvaceous beauty of glass, steel and timber that's an absolute gem of turn-of-the-twentieth-century station design. It's both supremely functional and heart-stoppingly elegant. As one rail historian put it, it's an 'Edwardian triumph of transport ergonomics'.

The only problem is that I'm not going to Wemyss Bay station today. I'm in Stranraer. As I step off the bus and gaze at the town's station building, words like 'triumph' and 'elegant' don't trip off the tongue. In comparison to the fine lines of the terminus at Wemyss Bay, the architectural attractions of Stranraer station don't just fade into insignificance, they are non-existent. Matching the flattened docklands in terms of bleakness, the giant corrugated-iron cattle shed that covers the platform has yet to be lovingly written about by appreciative admirers. It no longer wears the

'Welcome to Stranraer' sign it once did. The wind whistles, the ironwork creaks.

Any local resident arriving home by train is taken to this wind-whipped outpost. And, accordingly, any local resident arriving home by train has to make the grim walk back down the pier, the waves splashing over the sea wall and onto the tracks. Deadened and devoid of human activity, the scene is further haunted by the non-running of trains. Clumps of grass and moss have sprouted between the sleepers. The redundant, rusting cranes jealously watch each and every ferry sail in and out of Cairnryan in the distance.

If the station and its approach set a new definition for the word 'bleak' (or, at least, they do when buffeted by today's razor-sharp winds and ice-cold rain), how does the town centre itself fare?

I walk along the edge of the loch until I reach Agnew Park. Its many high-summer attractions are still in hibernation. There are no pedaloes for hire to navigate around the boating lake. There's a miniature train that does a double loop of the park but, echoing the actual railway, no services appear to have run for many a month. There's a pirate ship for kids to play on that sits grounded on a sandy island in the middle of the boating lake, but this can only be accessed by a drawbridge, which has been raised for winter. Padlocked too.

A pair of teenagers – girlfriend, boyfriend – make their own entertainment, egging each other on to see who can get closest to one of the park's swans. The swan's patience appears to be decreasing with every squealing approach from the teens.

On sunny days, I'm sure Stranraer wears more of a smile. But in meteorologically challenging times like right now, the frown is fixed, frozen. The doomy, gloomy intro to Morrissey's 'Everyday

Is Like Sunday' involuntarily plays in my head. A crow on a post shares a knowing look with me.

Oh yeah, pal. I know that song well.

I head inland, towards the shops, towards the heart of the town. My first stop is at what is surely Stranraer's most distinctive building, the Old Town Hall on George Street, topped by a spire-like clock tower. It is the home of Stranraer Museum, the repository of the history of old Wigtownshire. Well, sometimes it is. It's currently closed for refurbishment. My unlucky run continues. After the museum in Wick and the heritage centre in Mallaig both denied me entry, my thirst for local knowledge once again goes unquenched. History remains a mystery.

Many shops lie empty, vacated by both staff and customers. A glance in an estate agent's window shows that there are plenty of retail outlets, with flats above, that can be snapped up for a price on the sunny side of £60,000. Indeed, the town offers plenty for the eager first-time buyer, with an array of homes coming with five-figure price tags.

With whatever shops and cafés still open on a morose Saturday afternoon starting to make moves towards closing their doors, there's no need to voluntarily get buffeted any further by the elements. Not for now, at least. I turn on my heels and head for my hotel.

A huge white mansion facing the loch, the North West Castle Hotel isn't actually a castle. It was built in 1820 by the polar explorer Sir John Ross as a base for him in his native south-west Scotland between Arctic expeditions. But it certainly wasn't intended as a haven from which to isolate Ross from adventures, a place where he could clear his head of the stress of travelling through and over ice fields. Quite the opposite. Inside the 'castle', he built a facsimile of the cabin of his ship *Victory* simply to be able to explain to friends and guests about the processes and procedures of polar exploration. The cabin has survived and today forms part of the hotel's bar.

After passing through various owners' hands, in 1970 – and by then in possession of the McMillan family of hoteliers – a notable addition was made to the North West Castle. The head of the family, Hamilton 'Hammy' McMillan, installed an ice rink in the basement. Not one for figure skating or ice dancing; one specifically for curling, the sport often reductively described as 'bowls on ice'. Or, you could say, 'darts on ice', it effectively being a game of long-range, horizontal nearest the bull.

The rink proved to be a great investment, not just for the town but also for the Hamilton family. Hammy's son – also Hammy – grew up with it being his subterranean playground, in the process becoming rather good at the sport. He was crowned European champion on no fewer than five occasions during the Eighties and Nineties; in 1999, over in the Canadian province of New Brunswick, he became champion of the world.

And it didn't stop there. Hammy's own son – the third Hammy – won silver at the 2022 Winter Olympics in Beijing. He's not Stranraer's only Olympic curler. Vicky Wright won gold at the same Olympics, while Vicki Chalmers had previously taken bronze in Sochi in 2014. As at every Olympics, these medallists used stones cut exclusively from the unique quartz-free granite of Ailsa Craig.

Once checked into the North West Castle, I dump my bag and head straight downstairs to where it all started and where today, rather fortuitously, the Scottish Pairs Championships are in full swing. The clink and clunk of the stones, and the seemingly wordless calls and hollers between teammates, are my siren song.

Since yesterday lunchtime, 20 teams from 13 curling clubs across Scotland have been playing each other in a round-robin format. By this evening, eight of these will have graduated to tomorrow's knockout stages.

I take up position in the Alpine Bar located at one of the two ends – a perfect, slightly raised rink-side seat. There's a mural along one length of the rink, depicting snow-capped peaks, pine forests, ski chalets and cable cars. Waistcoated waiters pour gin and tonics and deliver hot paninis and fish suppers to the tables. This is a highly agreeable way to watch sport. An all-weather one too. We're as warm and toasty as those paninis.

The rink below is full, with four matches currently in progress. I've decided to back one of the local pairs. When in Stranraer and all that. Ian Kirkpatrick wears a Scotland jersey and is built like he could also represent his country in the back row of a scrum. Frazer Hare is shorter and bears an uncanny resemblance to the middle-aged Jimmy Osmond. He is also the local funeral director. Faithful to his trade, he's dressed all in black.

This is Frazer and Ian's fourth match of the championships. They've won all three so far and are leading in this one too. The undertaker is burying the opposition.

Curling is a game of contrasts. Players gracefully glide a quarter of the length of the ice before delicately releasing their stone, giving it a little tweak and twist as they do so, applying the curl that gives the sport its name. But that grace then evaporates as urgent commands are issued to their teammates, shouted requests to furiously sweep the ice to smooth it and thus keep the stone moving towards its intended target.

Each match in a pairs competition consists of six ends, with 16 stones released per end, and lasts in the region of an hour and a half. Whoever is victorious in tomorrow's final will have played seven matches since Friday afternoon, more than 10 hours of competition over the weekend.

The spurts of furious brushing aside, it's not the most physically punishing of sports, but it is still draining – hours of scooting up and down the ice inspecting shots, hours of brain-stretching tactical puzzles. It's a game of intricate subtlety and marginal gains, where tables can turn on the release of a single stone.

There's no crowd of cheering fans watching on. Everyone in the Alpine Bar, aside from the waistcoated staff and me, are insiders – either competitors or club administrators or spouses. These bar-room analysts offer plenty of under-the-breath comments.

'Why's he not given that a little more?'

'Why's he gone that side?'

'That's not what I would have done.'

These are the voices of people who devote their spare time to the sport. Their knowledge is encyclopaedic.

'Do you remember that shot he made in Garmisch in '92? Against Canada, it was.'

Frazer and Ian win another end. Their 100 per cent record looks like staying intact. The fate of some of the other pairs has already been decided. A silver-haired player walks across the bar, stopping to talk to a competitor a third of his age.

'You done for the day?' he asks. 'You're OK? You're through?'

The teenage lad nods. His place in tomorrow's knock-out stages, with the quarter-finals starting at 10 a.m., is assured.

'We're not,' says the more senior player, glancing down at the tray he's carrying. 'Hence we're on the beer.'

Down below on the ice, Frazer and Ian have just finished their final end, running out 7–2 winners against their competitors from Forfar. They are one of only three of the twenty pairs to win all their round-robin matches.

They'll be back in the morning, as will I. For now, though, I'm heading back into town to refuel. Options are a little limited. The Star Fish Restaurant on Charlotte Street wins out, mainly for the immodest quote on their sign: 'The Best Fish and Chips in Scotland'. For a country that, including all its islands, boasts more than 11,000 miles of fishable coastline, and which leads the world when it comes to battered cuisine, this is quite some claim. Of course, while the quote marks suggest them to be the words of someone impartial and independent, there's no attribution to their source. The name of Rick Stein or Nigella Lawson or a Hairy Biker doesn't accompany the quote. I suspect the restaurant's owner to be the author of this particular declaration.

While I wait for my order, I flick through this week's edition of the *Stranraer & Wigtownshire Free Press*. Although the front page concerns itself with the sentencing of a local man for a murder in the town, elsewhere its pages are largely crime-free. There's a piece about a fun farming day, another about a proposal for a 'rural mural' for the waterfront and a report about the removal by crane of a train stuck at Stranraer station since the line closed back in September. (There is also, just to bait me, a centrespread of readers' pictures of the Northern Lights when they visited this corner of south-west Scotland a few days ago. Missed them again.)

I've read elsewhere that the most recent arrests around here have taken place at the Craigryan port. Last month, £510,000 worth of cannabis was uncovered by a sniffer dog. Two days later, another cannabis haul, this one with a seven-figure street value, was retrieved. And, over the course of a few days last week, the equivalent of 132,000 pints of illegal beer was seized.

It seems that one positive by-product of Stranraer's main industry upping and leaving town is a reduction in crime. The problem of smuggling has migrated a few miles up the loch. Certainly the two coppers currently having a leisurely chat in the car park of Stranraer's police station appear to be in no hurry to apprehend any wrong 'uns.

One of the few presences on the streets tonight is a small gang of after-dark, no-lights BMX riders pulling tricks on some stone steps on Castle Square. They are unfailingly polite, though, apologising when one spills into my path. At least two of them appear to be in their early thirties. A single patrol car makes a perfunctory circuit of the one-way system, but the hatchbacks of the town's boy racers maintain a respectful distance, keeping their revving and wheel spins to a minimum.

Those supposedly nation-leading chips scoffed, I head back to the hotel. Its other bars are empty, silent and dark, but I can hear plenty of voices downstairs in the basement, where today's matches have long since finished. Indeed, the Alpine Bar is even fuller than it was this afternoon. Plenty of drink has been taken and a 'short curling' tournament – where competitors release their stones from just a few feet away from the target, with no requirement for any of that frenzied sweeping – is well underway. For some reason, a table has been placed in the middle of the rink. I soon find out why.

At the end of each match, both competitors walk to the table, pour themselves a dram of whisky from a decanter, toast each other, down it and walk off the ice. So, the further a player gets in the competition, the more matches he or she plays and the more drams he or she takes. It's a handicap system of sorts, one that presumably means the quality of play deteriorates the closer the competition gets to its climax.

Come the next morning, there are, unsurprisingly, some sore heads at breakfast. The quarter-finalists took things easier last night, but some of those already eliminated let themselves go. The hangover cures of choice – black coffee, Irn-Bru – are being served in the Alpine Bar. One pair, who've already checked out of the hotel, scrutinise their bill, struggling to remember charging particular refreshments to their room.

In their quarter-final, Frazer and Ian have been drawn against a father-and-son pair from Perth, the Rutherfords. Teenager Finlay looks like a young Kevin De Bruyne. It's the tightest match the Stranraer pair have experienced so far, with just one point separating the teams going into the fourth end. Frazer and Ian then begin to pull away, leaving the Rutherfords needing three in the final end to tie.

'Three's possible,' says one of the bar-room analysts, sipping his restorative Irn-Bru.

Possible, but it doesn't happen. The Rutherfords end up conceding, swapping handshakes with their conquerors before grabbing their suitcases and heading for the highway. Frazer and Ian's weekend extends still further.

***

Back out in the town, it's time for more sustenance.

It's not just last night's chippy that shows off its culinary credentials. As shown by the certificates in their window, the pie-makers/bakers John Gillespie & Sons won multiple gongs at the most recent Scottish Baker of the Year awards. Both their carrot cake and their potato scones were declared the best in

Scotland, while their Scotch pie took silver in the world championships. Stranraer's curlers aren't the only locals who've turned heads on the global stage.

(Rather curiously, the Gillespies' window display also features notices announcing the coming week's funerals, several of which will be officiated by Frazer Hare – once he's off the rink.)

Another eatery, the Fig & Olive café at the far end of George Street, isn't quite so decorated, but is still happy to display its achievements: a certificate announcing it to have been a previous winner of the Café of the Year gong, as determined by *Dumfries & Galloway Life* magazine. It's a popular spot with Stranraer's Sunday brunch brigade, lured here by its buttermilk pancakes, its bacon on sourdough, its eggs Florentine. I opt for a brick-like slab of flapjack.

The music's good here, too. Tom Waits is currently explaining to the patrons that it's his piano that's been drinking, not him.

Aside from the locals, the Fig & Olive also finds favour as a refreshment stop for weekend cyclists. The framed cycling jersey on the wall – and the wallpaper in the toilets that comprises pages snipped from *Cyclist* magazine, shots of evocative landscapes, hairpin bends and impossible climbs in the sunnier climes of southern Europe – tells them they're welcome.

Across the road is the café's spin-off business, a 'speciality grocer and deli' called F&O Larder. Further down the street this morning, the town's monthly craft fair is open for brisk business. Among the handknitted items and homemade candles, several stalls sell culinary delights, be those pies, cakes or, on one stall, a bewilderingly wide selection of local cheeses.

It strikes me that, should Stranraer wish to reinvent itself, rebadging as a foodie destination would be a fruitful avenue along which to venture, possibly based around an annual food festival, making it akin to a Scottish Abergavenny. Just look at how

Wigtown, 40 miles due east of here, dramatically increased its visitor numbers by becoming known the world over as a capital for secondhand bookshops, and has, accordingly, been officially anointed as Scotland's Book Town.

A number of regeneration projects, aiming for Stranraer to regain the groove it once might have had, have been mooted in recent times. These include becoming a hub for watersports, developing and expanding its marina, and the establishment of a marine research centre. All these loose proposals are, of course, based around the town's main geographical attribute – the loch – the scene of such limited activity of late.

There is one new initiative which, if taken up in serious measure, could also help to redraw Stranraer's identity. Last summer, a 250-mile cycle route was opened, linking Stranraer here in the west with the fishing port of Eyemouth in the east. This coast-to-coast route was named the Kirkpatrick C2C, after Kirkpatrick Macmillan, the Dumfriesshire blacksmith commonly heralded as the inventor of the bicycle.

The opening of the Kirkpatrick C2C followed the arrival, in 2022, of a Stranraer leg in the Tour Series, the multi-leg competition that welcomes pro cyclists to race around town centres across the land. The men's race was won by the then US national champion, Luke Lamperti, who led the accelerating peloton past such local landmarks as the Star Fish Restaurant, the closed town museum and the bike-friendly Fig & Olive.

Standing outside the café this lunchtime is a pair of cyclists about to mount their steeds, having fuelled up for their ride ahead. And it's that 250-mile ride that's ahead of them, across the Scottish borders to Eyemouth. The two women had opted for the eight-day Explorer option, rather than the four-day Challenger version. However, their arrival in Stranraer was later than they hoped. It was only Friday when they realised the trains didn't run all the way here, and so reached the start line a day late, having had to beg for a ride across from Edinburgh. The pair now only have seven days in which to complete the route, so will have to recoup a day somewhere along the way. Not today, though. This afternoon's ride will be a relatively modest 40 miles to the town of Newton Stewart.

When the route opened last summer, a local amateur cyclist by the name of Josh Wood was invited to see how quickly it could be completed. Josh did well. He reached Eyemouth within 24 hours: 52 minutes within 24 hours, to be exact.

However impressive this maiden ride was, that record will be expected to be broken several times in the coming years. It certainly will if the Kirkpatrick C2C comes on the radar of endurance cyclist Mark Beaumont. He holds the record for the fastest ride of the NC500 around the Highlands. Despite it being more than twice as long as the Kirkpatrick, Mark completed it in a time that was less than five hours more than Josh's time.

Today's cycling duo aren't fussed by such records; they want to take in some of the views at a more leisurely pace. The only issue is that the new route has yet to be endowed with proper signage and they don't know where the official start line is. As it's a coast-to-coast route, I suggest they head down the hill to the loch, to the promenade where yesterday it was blowing a hooley. At least the weather is more amenable today, I blithely offer.

As they freewheel down the hill from the café, the first drops of what will become an afternoon of persistent rain can be felt. The weather gods aren't making things easy for their epic jaunt.

Nor for mine. I pull up the collar of my jacket and head back towards that desolate concrete jetty and the bus replacement service.

4

TALES FROM THE RIVERBANK

Newcastle Airport–South Shields

Chania, Antalya, Marrakech, Dubai…

These are destinations which, on a sharply cold early morning on Tyneside, feel impossibly glamorous, impossibly warm.

Here at Newcastle International Airport, I'm not heading into the skies. Instead, I'm shuffling across the concourse. Past the 24-hour branch of Greggs, where four members of His Majesty's Border Force are currently tucking into their start-of-shift sausage sandwiches. Past the branch of WH Smith where I once witnessed Clare Balding spend 20 minutes reading that day's *Racing Post* cover to cover rather than buying it. And then down the curling slope to the Metro station, the most northerly point on Tyne and Wear's dedicated rail network.

For Chania, Antalya, Marrakech and Dubai, see Bank Foot, Felling, Simonside and Tyne Dock… For the next hour or so, we'll be riding through Newcastle's suburbs and centre, before crossing the river and heading for the coast. Destination: South Shields.

First opened in 1980 between the stations of Haymarket and Tynemouth, the Metro extended to South Shields four years later. Further extensions have meant that it now comprises 60 stations set along 48 miles of track – or, rather, 78 kilometres, the Metro being the only rail network in the country that refuses to use imperial measurements.

There are only a few other passengers on this early-morning service: a couple of air stewardesses, the odd just-landed business type ready for a day of hard-bitten negotiation and an American family who get on board just as the beeps announce that the doors are closing. The mother asks one of the ticket inspectors if this is the correct train to 'New Castle'.

'Aye, pet. All trains stop at the promised land.'

The square, squat train, in its familiar black-and-yellow livery, quickly fills with schoolkids and commuters as it rattles through the city's northern suburbs. By Kingston Park, the third stop, it's already standing room only in this carriage. The various smells linger and converge. Just-extinguished cigarettes. Cheap deodorant. The tang of hangover-shortening energy drinks. The whiff sits on the air, the outside temperature too cold to allow any windows to be opened.

Across the flatlands of Newcastle's northern suburbs, across innumerable barrier-free level crossings. Car-bound commuters just have to wait; the Metro takes priority, the main artery pumping workers into the heart of the city.

The schoolkids spill out at South Gosforth and the carriage thins for a stop or two. At West Jesmond, they're replaced by university students, silent compared to the chatty schoolkids, their ears cocooned in headphones.

Between West Jesmond and Jesmond, I glance up at a shallow curve of houses through the bushy embankment. This is a very significant street in Newcastle's cultural history. This is Lily Crescent where, in 1979 in one of the bedrooms of number 16, *Viz* was born. The comic – which, from such small origins, brought the nation such unforgettable creations as Sid the Sexist, Billy the Fish, and Buster Gonad and His Unfeasibly Large Testicles – would, at its peak in the early 1990s, shift more than a million copies of each issue.

Accordingly, from the proceeds of a comic started in his bedroom in his parents' house, Viz's founder, Chris Donald, became wealthy enough to live out a particular dream of his: setting up home in a converted railway station, which he did by swapping the Newcastle suburbs for rural Northumberland. Chris didn't stop there. He reportedly bought several more decommissioned stations, a stretch of the old Alnwick–Cornhill line and even a locomotive. Unsurprisingly, railway devotees got unbearably excited that he had designs on reopening the line, but any plans to do so have yet to be made flesh.

Chris's fascination with railways was surely cultivated when the Donald family moved into Lily Crescent in 1970 when he was 10. 'Moving there was a bit like *The Railway Children*,' he once told the *Independent*, 'except my brother looked nothing like Jenny Agutter. And still doesn't.'

The line was just a few yards from their front door and would get even busier, five years after Viz's launch, with the coming of the Metro. By then, making lewd comics had replaced Chris's trainspotting hobby, from which he'd retired in 1978 upon reaching adulthood. 'I decided to walk away,' he later wrote in the *Oldie*, 'to rinse out my flask and hang up my binoculars for good.'

After Jesmond station, the Metro heads into the darkness, burrowing and burying its way underground for the stations that service the city centre – Haymarket, Monument, Central Station. With no view out of the window, I look around at my fellow passengers, all gazing down at their phones. The man sat opposite – with neatly parted hair but sad, bloodshot eyes – is watching various clips of US police officers pulling over errant drivers on freeways.

Next to him sits a lad in his mid-teens playing a game on his phone. He's wearing head-to-toe Sunderland FC-branded leisurewear. His tracksuit bottoms show his initials: TO. Clearly a scholar in the club's academy, he's off for another day both on the training pitch and in the classroom. Across the aisle sits his dad, chaperoning him to make sure he doesn't miss the day, that he doesn't damage the opportunity of a lifetime. The father is constantly on his phone, talking in hushed tones. He's possibly the boy's agent too. I surreptitiously Google the lad and discover he's Trey Ogunsuyi, a young striker who's been at the club since he was 10 and who has represented the Belgium U18s side.

Even international footballers take the Metro. With their dads.

I next notice a man, with short ginger hair and a neat ginger beard that's just starting to silver, standing next to the driver's cab at the front of the train. He's wearing a Metro-badged jacket and is holding a driver's handbook of rules and regulations. I leave my seat and start asking questions.

A driver himself, and an instructor of drivers too, today he's assessing the performance of the man at the controls of our train, checking for speeds, early observance of signals, that kind of thing. It turns out these regular assessments are necessary.

'You can be driving for up to nine or ten hours a day,' he explains to me. 'Four and a half hours on, half an hour break, and then another four hours on. Everyone thinks it's an easy job. It isn't. You need total concentration at all times.'

After Central Station, where the American family take their leave in unquiet fashion, the train bursts out of the darkness and into the sunshine, clearly anxious for a hit of Vitamin D. It's the best vista on the entire line, the stretch where the Metro crosses the Tyne. Just downriver is the Tyne Bridge itself, and beyond it the distinctive architecture of the Glasshouse International Centre for Music (the new name for the Sage), its shape and texture resembling that of a giant armadillo.

'Do you ever get bored of this view?' I ask the assessor.

A shake of the head.

'You never see it. Eyes to the front. There's an important signal coming up. Really important. You see that green light?'

He points to a light at the entrance to a tunnel on the southern bank of the river.

'If that were yellow, it's basically saying "You're not getting into Gateshead station." And you've hardly got any time to come to a stop before this light here…' He points to a yellow light just a couple of hundred metres on. If the earlier one had been yellow, this would be red.

He nods to himself. 'Total concentration.'

We're back into the darkness, underneath Gateshead. This means there's no chance of catching a glimpse of the Brutalist multi-storey car park off which Michael Caine's character Jack Carter despatches a crooked businessman in *Get Carter*. It later turns out there's another reason why I can't catch a glimpse of it. It was demolished in 2010.

We head back into daylight and past Gateshead Stadium, heading east through south Tyneside towards the coast. Trey the footballer continues his game, his father continues his softly spoken conversations. The lad's prospects at 17 are rosier than they were at that age for the most famous footballing son of our next station stop: Felling.

Chris Waddle was famously working in a sausage-seasoning factory when Newcastle United, the arch rivals of his favourite club Sunderland, plucked him from non-league obscurity and made him a Second Division player. They paid the 19-year-old's club, Tow Law Town, the princely sum of £1,000 for his services. He would go on to play for England 62 times (including in a World Cup semi-final), win three French league titles with Marseille, play in two FA Cup finals and be named Footballer of the Year in 1993. Not a bad rescue act.

In his junior days, Waddle played for Pelaw, another residential area of Gateshead and where I have to change trains. This one will continue to Sunderland and beyond; I need to wait just a couple of minutes for a service on the Metro's 'yellow' line to take me to South Shields.

Pelaw didn't exist before the railways came. It was just bridle paths and fields until the Cooperative Wholesale Society Ltd – aka the Co-op – decided to place much of its manufacturing base there at the turn of the twentieth century. A mile-long row of red-brick factories were built, housing all manner of trades, from drug manufacture to printing, bedding to grocery-packing. A labour force was drafted in from the Co-op's stronghold of Lancashire, transforming the previously rural area into a noisy, productive centre of industry. Those brick buildings are mostly all gone now, though. The last of Pelaw's factories to face the wrecking ball was the shirt factory, which bit the dust in 2011. A supermarket now sits on the site. But its sign isn't the pale blue of the Co-op. It's the royal blue, yellow and red of Lidl.

Chris Waddle wasn't the only world-class sportsman to emerge from south Tyneside. Born exactly two months before his fellow Sunderland supporter, Steve Cram – the 'Jarrow Arrow' – was one of this country's greatest-ever athletes, a world champion, a two-time European champion, a three-time Commonwealth champion and an Olympic silver medallist. Also, for a period of eight years from the mid-1980s onwards, no human in history had ever run a mile faster than him.

Running is in the blood of south Tyneside. Another Olympic medallist, Brendan Foster, hails from nearby Hebburn and was the founder of the Great North Run, one of the world's most prestigious half-marathons, which weaves its way from Newcastle city centre out to South Shields.

Of course, Cram's birthplace of Jarrow is more famous for a journey by foot that was distinctly further than his favoured 1,500 metres. Over 27 days in the October of 1936, around 200 men marched from the town to London to protest about Jarrow's deplorable economic conditions – and, by extension, its moribund employment opportunities – since the closure of a major shipyard a couple of years earlier. In 1936, those who worked in the ship-building industry were three times more likely to face unemployment than the national average.

On reaching Westminster, a petition was handed in to the House of Commons via the Jarrow MP, Ellen Wilkinson, insisting that 'work should be provided for the town without delay'. While, to the crusaders' dejection, the Commons failed to debate the petition and its demands, the depth of the reception that they received as they strode towards the capital was impossible to ignore. The symbolism of their resolve and determination would form the foundation of sweeping social change the other side of the impending war.

After Jarrow, and just before we reach the next station stop of Bede (named after the area's most famous monk, the Venerable Bede), sits the current iteration of south Tyneside's contribution to the rag trade: the Barbour factory, where waxed jackets are produced for retail outlets in 55 countries across the world. As well as its products religiously being worn by Hollywood style icon Steve McQueen whenever he went motor racing, Barbour is of course also the outerwear of choice for those who fancy themselves to be in close proximity to the upper classes. The factory's location offers an uncomfortable juxtaposition. There's no such proximity to the upper classes, close or otherwise, here on south Tyneside. One in three children is from a household in poverty, while a quarter of the population lives in one of the 10 per cent most-deprived areas in the country. Perhaps a new crusade to London is needed.

At Bede, a group of gobby teens get on, relentlessly effing and jeffing despite the presence of several senior citizens and a handful of pre-school kids. The childminders are sending daggers to the youths, but they're oblivious to us all – and to their behaviour. They're lost in their own little world, where nothing matters more than deciding which ride will be the first they'll go on at the fairground in South Shields and which drinks they'll be downing before doing so. (The most popular answers are 'the fucking Matterhorn' and 'fucking Strongbow'.)

The trains into South Shields don't stop in quite the same place they used to. Until the summer of 2019, they ran to King Street, but now come to a halt a hundred or so metres earlier, up above Keppel Street. The new station is airy and bright and modern, and comes with a pair of escalators to ease passengers' onward passage.

There's a queue at the top, though, the reason for which soon becomes clear. A couple of the noisy youths are trying to ascend the down escalator. It soon becomes obvious why. At the bottom are a pair of police officers, whom the youths are clearly trying to avoid, possibly for misdemeanours more serious than riding a few stops on the Metro without a ticket. They reach the top and hide around the corner.

The voice of one of the officers floats upwards. 'I saw you, Sean. I know you're there. I'm not going to chase you up and down the escalator.

'Either come down or I'll go and have another chat with your mam.'

My first stop in town is the museum on Ocean Road, both for culinary nourishment in its café and historical nourishment via its exhibits and display boards. Having been welcomed in by a rather threadbare stuffed lion, 4,000 years of south Tyneside history are subsequently unveiled. I learn that, from the fifteenth century onwards, South Shields was a major centre for the harvesting of sea salt, an industry that ran alongside its buoyant fishing heritage.

But it's in the nineteenth century that the town's industrial might was truly unleashed, focused primarily around shipbuilding, mining and glass making. Indeed, so strong was the former that, by 1861, one in three of South Shields' adult males were employed in its shipyards. These were boom times: the 1801 census records the region's population as being a tad more than 14,000; by 1901, it was 12 times that.

I also learn that, before the dawn of the ice cream van and its sickly chimes, local gelato institution Minchella's would sell their wares in mobile fashion via horse and cart. Further enlightenment comes with the revelation that, five years ago, the 2,000th branch of Greggs opened right here in South Shields. Take those plaudits wherever you can.

I wander through the town centre, under the old Metro bridge and towards the river. Across in North Shields, the cruise liner

Balmoral, bedecked in the blue and white of the Fred Olsen company, sits in port on the opposite bank of the Tyne, readying itself for a five-night cruise of the Norwegian fjords. Despite there being North Shields and South Shields, the latter is known locally as 'Shields', as though North Shields, just a few hundred yards away across the water, doesn't exist.

The former hunting grounds of long-deceased shipwrights – Robert Wallis, Brigham & Cowan, John Readhead – now lay silent, either turned into car parks or open leisure spaces or still awaiting the dawn of their next life. And there is some new life in this part of town. For instance, take The Word, 'the National Centre for the Written Word', which stands in a striking circular building next to the town's market. Arranged over four floors, the first impression is that 'the National Centre for the Written Word' is a fancy-dan phrase for a library with an in-house café and shop. Further investigation, though, reveals a range of exhibitions, workshops, book clubs and even chess sessions.

Most are using it as a library, though, whether just popping in to see if the new instalment of Richard Osman-penned cosy crime is in stock or lingering a little longer. At one table, a man appears to be munching his way through a Tupperware container of mussels while he charges through the latest literary effort by *Strictly* prancer Anton du Beke. This is much to the annoyance of the senior citizen sharing the same table who's earnestly under-taking some local history research. Whether the choice of snack or the choice of reading matter is the source of annoyance is never clarified. Both, I suspect.

I disappear into The Word's extraordinarily well-stocked selection of music books, where I could happily spend the rest of the day, if not the rest of the week. There'd be plenty of paninis and artisan coffees in the café downstairs to survive on.

Instead, though, I need to make my way south, where a figurative call to prayer reminds me to undertake my own local history research.

A 15-minute walk from the town centre, the Al-Azhar Mosque on Laygate makes claim to being the UK's first purpose-built mosque, a claim surely challenged, it has to be said, by the more attractive Shah Jahan in Woking (where, fact fans, Paul Weller's mum used to be the caretaker). Whichever came first, the Al-Azhar does have an extraordinary boast that no other mosque in the world can make. On one Saturday in the summer of 1977, it was the crucible for the blessing of Muhammad Ali's wedding.

Yes, *that* Muhammad Ali.

It's a story that appears too tall to consider, were there not plenty of documentary material available to disprove the doubters. Ali had been invited by the South Shields-born former boxer Johnny Walker, who'd met him in Chicago and asked for assistance in raising funds for boys' clubs on Tyneside. Cue, that July, a British Midland plane carrying Ali, his wife Veronica, their 10-month-old daughter Hana and an entourage of 11 others, descending out of the skies at Newcastle Airport.

After landing, Ali took an open-top bus ride through South Shields, waving to well-wishers in a rather less formal way than Elizabeth II, celebrating her silver jubilee, had done on the same open-top bus, on the same streets, just the day before. The queen one day, the king the next.

Ali then visited Ron Taylor's Boxing & Wrestling Academy, casting an expert eye over a pair of teenage scrappers. 'I wanna box! I wanna box!' he called from the sidelines, before climbing into the ring, sparring in his shirt and tie with one lucky, wavy-haired lad.

Then came the marriage blessing at the Al-Azhar Mosque. 'Somebody showed me a picture,' Ali told a local television crew, 'and it looked like a beautiful place. It looked like it was built to be what it is.' Ali had 'married' Veronica in Zaïre ahead of 'the Rumble in the Jungle' in 1974 while he was still married to his second wife. He and Veronica then got officially hitched in California three years later, a month or so before their trip to north-east England. The mosque was packed that day. So too were the surrounding streets. Around 7,000 came for a glimpse of the king, for a flash of his smile, for a snatch of an off-the-cuff quip.

The extraordinary events of that summer's day back in 1977 are recalled and examined in a documentary film called *The King of South Shields*, made by a local filmmaker by the name of Tina Gharavi. Well, kind of local. Of Iranian heritage, Tina grew up in and around New York City, making her a highly unlikely chronicler of the social history of South Shields. But, after visiting her parents, who were at the time living in the Midlands, she successfully applied for a job at a college in Northumberland, teaching television production. North-east England was quite an alien landscape, as she tells me when I pay her office a visit.

'It was very different from New York. I was fascinated and so interested in everything I found. The people, the history, the accents... I could barely understand anyone. I was just interested in the social history. I learned about the miners' strike. It was much more interesting than New York. I knew New York too well. It was almost boring to me. I grew up there, or near there, from the age of twelve. What you know is not too interesting.'

After two years away studying for an MA in France, the magnetic lure of the north-east was too much and Tina returned to take a teaching role at Sunderland University. But it was a certain town eight or so miles to the north that captured her heart.

'I went to visit South Shields and fell in love with it. It was like a sleepy 1950s seaside town with quirks and character. And the coastline is so beautiful. I bought a house in the town and I'd see these Yemeni men in their seventies, eighties and nineties at the post office or at the doctors.

'I bumped into an actor I knew – a guy called Darren Palmer. He told me about the Yemeni community. I asked him about the mosque.

'"You know Muhammad Ali got married there?"

'"What are you talking about? You're mad. That's not a thing."'

Tina took herself off to the local library where the records confirmed one of the most unlikely stories in the life of the world's most famous boxer. Stumbling on this tale, yet to be told in a documentary and with plenty of archive footage available, was gold dust to a filmmaker. 'It led me to meeting him,' she smiles, 'and becoming very good friends with his daughter Hana, who's in the film.'

Pinned to the noticeboard above Tina's desk is a photo of Ali flying into Newcastle back in 1977. Another photo from the visit – one that was the main image of both the documentary's promotional poster and DVD cover – shows a young boy gazing up at Ali in wonder and devotion. A beatific glow washes across the boy's gentle face.

'I thought about what that would have been like for that kid, what would it have been like to meet your hero – because Ali was my hero too.' Tina tracked down that young boy for the film, now in middle age, the beatific glow faded somewhat. His recall was poignant. 'I just remember thinking, *The champion of the world. What them hands have done...*'

The King of South Shields hasn't been Tina's only project within the town's sizeable Yemeni community. Another endeavour – encompassing a documentary, an oral history project, a book, workshops and a video installation at Baltic, Gateshead's centre for contemporary art, which involved the men's stories being relayed on a row of vintage TV sets that were sourced from the local community – is *The Last of the Dictionary Men*. It's Tina's attempt to record the life experiences, simultaneously extraordinary and ordinary, of the community's elders before their entire generation slipped away. These were men who served in both the Merchant Navy and the Royal Navy during World War II before settling into quiet existences on quiet streets in quiet South Shields.

'After 9/11, these Muslim men were just seen as a threat, despite the fact they'd live in Shields for many years. They'd been good citizens; they'd married and integrated. Theirs was a very positive immigration story, one which I thought I should try to tell, to capture.

'I knew these men were disappearing, that they were fragile. For a while, they were always like, "Why do you want to tell my story?" They thought I worked for social services or the tax office as I was asking about when they got married, how many children they had… Their story was now being, in some sense, recognised. Previously it had either been abused or neglected. These men had been in the Battle of the Atlantic. Seven thousand Yemenis from Shields died in the Battle of the Atlantic. That's a huge number.'

The first recorded reference to a Yemeni presence in the town, in the pages of the *Shields Gazette*, came in 1890. They came to serve in the Merchant Navy and in south Tyneside's shipyards. They came and they multiplied, often with the local white population.

'Twenty per cent of the Shields population have a genetic connection to the Yemeni community. They just might have blond hair and blue eyes. The British see themselves as something very homogenous – and that's about the least accurate thing you can say about the British.'

It turns out the Yemenis weren't the first Arabs in Shields. That came much, much earlier – around AD 170 in fact. 'Seventy men from the modern-day Tigris River, from modern-day Iraq and Iran, were conscripted into the Roman army,' Tina explains. 'These men, the Tigris bargemen, knew how to move stone on rivers in order to build the fort here in Shields. The fort is called Arbeia. Arbeia means "land of the Arab".'

The telling of the history of Arabs here on Tyneside, whether from Roman times or from the late nineteenth century onwards, had largely been ignored before Tina rode into town. Indeed, on my circuits of the museum earlier, the only mention of the Yemeni community I could find was a brief mention of their cuisine as part of a temporary exhibit about local food. As Tina says, neglected. And so much more of a story than that one – albeit extraordinary – day in 1977.

Today at the mosque there are no such crowds, no such super-star cameos. It's just time for the usual midday Dhuhr prayers, so a stream of men of all ages start to arrive – by foot, by car, by taxi or, in one person's case, freewheeling on a bicycle, the chain of which has become disconnected. Near the mosque's entrance, a quartet of pro-Palestinian activists attempt to hand out leaflets for a forthcoming march against the bloodshed in Gaza. Not a single person arriving for prayers takes one.

Across the road, on a patch of fenced-off grass too small to be called a park, a pair of border collies, oblivious to the ongoing warfare in the Middle East, chase a rubber ball in the sunshine. In a nearby block of flats, a pair of painter-decorators are having a heated argument, their potty-mouthed words escaping through an open window.

From the mosque, I continue my way eastwards, passing through the suburb of Chichester (pronounced *Chai*-chester), the location of the many, many novels of local lass Catherine Cookson. I wander through the neighbourhoods of Westoe and Harton, both of which do nothing to disprove my theory that the wider its roads, the more affluent an area (dual carriageways notwithstanding). Here, neat Victorian terraces and handsome villas twinkle in the sunshine on generously proportioned avenues.

My destination is Harton Cemetery, a vast resting place with thousands upon thousands of graves and headstones. Some are startlingly well maintained, their dark-granite headstones buffed to a shine. Others have fallen into chronic disrepair, the deceased no longer having any surviving relatives who were actually around during their lifetime and thus remember them. Subsidence is an issue in several parts of the cemetery.

A widow quietly chats to her late husband as she tops up the bird feeder above his grave. A grateful squirrel hops onto the feeder, leaping from a neighbouring headstone. Not everyone's respectful. A pair of gulls are pecking the seeds out of an arrangement of sunflowers, while a speeding, headphones-on cyclist is taking a racing line on the corners of the cemetery's avenues as if he were descending an alpine peak in the Tour de France.

Sturdy, solid north-east names can be found on headstones right across these plots: Armstrong, Stephenson, Brewis, Charlton. On the far side, in the quietest section of a quiet cemetery, lies the Muslim section. Here, what's conspicuous is the proliferation of headstone names that hint at the depth of integration in Shields over the generations, over the last century or more.

Elizabeth Zenib. Tracy Majeed. Ronald Ahmed. Thelma Mufti. Mohamed Prendergull. Susan Saleh. Margaret Basha…

Although segregated in their own section in the furthest corner, these names are proof of the fluidity of the local population during their lifetimes. These too are sturdy, solid north-east names.

I wander on, over towards the coastline. It's time to eat.

Colman's Seafood Temple is my destination, a restaurant born out of one of the town's most legendary of local chippies, one that's been in operation since 1926. This comparatively new venture stands on the site of a bandstand formerly known as Gandhi's Temple. No one knows why it was called that. Unlike a certain former heavyweight boxing champion, it's not recorded that the Indian leader ever paid the town a visit.

The *Observer*'s food critic Jay Rayner recently dropped by the Seafood Temple to judge its fare and left for London a devotee. The sea bass – 'the length of my arm' – received hearty praise in his review, as did most of the menu. 'You can come here for something light and dainty. Or you can come here for something that will harden your arteries at twenty paces. If you're planning a walk on the beach afterwards, leaning into the wind, do go for the latter.'

The Seafood Temple is suitably shaped; it looks like an ocean-going liner. The bandstand represents the rounded stern (and is now home to an oyster bar), while the sharp lines of the 'bow' give diners the feeling that they're just about to be launched into the waves, cutting through the North Sea's cold waters for distant, exotic ports.

I'm not about to be one of its 'passengers', though. It's reservations only (possibly since Rayner's gushing visit) and I don't have one. I have to make do with a takeaway instead. A chip stottie and mushy-pea fritters.

Fortunately, the weather is more forgiving than it was on the day Rayner visited. I eat my dinner on what should rightfully be called a boardwalk. It might be constructed from concrete rather than wooden boards, but its elevated position above the beach is made for strolling, and its benches for canoodling couples. There are no couples here this evening, though, canoodling or otherwise. Instead, it's just me and them gulls. They line up in an orderly queue, waiting for a chip to fall from my stottie.

I watch the waves gently tumble onto the golden sands of Sandhaven Beach, the surfers larking around in the breakers, the dogs chasing crows. This could be Coney Island, waiting for its high-season trade. Perhaps that's the appeal of the place to Tina, the former New Yorker.

I wander up Sea Road to Ocean Beach Pleasure Park, where the screams exaggerate the fairground rides' mild peril. I fail miserably with the wonky guns of the shooting gallery and receive moderate whiplash on the dodgems.

The sun heads low and the Friday-night kids have come out to play. There are angsty teenage tears in the arcade, candy-floss-flavoured wails of regret and promises of revenge. 'Why would he go with *her*? I'm gonna punch her lights out…'

The air in North Marine Park is scented by numerous joints being lit, by furtive smoking in the bushes. A lad on a modestly powered motorbike pulls a wheelie along the entire length of

Ocean Road, speedbumps and all. His pillion passenger, whose backside is pretty much scraping the tarmac, throws both arms in the air, like he just don't care.

This could be Coney Island, baby.

I leave them to it and take the Metro back out of town, imagining it to be the D train back to Manhattan. The Tyne will be my East River.

I nab that precious front-row seat as we roll off towards the horizon. If I wanted to spot the trackside signals that I learned about on my outward journey, I wouldn't be able to. The horizon, the window and the carriage are all ablaze with the brightest, Fanta-orange surge of retreating sunlight. It's blinding. The train's controls have clearly been set for the centre of the Sun.

My own controls are somewhat less ambitious. I'm going to Middlesbrough.

— 5 —

VAMPIRE WEEKEND

Middlesbrough–Whitby

Many of the destinations on my countrywide itinerary are among those less frequented by the casual traveller. They are places rarely visited without a reason. Not so today's port of call, Whitby – a magnet for visitors by the thousand all year round.

The town's popularity, though, can't be measured by the meagre number of passengers waiting to take this morning's first train there from Middlesbrough station. To be fair, it is 6.54 a.m. on a Saturday. There are only a dozen or so of us heading that way this early, although this would be two fewer had I not checked that the young couple on the platform busy being infatuated with each other were booked on the service just about to depart. The young man's hair touches down to his belt and he's holding what can only be described as a wizard's crook. This is not a typical scene at Middlesbrough station.

I call out to them. 'This is the Whitby train.'

'How did you know we're going there?' the man answers, tucking his hair behind his ears and his crook under his arm.

Just a hunch. All 12 of us are up this early and heading for the coast for one reason: the Whitby Goth Weekend.

An alternative-looking couple in their thirties have managed to get their three kids up early for their day trip. The kids don't look remotely alternative, but they're clearly obeying a three-line whip from their parents regarding today's clothing. All three wear Adidas tracksuits. Crucially, though, all three wear *black* Adidas tracksuits.

The eldest child, the daughter, slumps her head on the table in front of her and promptly falls asleep. Her mother looks like she could passably be the frontwoman of All Above Eve, while her father's fingers and wrists display numerous examples of the silversmith's art. Later during the journey, he'll pull a small silver tin from his trouser pocket and take a couple of sniffs of snuff.

The train sleepily slides out of Middlesbrough, the town still snoozing under a heavy grey duvet of cloud. Out of the window, its landmarks slip past: the Transporter Bridge, a high, wide and handsome feat of engineering once described by the poet Ian Horn as 'a giant blue butterfly across the Tees'; the docks' clock tower, which all operations here on the Tees would have worked to; the Riverside Stadium, home of Middlesbrough FC.

The train heads through its southern suburbs, the sun doing its best to push that duvet of cloud aside. The guard issues an announcement as we approach Marton, one that he'll repeat at most of the 15 stations between here and Whitby.

'For passengers leaving the train here, please be advised that only the doors of the middle carriage will be unlocked. All other doors will remain locked.'

A pause.

'How do you know if you're in the middle carriage?' he continues. 'If you can see me, you are.'

The train grinds on through the remnants of Middlesbrough, over deserted dual carriageways, alongside dew-encrusted meadows, through gnarly woodland. Past Nunthorpe, the coun-tryside opens up, the countryside that makes this particular stretch of the national network – the Esk Valley Line – one of the most desirable to ride on. The impressive Cleveland Hills rise to the south, while just to the north is the steep, nobbly peak of Rosebery Topping, a pyramid of sandstone with the sun now appearing over its silhouette.

The next landmark is the nearby Captain Cook's Monument. Born in Marton, Cook went to school in Great Ayton, the village in the shadow of Rosebery Topping, onto the slopes of which he would often retreat as an adolescent. He then undertook a three-year Merchant Navy apprenticeship in Whitby; after the success of his later voyages, the town took him as one of its own. Cook would have loved the Esk Valley Line, linking the formative loca-tions of his life before he became the celebrated ocean-going explorer.

The wizard's-crook-toting young couple from Middlesbrough station are also catching up on sleep, also using their table as a pillow, their generous hair spilling all over it. They don't know what they're missing. Out of the window is a landscape they'd surely appreciate. Its nooks and crannies and woods and small valleys create a landscape that shouts 'Here be hobbits'.

The Esk Valley Line is a little gem, a little secret, hidden from view from the rest of the world. It's exclusively rural between the Middlesbrough suburbs and the coast, its stops serving only small villages and hamlets. Kildale station feels particularly remote, like one of those halts on the Far North Line at which just a handful of people get on in any given year. Buildings are boarded up, roof tiles are askew and Japanese knotweed runs amok, bringing the derelict structures into nature's grasp.

It might be the last weekend in April, but the windscreens of cars and vans parked at secluded farms are iced up. Lambs bounce about in the fields, defrosting themselves. The service only runs five times a day, but they're already impervious to the train's noisy grunt and grind.

But, still, there are only so many bouncing lambs that can entertain sub-teen boys dragged out on a day trip that's their parents' idea of fun. The two sons in that family of five want to listen to some music on their phones. I keep an ear out to hear if the three-line whip they've been issued with extends to today's listening pleasure, expecting the carriage to soon be filled with the sound of The Damned or Fields of the Nephilim. Instead, they call up the back catalogue of Michael Jackson, which prompts a history lesson from their parents that attempts to trace the tangled roots of the Jackson family tree while avoiding the thornier rumours discolouring the King of Pop's reign.

The River Esk makes its first appearance between Castleton Moor and Danby, and will accompany us, guiding us, all the way to the sea. It takes a leisurely route, winding and bending and winding some more over rocks, weirs and waterfalls, crossed by the railway tracks innumerable times. (I say 'innumerable', but later tonight, electing to swerve the fleshpots of Middlesbrough and stay in my hotel room, I'll get out a map and count how many times the line spans the river that gives it its name. I make it 18.)

At Glaisdale station, with its deserted signal box now in the control of invasive ivy, our guard is back with a potentially lifesaving announcement: 'Please do not use the pedestrian crossing across the tracks until the train has left the station.' Those pedestrians might be en route for the village's Victorian Museum of Science; not that human traffic towards it is ever heavy. It's not permitted to be so, as the museum's website pronounces: 'Visits are limited to between two and four people, last approximately two hours and are by appointment only. (Over 18s only.)' Youths and pre-teens are therefore deprived of learning about the electro-static generator, the electric telegraph, X-rays, cathode rays and, most thrillingly, Dr Frankenstein's laboratory.

The river thickens and widens the closer we get to the coast. The bridges lengthen accordingly. The Esk is where TV angler and Middlesbrough native Bob Mortimer fished for the very first time. He revisited its waters in the company of his chum Paul Whitehouse for the 2020 Christmas special of *Gone Fishing*, where the pair went in search of grayling and salmon. Whitehouse caught a small sea trout here, one he described as being 'the colour of Yorkshire tea'.

The pair began the episode not aboard a train on the Esk Valley Line, but riding a steam-pulled service on the North Yorkshire Moors Railway. The two lines meet at Grosmont, where a couple of our passengers, preferring the Victorian age of steam to the Victorian age of vampires, get off.

After the villages of Sleights – where the Salmon Leap Hotel offers the promise of athletic fish action on the river – and Ruswarp, the train passes under an impressive brick viaduct before drawing into Whitby. As it readies itself to join the salty waters of the North Sea, the Esk has now matured into a wide river. Beyond it, up on the town's East Cliff, the silhouette of Whitby Abbey broods under darkening skies.

It's not even 8.40 when the train comes to a stop. As goths aren't known for being early risers and as the pre-breakfast streets of Whitby will be empty and quiet, the day's theatre yet to begin, I make a snap decision. The last couple of hours were so glorious, and so cheap is the fare (a full £2.90 each way), that I elect to stay on board, taking in the tremendous countryside all the way back to Middlesbrough, before heading straight back out to the coast again. I'll still be back here by lunchtime.

Three minutes later, the doors close and we head back upstream. The journey unravels in reverse, fresh views and fresh perspectives around each bend. The lambs are still bouncing, the cars have defrosted, the day is awakening. We approach Rosebery Topping from the opposite side. It looks dramatic whichever direction you come at it from.

When we (me, plus a handful of Whitby residents escaping the goth invasion for a day of shopping) arrive in Middlesbrough, the day has fully awakened. Platform 2 is now thronging with passengers, many jostling for position in order to secure a seat on the Whitby service due to leave in seven minutes' time. From their attire alone, it's clear that everyone is going all the way to the coast. The fastest member of each party is primed and ready to bag that all-important table for them and their companions.

I've been in situ next to this window since before 7 a.m., so I'm sorted, but so popular a draw is the goth weekend that the train is oversubscribed; several on this service will be forced to stand the entire way to Whitby. As we head back out – back past the Transporter Bridge, the clock tower, the football stadium – those waiting on the platforms at Marton and Nunthorpe and Great Ayton wear pained expressions when they see the standing-room-only service pull in.

If the earlier train hummed with a gentle peace, the 10.19 service is an altogether livelier affair. By comparison, it's practically a carnival. Prosecco is popped and hip flasks are handed around. The muted conversations of the earlier train ride have been replaced by free-flowing banter tossed around the carriage. Strangers are strangers no more. The tribe is everyone's tribe.

'I love your hair,' one woman calls out from her seat towards another woman standing up, before they embark on a conversation about the best hair-dye brands for the richest shade of burgundy. Similarly, two men are discussing the cheapest website for Victorian-style top hats. I feel distinctly under-dressed – in that I'm not dressed-up at all. Another conversation, between two young goths who weren't even born at the time of the band's heyday, place New Model Army's albums in order of preference.

The more hardcore revellers swap memories of Goth Weekends past ('Dream Disciples definitely played in '97. I remember because I was snogging Blackpool Robin throughout!'), while notable festivalgoers no longer with us are lamented ('He never looked the healthiest specimen, but fifty-four is no age').

This year marks the 30th anniversary of the festival, a gathering initiated in 1994 when a Barnsley-born goth called Jo Hampshire corralled, through the pages of the *NME*, like-minded souls to spend the weekend at Whitby's intimate Elsinore pub to celebrate goth culture and the town's gothic atmosphere. The expected number of attendees was around 40. Two hundred turned up.

A year later, so the *Whitby Gazette* reported, the number of attendees reached four figures, with the idea of making this an annual pilgrimage having fully taken root. Within three years, it had become a twice-yearly event. That year, 1997, the *Gazette* tried to placate concerned local residents about this double invasion: 'Many of the goths are professional people and they were generally well received last year.' Further reassurance came with the news that the Revd Graham Taylor, the vicar of St Mary's Church up on Whitby's East Cliff, next to the ruined abbey, would be 'conducting a special service for the goths'. How full his pews were remains unrecorded.

Many thousands now descend on the town, clad in black and often heavily made up. No more an expression of a small subculture, the festival is a firm fixture of the Yorkshire coast's cultural calendar. A 'Mecca for goths' is how Jo Hampshire has described the pilgrimage. 'The town has taken us into their hearts,' she told *TNT* magazine. 'Locals love talking to the goths. You see pensioners getting their photos taken with them all the time.'

When my train stops at Grosmont for the third time this morning, a less than cheery pensioner gets on board, trailing a basket on wheels behind her. I give up my seat for her. I've been sat down long enough. She doesn't thank me though.

'I had no idea it was this weekend,' she says with a sigh. 'How is it time for this again?'

However, within a few minutes, she's chatting away to the Chinese goth sat next to her, fascinated by her armfuls of tattoos and multiple piercings. Jo Hampshire was right.

Whitby looms into view again; the town clocks are still yet to strike noon. The train releases its black-clad human cargo. Four lads on the platform wait to get into an emptying carriage. 'Here we go,' says one, eyeing up the new arrivals. 'Here's a load more for the freak show...'

If the train was busy, so too are the narrow, cobbled streets of Whitby. Were someone in a hurry, they wouldn't be able to be. The town is full of interlopers. Many, many interlopers. And they're slow-moving. This is the weekend for those who believe there's something of the night about them. And aren't they keen to let the world know.

Along the cobbles of Church Street, a fashion parade is effectively taking place, with the most extravagantly dressed only too pleased to pose for photos. There's a gaggle of amateur and semi-pro photographers organising semi-formal set-ups in front of particular vistas or in the entrances of tight alleyways. And there's a definite correlation between men of a certain age with long lenses and women of a younger age dressed up as blood-sucking sirens. These photographers are certainly far less interested in the countless men of their own age done up like undertakers.

'Fancy-dress fuckers,' mumbles one young male goth as he passes a couple pushing a vintage pram, inside which is a blood-covered doll. 'It's a lifestyle,' he grumbles to no one in particular, 'not a weekend hobby.' As a commitment to his tribe, he wears a vial of blood on a leather necklace. I suspect it's Ribena.

Whitby is the international capital of the goths for one reason, one man: an Irishman by the name of Abraham Stoker, better known as Bram. His most celebrated work, *Dracula*, was partly set here and, ever since – and especially in more recent years – the town has been Goth Central. Had Stoker chosen to have his protagonist arrive either up the coast in Staithes or down the coast in Robin Hood's Bay, things in Whitby would be somewhat sleepier on two particular weekends of the year.

And it's *Dracula*, that nineteenth-century slab of gothic horror, that provides the glue this weekend, the intersection of a Venn diagram involving pale-faced, kohl-wearing goths and hopelessly devoted Victoriana enthusiasts. The latter, usually in late middle age (at least they are here today), are disciples of the steampunk movement, that strange amalgam of Victorian culture and retro-futuristic science fiction. The men are instantly identifiable by their uniform of top hats, goggles and imaginatively sculpted facial hair. God knows what that grumpy young goth thinks of *them…*

Certainly, the definition of goth appears to have widened over time. The handle used to be the reserve of young folk who would haunt the market squares of provincial towns after dark, with their unsubtle make-up, home-dyed hair and communal bottles of high-strength cider. At least when applied to this weekend's antics, 'goth' now seems to mean 'any alternative types whose favourite colour is black, regardless of the depth of their love for and knowledge of the Sisters of Mercy'.

Progress continues to be slow on the town's pavements and streets, whether paved or cobbled. An older woman on a mobility scooter is getting nowhere fast against the flow. 'Hello? Can you not see me?' she yells. 'I knew I should have stayed indoors this weekend…'

Passage is even slower on the famous 199 steps up to the abbey and St Mary's Church on East Cliff. I'm reminded of those pictures of latter-day Everest climbers patiently queuing on the mountain's slopes, a human snake inching its way towards the peak and a photo opportunity. 'Let's just stop here and admire the view,' says one out-of-puff goth to his wife, reaching for his vape as though it were an asthma inhaler.

There are photo opportunities a-plenty at the summit of East Cliff, the graveyard offering an immediate backdrop of not only plentiful tombstones, but also of the town and harbour down the hill. No photos are permitted inside the church, where a make-shift sign pinned to the door hopes to relieve those working here of having to answer an eternal question.

PLEASE DO NOT ASK STAFF WHERE DRACULA'S GRAVE IS AS THERE ISN'T ONE. THANK YOU

Across the way, in the English Heritage gift shop, the celebration of Stoker's most enduring character couldn't be described as slight. They've gone all in, with many and varied gifts using the Dracula name. Fancy a tipple? The Castellum Dracula wine range comes as a merlot, a rosé or a sauvignon blanc. On a tight budget? A leather Dracula bookmark will do the job, with the 'Dracula' design echoing the 'Batman' logo. A bit chilly? Warm up with a Dracula hoodie, featuring the same logo.

The rest of the stock is thoroughly goth-appropriate too, with the same dark and brooding silhouette of the abbey reproduced on fridge magnets, tea towels, coasters and pencils. There are also bat cuddly toys and a 'Freaks Like Me Drink Tea' mug-and-spoon set. For those whose gothic sensitivities can't cope with today's bright sunshine, a Victorian-style black lace parasol can be yours for £42.50.

A man with a soft southern Irish accent is asking one of the shop assistants how much a bottle of Mr Fitzpatrick's Blood Tonic Cordial is, swiftly and precisely converting it to euros. His voice brings the Dubliner Bram Stoker back to the forefront of my mind, wondering how astonished the author would be if he were able to somehow join the crowds today and witness the lasting legacy of his most famous work. A commercially astute man (he served as the business manager of London's Lyceum Theatre for nearly three decades), he'd no doubt be gazing around the shop, his brain a whirl with mental arithmetic as he calculated the percentages due to him from sales of all this merchandise.

He'd be getting no royalties from the various editions of *Dracula* that are piled up into a mini mountain of one of the tables in the shop. There are at least a dozen different versions, from basic paperbacks to luxurious hardbacks with ornate engraved covers. A back-to-life Stoker wouldn't be able to claim a penny from them, though. The copyright expired in 1982, 70 years after his death, a deadline that then permitted a slew of Dracula-themed movies, for which Stoker's estate also couldn't claim a penny.

I assume – although, to be absolutely watertight on this point, I'd need to seek legal advice – that he or his estate wouldn't be due a cent on any of this Dracula-branded merchandise here in the gift shop, either. While that might, understandably, make Stoker's blood boil, his compatriot in the queue is of a sunnier disposition. Happy with the conversion rates, the Irishman has matched his Blood Tonic Cordial with a bottle of Whitby Gin, the 'Prince of Darkness edition'. 'Those'll go well together,' he says to the assistant before heading back down the hill, his bottles clinking together with each step descended.

It's not just English Heritage making the most of the commercial opportunities afforded by a 130-year-old gothic horror novel. There are several permanent goth-friendly shops on Silver Street back down those 199 steps and over the river, suggesting a sizeable-enough year-round clientele, one that turns up more often than two weekends a year. Also, by my estimation, the most popular ice cream this afternoon is – but of course – black vanilla in a black cone.

Back on the other side of the Esk, I seek out the Quayside chip shop, not for reasons of sustenance but because, in a past life, the building housed the local library. It was here that Stoker named his main character, finding the name Dracula in William Wilkinson's *An Account of the Principalities of Wallachia and Moldova*.

The chip shop would be one of the lynchpins of any Dracula-themed guided tour of the town, but signs explain that 'Dr Crank' isn't hosting his tour today, suggesting – with such a huge customer base on tap – a wilfully alternative take on running a commercial venture. Instead, further along the quay, is the Dracula Experience, described by the *Daily Mirror* as 'an eerie, spine-chilling show ... gripping'. There's a further recommendation: 'as seen on TV's *Wish You Were Here*'.

The Dracula Experience ends with patrons being sent out through its back entrance onto a back street. None of them look particularly scared, enlightened or entertained. From here, I make another sturdy, sinew-sapping climb, this time up the West Cliff. At the top, at number 6 on Royal Crescent, is the apartment in which Bram Stoker stayed during his time in Whitby and in which he conceived his masterpiece.

You can imagine him, on a blustery Whitby night, staring out to sea through his telescope, trying to catch a glimpse of a fishing vessel attempting to make safe harbour in the swell, and then hearing the cheers of its crew as the boat passed between the twin piers and into the welcoming waters of the Esk. Such a night would have been the inspiration for the conditions in which he imagined the *Demeter*, the schooner on which Dracula had travelled to the Yorkshire coast, somehow making it to harbour in the most violent of tempests with its entire crew deceased.

'The searchlight followed her,' Stoker would write, 'and a shudder ran through all who saw her, for lashed to the helm was a corpse, with drooping head, which swung horribly to and fro at each motion of the ship ... A great awe came on all as they realised that the ship, as if by a miracle, had found the harbour, unsteered save by the hand of a dead man!'

The momentary relief of the onlookers was soon replaced by further unease as the schooner came to a juddering halt among gravel and sand.

'The very instant the shore was touched, an immense dog sprang up on deck from below, as if shot up by the concussion, and running forward, jumped from the bow on the sand. Making straight for the steep cliff … it disappeared in the darkness.' The shape-shifting Count Dracula had arrived in Whitby.

Parts of the apartment aren't dissimilar to how they would have been in Stoker's day, including the telescope still pointing out to sea. But this is no museum piece. Flat 4 – aka 'Bram's View' – is bookable self-catering accommodation, whether for three- or four-day breaks or an entire week. Past renters have, judging by their online reviews, got into a Stoker state of mind while staying within its four walls. 'I managed to reach chapter twelve of the novel,' says one. 'We had to watch at least one of the *Dracula* movies while we were there,' chirped another. The apartment downstairs from Stoker's lodgings is currently for sale, should you fancy a permanent arrangement.

Just near the Royal Crescent, pointing out to sea just like Stoker's telescope, is a statue of James Cook. Invariably, and despite the captain's complete lack of goth credentials, photographers are arranging impromptu photoshoots in front of it. I'm again imagining long-dead historical figures paying a visit to the twenty-first century. What the straight-backed Cook would make of all this black-clad ballyhoo is anyone's guess. I suspect it wouldn't be too positive.

Without Bram Stoker, without Dracula, without the church and the abbey ruins up on East Cliff, would the Whitby tourist industry be leaning much more on the captain's story to entice visitors here? We certainly wouldn't have a mass of goths descending on the town for two weekends a year, pushing prams of bloodied dolls through its streets and performing for the massed cameras. But would a celebration of someone who frequently ordered violent confrontations with indigenous peoples, and who – inadvertently or otherwise – laid the foundations for future British colonial rule, be at all appropriate? Perhaps Stoker and his boy Dracula have actually taken some heat off Cook's reputation within the town, the limelight diverted elsewhere.

And, thanks to film and TV adaptations over the years, the appeal and allure of the count show no sign of abating, of diminishing. If anything, his beguiling hold remains as strong as that over his victims. As Steven Moffat, the co-writer of the BBC series *Dracula* alongside Mark Gatiss, has observed, the book is 'the first time that evil gets to be attractive, and evil gets his name on the cover'. Dracula is the anti-hero who's sunk his teeth deep into his admirers, a figure that fittingly refuses to die.

As rainclouds as dark as the count's cape swoop in from the North Sea, I decide to take my leave and head for the station, not even stopping for a black vanilla ice cream en route. I've travelled to the heart of darkness and now I'm ready for my fourth journey today along that glorious Esk Valley Line. And as I do so, I can reveal the final scores in today's fashion stakes:

Bauhaus T-shirts: 2
Sisters of Mercy badges: 0
Top hats and frock coats: bloody thousands.

— 6 —

'BYE BYE, MUCKY LEEDS!'

Leeds–Morecambe

'm on my own but not alone.

I'm sat here in a train carriage at Leeds station, awaiting the departure of the 12.18 to Morecambe. Young Alan Bennett – 10 years old, bespectacled and sporting the same fringe he'll be gifted with throughout his life – is sitting next to me. Opposite, squeezing three abreast, are his parents Walter and Lilian, and his big brother Gordon.

But Alan and his family are invisible. They're invisible, because they're imaginary. And they're imaginary because it's been 80-odd years since they took this journey, from their home city of Leeds to Morecambe on the coast of Lancashire, travelling westwards from the white-rose kingdom into the lair of the red rose. They are travellers from the past. Last week, 10-year-old Alan turned 90.

Back then, unknowingly entering the last year of the war, they would have been waiting for the blast of whistle and gush of steam to signal their departure. Today, the beep-beep-beep of the closing doors and the loudening grunt of the diesel engine is the cue to leave.

In the Bennetts' day, many other Leeds families headed to the Lancashire coast for a week, or at least a few days, on its beaches.

Alan and his folks were far from an anomaly. And there were reasons why they ventured west, despite the Ridings having plenty of fine resorts of their own: Scarborough, Filey, Bridlington...

For starters, the west-facing coastline offered the prospect of rich, romantic sunsets on a nightly basis. Plus, their crossing of the border into enemy territory possibly emitted the feeling that they were somehow going abroad, going somewhere *other*, that time spent on the other side of the Pennines was the equivalent of crossing the English Channel.

To be fair, the Bennetts themselves did also head to the Yorkshire resorts on occasion; Alan calculated later in life that, being a May baby, he may well have been conceived in a guesthouse in either Filey or Scarborough in high summer. Gordon, another May baby, too.

But Lilian Bennett appeared to favour the Lancastrian resorts. Morecambe – more refined and less brash in the eyes of this woman whom her son would later describe as possessing a 'natural preference not to want to attract attention and to get by unnoticed' – won the day over bold and brassy Blackpool.

Lilian's attraction to Morecambe may well have been transferred to the character of Mam in *Sunset Across the Bay*, Alan's television play from 1975. It deals with the migration of a retired Leeds couple who opt to see out their time in Morecambe. Alan's own parents also made a permanent move west, albeit not as far as the coast, plumping for a village in the Yorkshire Dales instead. What the fictional couple in *Sunset Across the Bay* find in Morecambe, though, is the claustrophobia of retirement, especially in a town where no one yet knows your name. The future wasn't as rosy as they might have hoped – this despite Mam calling out, as their coach heads onto the M62 on their departure, 'Bye bye, mucky Leeds!'

In their day, on their journey, the Bennetts' carriage would have been full to bursting with excitable holidaymakers. Today, ours is decidedly roomy, only about a third occupied. And almost all of those dragging suitcases on board are at holiday's end rather than its start, having flown into Leeds–Bradford airport this morning before embarking on the final leg towards home.

The train leaves the station and traces the line of the River Aire, a two-carriage affair gamely overtaking the LNER service to King's Cross and moving smoothly through twenty-first-century Leeds's architectural mix of futurism and Victoriana. The stone of the high cutting denies a view across to the Bennetts' home patch of Armley.

Not all the holidaymakers are returning from their travels. There is one retired couple heading for the coast, as revealed by the husband's near-instant question 'What time do we get into Morecambe?'

They could be creations from Alan Bennett's pen. He: small, hawkish, milk-bottle glasses magnifying his pupils; she: tidy, petite, garlanded by modern jewellery, nervously checking her watch every two minutes. Their travel documents are carefully ordered in a clear plastic wallet that sits on their table, awaiting approval from the guard. In 40 minutes' time, on the stroke of 1 p.m. and not a minute before, foil-wrapped sandwiches will emerge from a small backpack, ready for consumption.

Lilian Bennett would certainly approve of this. Back in the day – a time of rationing, of course – the budget-conscious Bennetts brought their own food, not just for the journey but for the entire length of their stay. It would be packed into cardboard boxes that they would keep in their boarding rooms. 'I was a bit ashamed of this as a child,' Alan would later admit. 'I thought it was evidence of our lowly status, that we didn't have full board. We just had breakfast.'

At Shipley, a pair of retired men – daytrippers from the show of their modest luggage – get on board. They're joined at Bingley by another couple of pals who take their seats opposite me, rather rudely sitting in the laps of the imaginary Bennetts.

'There's a fifty per cent chance,' says one. 'I'm more optimistic than I was.'

It takes me a little while to realise they're not discussing the likelihood of rain on today's excursion. They're evaluating Leeds's chances in tonight's second leg of the Championship play-off semi-final against Norwich. The first leg was goalless.

By the time we reach Skipton, though, that rain has started falling. At Gargrave, a couple wheel their cases off the train, their holiday over. The man with the milk-bottle glasses studies their tans, possibly with envy.

Outside the window, the landscape of the Dales is an undulating delight, the hills an everlasting lattice of dry-stone walls. You can understand why Mr and Mrs Bennett ultimately left Leeds, mucky or otherwise.

The quartet of retired gentlemen walkers get off at Hellifield. Perhaps they intend to amble to Long Preston, from where, having taken stout refreshment in the Maypole Inn, they'll catch the train back east, back home, and be in a favourite armchair before kick-off this evening. I'm a little jealous, if so.

Other east–west train routes across northern England – say, services into Manchester from Leeds, Sheffield or Barnsley – burrow deep into the limestone of the Pennines. We don't. We head up, over and around rather than pushing through and under. After Long Preston, our train branches off north-westwards, away from the storied Settle–Carlisle stretch and off in the direction of

Giggleswick instead. We trace the northern outline of the Forest of Bowland, heading for Bentham, the town that gives the line between Leeds and Morecambe its name. Why's it called the Bentham Line? What's that station got over any of the others? Why not the Giggleswick Line? Or the Wennington Line? No one seems to know, not least the guard for whom it's their place of daily work. He just shrugs when asked.

Me, I'd petition to call it the Bennett Line.

It's a little wilder up here in the Forest of Bowland than in the picture-postcard Dales. There are fewer towns and villages, and the geography is sharper, stonier, less rolling. Befitting its name, it's more wooded too. But the miles and miles of dry-stone walling remain immaculate.

After Wennington, we coast downwards, over the M6, the motorway's traffic the first vehicles we've seen for about an hour. Very soon after, we arrive in Carnforth, home of – of course – the country's most famous station buffet. Indeed, the whole town is known for one thing and one thing alone: the filming of a certain movie scene, the denouement of an illicit and fleeting love affair.

'What's that film?' a squeaky voice behind me pipes up. '*Close Encounter*?'

There's an extended silence in the carriage.

'*Brief Encounter*!' the voice squeaks to a travelling companion. 'Why didn't you correct me? You've made me sound stupid.'

She lets out a chuckle. She's not embarrassed. The carriage is fairly empty now and I'm probably the only one within earshot – although Mr Milk Bottle Glasses shares a conspiratorial smile. He heard too.

So synonymous is Carnforth station with the 1945 film that you expect all its occupants to be wearing trilbies and smoking unfiltered Capstans. It's therefore something of a shock to see someone in a shell suit and drinking a can of Red Bull while standing next to a 'Home of Brief Encounter' sign.

A detour back and forth across the River Lune, in and out of Lancaster, removes a smattering of university students from the carriage. Just a handful of passengers are left for the last two station stops – Bare Lane and, at the end of the line, Morecambe.

We're on time, much to the pleasure of the watch-checking half of the couple opposite.

I help them off with their suitcases. Mr Milk Bottle Glasses gives me another smile. 'Let the good times roll…'

Eighty years ago, once out of the station, the four Bennetts – struggling under the weight of those cardboard boxes of food supplies – would have staggered towards the northern edge of town. Here, presumably, nightly rates were less onerous on the shallow pockets of butcher Walter's wage than those of boarding houses closer to the action. (As it was, Walter didn't always stay the full week; it was mostly just a few days of separation between him and the meat counter at the Co-op.)

The Bennetts, semi-frequent visitors to Morecambe, knew where they were going. I don't. I turn right out of the station, heading towards the town's Arndale Centre.

There are 23 Arndale Centres in the UK, Arndale being the name of the company that built them, a compound of the names of its two founders, the entrepreneurs Arnold Hagenbach and Sam Chippendale. Often portrayed as dazzling symbols of post-war modernity, many Arndale Centres have seen better days. It's certainly not unfair to place Morecambe's mall in this bracket. If it represents the pulse of the town, this is a place where the heartbeat is decidedly slow. A third of its units are vacant. Of those that are occupied, the discount bookshop The Works is the most upmarket store. 'Get Lucky' plays over the PA, possibly ironically. Around the corner, The Jam's 'That's Entertainment' spills out of a charity shop's speakers, an anthem of urban neglect, with its ripped-up phone booths, smashed glass and screaming sirens.

It's the luck of the draw, or the misguidance of instinct. Had I exited the station and headed straight ahead rather than turned right, taking the shortest route to the seafront, I'd have been greeted by an altogether very different first impression: a wide, sun-kissed promenade, golden sands, a view across the bay towards the southern fells of the Lake District, an array of public art and, to the left, the curving magnificence of the art deco Midland Hotel.

One of those examples of public art is the much-photographed statue of the town's funniest son: Eric Bartholomew, aka Eric Morecambe. It's arguably the most recognisable statue in the entire country, one instantly identifiable from its dancing silhouette alone. During daylight hours, it rarely goes more than two minutes without being approached by someone ready to snap it.

Eric's birthplace, a modest house on Buxton Street, is equally modestly celebrated. Unlike the childhood homes of those other major contributors to post-war British culture, Lennon and McCartney, the house hasn't been placed in the tender care of the National Trust. Its front door remains closed to fans fancying a poke around. The man is, though, namechecked across the town. Eric's Café sits across the road from that bronze statue, while the Morecambe branch of Wetherspoon's is named The Eric Bartholomew. The Eric Morecambe House care home brings sunshine to those in the late evening of their lives.

Morecambe has a new local hero these days: one Tyson Luke Fury. Despite being born in Manchester and growing up in Cheshire, the boxer has made Morecambe home for him and his family. 'I love it,' he told an ITV documentary crew. 'I would never leave Morecambe. It's true beauty. If the weather was better, every house here would be a million quid.' His love for the place, his keenness to do right by it, can be measured by him once contemplating standing as its MP.

Fury's first foray into the local property market was a two-bedroom bungalow, before upsizing to a larger home on Morecambe's northern outskirts, a five-bed property overlooking the bay. Upsizing was necessary with a rapidly growing family. And continued to be. Home is now a new-build mansion on the southern fringe of town, a house large enough for Tyson, his wife Paris and their seven children: Venezuela, Prince John James, Prince Tyson II, Valencia, Prince Adonis, Athena and Prince Rico.

I take a stroll to have a gander at the house, on the way passing the Mazuma Mobile Stadium, home of both Morecambe FC and a Fury-owned gym. While the Fury homestead does speak wealth – most notably the pair of stone lions out front – it doesn't do so hidden within the depths of a gated community. It's right here, in full view of the passing B-road; no high fences or leylandii to obscure, to camouflage. Only a single 'CCTV in action' sign suggests someone of import lives behind its walls.

Fury has not courted the sanctity of seclusion. The house is just along from a caravan park while, four doors down, a neighbouring bungalow has been reclaimed by nature, the foliage of bushes consuming the house. A rusting tractor, along with the remnants of both a caravan and a campervan, are also being eaten by the encroaching plants. The Fury homestead, in comparison, is immaculate.

A small Peugeot zips past, its driver giving two flyweight parps on its horn towards the house, towards the local hero. Fury won't hear the two-note salute, though, He's more than 3,000 miles away right now. He and his entourage are currently in Riyadh.

In two days' time, Fury will be taking part in what can justifiably be called – in, of course, the most over-hyped, never-knowingly-undersold sport of them all – the fight of the century. The last time that the right to be crowned the undisputed heavyweight champion of the world was contested, the last time all four title belts became the possession of just one man, was back in 1999 when Lennox Lewis achieved the feat. The hype this time around keeps amplifying; the fight has already been postponed twice. The noise around it is now deafening.

Serious boxing history will be made in Saudi Arabia on Saturday night. Whether the holder of three of those belts, Ukraine's Oleksander Usyk, will add a fourth to his collection, or whether Fury will bring them back to Morecambe, will be decided in 48 hours' time. If it is the latter, you can expect many more people driving past this pile on Oxcliffe Road, honking their horns in salute, a chaotic, unsynchronised fanfare.

But, whether in possession of four world title belts or not, Fury won't change. He won't move to Vegas or Dubai.

'I don't really do much, other than stay in Morecambe Bay,' he told the *Guardian*'s Donald McRae. 'I very rarely even go to Manchester any more. I don't like holidays. I've no interest [in them] because it's headaches and hard work. Imagine going to the airport with seven kids, dragging all them cases.

'My idea of a good day is getting up early, going for a run, dropping the kids off at school, and then I found this really long walk. There's nobody on it, so I can take the dog for a walk in privacy.'

Fury doesn't always keep his distance, though. He can often be spotted doing the family shop in the local Asda, or taking training runs along the prom. The town's residents are his people. And he is their man.

Whether inspired by him, or hopeful of an accidentally-on-purpose encounter, the prom is well-used by runners. And by cyclists and dog walkers, too. During my time in Morecambe, I'll come across three different dogs all called Tyson (who knows, perhaps back in the day 'Eric' was the most popular name). The last dog was the best, a bouncy cockapoo. Another cockapoo lives with him. He's called Fury.

'I got him six months after Tyson,' his owner explains. 'There was only ever going to be one name for him.' (This reminds me of the time a friend of mine was walking through Bristol city centre. 'Luther, come here!' an exasperated mother called out to her toddler son. 'Sit back in the pushchair next to Vandross...')

From Fury's gaff, I saunter back towards the town centre through the West End, a once-thriving neighbourhood that's faced many economic and social challenges during these decades of decline. It's livening up for the evening, but today's cast of characters are the kind you'd speed up your step to move away from. Here, eye contact lingers longer than it should, and smiles possibly betray true intent. One man, his breath stiffened by drink, approaches with an 'Alright, pal?' greeting. It feels less a concern about your general well-being and more a confirmation about whose territory you're on. Another man is hoarsely shouting through the entrance door of the Co-op.

I'm reminded of a couple of lines in David Seabrook's spooky, extraordinary book *All the Devils Are Here*. Although writing of the inhabitants of another seaside town, Margate, his words fit the here and now. 'There are the young men of the front, this front, all bare arms, body art and fast-working furious faces, faces that ought to be spouting water from the walls of Gothic buildings. But they're here, and they speak, spraying spittle.'

Another man is pissing against the door of a church. Someone else is riding a mountain bike round and round in the middle of the street, his wheels tracing circles. Vulture circles. This is definitely not the place to pause on a street corner to jot down notes about how this is definitely not the place to pause on a street corner to jot down notes. Keep those thoughts for later. Set them in ink once in safer lands.

And safer lands soon arrive. While my budget doesn't quite stretch to a stay at the Midland, it does at least allow me to dine there. The hotel was built in 1933 and so named because it was constructed by the London, Midland and Scottish Railway as an upmarket residence for Morecambe's better-heeled visitors. Grade II-listed, it's a very fine example of the art deco style, being renewed and refurbished in 2008. Along with the Eric Morecambe statue, it's a true icon of the town, a striking white beacon on the seafront.

Alan Bennett's family could never have considered staying there; they probably just gazed at it from the outside, almost certainly never to cross its threshold. I'm gazing at it from the outside too, admiring its gentle curves. But I can't help but notice that it's not quite as strikingly white these days, even in today's bright light. It could definitely use a lick of paint. 'Off-white' would be a generous description; 'chewing-gum grey' is closer to the mark. But this is understandable. It is, after all, the building in Morecambe that's closest to the sea, the first line of defence here on the seafront, the first to be hit by onshore winds and salty spray.

The Midland's interior doesn't let itself down, though. It's cool, calm and kind of timeless inside, and is where television adaptations of the novels of Agatha Christie have been filmed. Thankfully, there are no murders waiting to be solved this evening – just a fine dinner in the rotunda restaurant. The food – a sweet potato and coconut curry, a glass of Madri – hits the spot, as does the view. The floor-to-ceiling windows offer a glorious panorama across the bay towards the Lakeland fells, behind which the sun is preparing to set.

There's plenty to see at ground level too, as Morecambe continues to make full use of its seafront. A woman on a pair of roller skis pushes her way along the prom, just before a man on a fat-tyred electric bike hoves into view. He pulls a wheelie and the bike slips out from under him, throwing him chest-first onto the unforgiving tarmac. His embarrassment is heightened by a pair of patrons in the hotel's outside drinking area serenading him with beer-flavoured laughter.

On the next table, an elderly man and his 60-something son enjoy their weekly meal together. This evening, while gazing across the bay, they're debating just how far away the sun is. 'I wouldn't know if it were a million miles or twenty-two million,' concedes the father, gamely sawing away at his venison steak.

The descending sun moves from yellow to a deeper hue, burning orange over the western edges of the fells. It's a long goodbye, a slow retreat, as its tangerine glow meets the shadows of the incoming tide. And that incoming tide can't be contemplated without thinking of the 23 Chinese cockle-pickers who died here on the bay's cockle banks in 2004, enveloped by the sea, unable to escape.

After dinner, the lightshow isn't quite over. The sun has disappeared behind the westernmost peaks, but pinks and purples illuminate my passage to The Eric Bartholomew. I head there in the hope of catching the second half of the Leeds game, but they're not showing it. I'm advised that another pub around the corner will have it on. With Leeds three-up at half-time, I expect a boisterous atmosphere inside. But not a single soul is paying attention. Were this 80-odd years ago, during the great holiday migration from the West Riding, this place would be packed to the rafters with Leeds fans, the roof raised when their side's fourth goal goes in.

Although, of course, that would have been half a century before Sky Sports was invented.

Instead, I turn half an ear towards the chat on the next table where the most vociferous drinker is loudly praising the charging capacity of his Tesla.

'Much better than I thought. Haven't run out of juice on the motorway yet.'

His short-sleeved shirt is struggling to contain his muscular upper arm, upon which a series of numbers is tattooed. I presume this to be the date of his wedding or of a child's birth, but no date contains eleven digits. It turns out to be a mobile number. Above it is the name of a building firm. It is the most imaginative way, but also the most baffling, to advertise your services. Bicep as billboard.

I wander back to my B&B further down the seafront, past a karaoke bar where inside someone is murdering – *murdering* – Rod Stewart's 'Baby Jane'. The B&B is a traditional establishment that saw better days a fair time ago. My single room with its single bed – one that has all the structural integrity of blancmange – at least faces west: to the sea, the bay, the Lake District. But my stay here certainly can't be mistaken for a solid night's sleep cocooned in comfort in one of the Midland's £200+ rooms. The bedside lamp flashes intermittently, the floor emits a creak when even a sock falls on it and the mattress keeps sinking low, low, low. And there's a set of traffic lights right outside, so the impatient revving of car engines waiting for the light to turn green becomes the soundtrack to my attempt to summon sleep.

When I check out the following morning, puffy-faced and bloodshot-eyed and eager to beat a retreat, I notice – which I hadn't done last night after dark – that the B&B is wrapped in scaffolding. Perhaps, like Morecambe itself, renewal for this wobbly establishment is on the horizon. Better times to come. Better times to return.

I'm ahead of schedule, so take a final circuit of the town. While I do so, I phone my friend Liz, the only person I know who's from, or has lived in, Morecambe. She spent the first 18 years of her life here in the town, after which she escaped to the West Country a couple of years into the new millennium, and where she's been ever since. I want to get her take on the town. For me, it appears to occupy some kind of purgatory, stuck somewhere between the hope of rebirth and the reality of decline.

'When I was growing up in the Eighties,' she says, 'I think it was already seeing a big decrease in visitors. The ones who did come – and still come – are those who came as children. They all still flock for those Morecambe Bay sunsets, fish and chips by the Clock Tower and a 99 from Brucciani's on the prom.

'I'm northern, so I don't have much time for sentiment and self-indulgence. I could not get out of there fast enough in 1998, and not in a million years would I have returned to Morecambe after university. I was always drawn to the brighter lights of bigger cities. Don't get me wrong, I loved coming home from university, but it just didn't have the employment opportunities. Plus, all my school friends had dispersed all over the country, so there wasn't much to entice me back in 2002.'

Liz remembers 'a weird mix' around the town when she was growing up. There was the older generation still clinging on to the memories of the town's heyday, despite 'the best-known landmarks from those heady days – the Winter Gardens Theatre and the Midland Hotel – having been shuttered up and left to rot'. There was also a sizeable and burgeoning younger population. They were catered for in a number of ways: the Western-themed fairground known as Frontierland ('how no one died there is beyond me'); the Polo Tower, a tall, thin tower with a viewing area at the top and which was sponsored by the manufacturers of the famous minty sweet; and an indoor/outdoor swimming pool with a wave machine called Bubbles.

All are now long gone, demolished, turned to dust. The site of Frontierland remains flattened, its future still unwritten. At least it's bounded by bright-blue fencing, along the length of which is displayed equally bright artworks and paintings by local young artists. They lend a splash of modernity to the place.

Also gone is the Dome, Morecambe's main music venue during Liz's youth. 'I saw Pulp there just after they'd released "Common People". Oasis and Blur also came, but I wasn't quick enough to get tickets. The Radio 1 Roadshow would set up outside too.'

Liz's verdict on the town doesn't mirror Tyson Fury's evangelism about the place, but it does chime with my impression: that Morecambe remains in some kind of limbo, clinging on while waiting for the developers' dollars.

'It's an odd one, as the Midland and the Winter Gardens have been completely restored, and the prom has had some serious investment. There's also now a train that runs along the prom, a trampoline place, bowling, a cinema... So, it's definitely seen growth in some areas, but places like the West End are still woefully run down. It's an eyesore. I think everyone's just hoping that the Eden Project will finally happen and will inject some much-needed life and prosperity into the town.'

The opening of a second Eden Project, on the site of the old Bubbles pool, has kept the town's population in suspense for many a year. Its promise to 're-imagine Morecambe as a seaside resort for the twenty-first century, inspiring wonder and a connection with the natural world' is still waiting to be fulfilled. Plans were first unveiled back in 2018, and planning permission granted by Lancashire County Council in 2022, but, a further two years on, site investigation work has yet to begin. The latest word is that the project could be 'edging towards' opening in either 2027 or 2028. *Could be edging towards.* Talk about hedging your bets.

Even without an imminent arrival for Eden Project Morecambe, Liz still finds reason to head back up the M6 on a fairly frequent basis. 'I return there every two or three months as I want my elderly relatives to see my four-year-old as much as possible. Morecambe is turning a corner, I think, but taking its sweet time over it. Its appeal for me, now, is nostalgia. I want my son to know where I grew up and where his grandad lived. And to appreciate those epic sunsets…'

I'm turning a corner too, away from the bay and towards the station, where the prospect of retrieving some shut-eye on the train out of town awaits. Well, an hour or so's kip once I've changed trains at Lancaster, at least. I'm changing trains as, like Walter and Lilian Bennett, and like Mam and Dad from *Sunset Across the Bay*, I'm not returning to Leeds.

I am heading inland, but to the Derbyshire peaks instead. First, though, a town called Manchester.

HIGHER GROUND

Manchester Piccadilly–Buxton

Manchester Piccadilly is a proper railway station.

The city's main terminus after the closure of Manchester Central (later known as the exhibition hall GMEX) in the late 1960s, Piccadilly is by no means an architectural gem. Its appeal is in what it offers: the potential, the possible.

It sprays passengers in each and every direction. East to the various cities and counties of Yorkshire. West to the Lancashire coast, Merseyside and north Wales. North to Newcastle, Glasgow, Edinburgh. South to Birmingham, Cardiff and London. It's quite possible to believe that, from its 14 platforms, you could get anywhere from here – or, at least, close to anywhere – in a single hop.

Of course, that also means that trains arrive here from anywhere – or, at least, close to anywhere. It can be one busy place.

And, this Friday lunchtime, it seems to be carnival time. Or at least the station's employees think so, blowing their whistles with all the fervour and frequency of a round-the-clock partygoer on the streets of Rio. Adding further carnival colour, an amateur musician plonks himself down at the public piano on the concourse and picks out the notes of Professor Longhair's 'Go to the Mardi Gras'.

These days, Manchester is party central for the weekend brigade and spirits are already high for those stepping off the constant flow of incoming trains. For them, hedonism awaits. The watering holes of the city welcome all-comers with open arms and generous drinks offers.

But there are plenty of passengers this lunchtime who are heading in the opposite direction. Outwards and beyond.

A family of six, the attire of the female members suggesting a connection to the Church of the Latter-Day Saints, weave their way through the chaos of the concourse. The four young children gaze around at the exuberance unfolding before them. Their parents hurry them up; the next train to Liverpool Lime Street leaves from faraway Platform 14 in six minutes. The family continues its snaking path through the hordes, a human chain. A pair of middle-aged women are also in a hurry to make their connection. As much as the busy concourse allows, they jog towards the waiting Norwich train. 'Oh, it's like *Race Across the World*, this,' chuckles one of them. Those taking the train to Manchester airport have the luxury of a travelator on their platform. One holidaymaker sets his suitcase down and attempts to moonwalk. He and his fellow passengers will glide to the airport terminal, as will those heading for Euston or Edinburgh, thanks to the smoothness and comparative hush of electric-powered travel. Those of us striding towards the 12.51 to Buxton will be noisily grinding our way to our final destination, taken there by the rumble and grumble of diesel.

If trains had rear-view mirrors, that's where we're leaving Manchester and its increasingly futuristic skyline, one that's in a state of constant redefinition as the next sharp-as-a-blade tower heads towards the heavens. Instead, we motor on through the city's southern suburbs.

Through Levenshulme, cradle of comic actors Arthur Lowe and Beryl Reid, the architect Norman Foster and original Oasis drummer Tony McCarroll, who grew up here a mile or two from the bolshie Gallagher brothers of Burnage.

Through Heaton Chapel, whose most famous son, John Alcock, was one half of the piloting pair to first fly across the Atlantic.

Through Stockport, hometown of Labour deputy leader Angela Rayner, actors Craig Cash and Joanne Whalley, and 10cc and their famous Strawberry Studios. The imaginatively named Stockport Viaduct carries us up over the M60 and half of the town centre, high above the new Stockport Interchange. The latter is described by the developers as the town's 'gateway to the region' and 'a key part of Stockport's £1 billion regeneration'. In this case, 'interchange' appears to be a posher way of saying 'bus station'.

As we cross Cheshire, other trains heading in the same direction, especially those bound for London, speed blurrily past, heading south at a true lick. Ours not so. We're the stopping service into one particular corner of the Peak District. And I've no problem with our comparative dawdle.

In this half of our carriage, we all sit facing the direction of travel, as if we were on a bus or an airliner. With no table seats, random or spontaneous conversations can't break out between those sat opposite each other. Everyone keeps to their own. When a conversation does occur, the comparative silence means it's hard not to eavesdrop. From seats in front of me, there's talk of NHS waiting lists ('Maybe I should ask our vet to do the procedure. Our cat got her op the same day she was diagnosed'); from behind, affairs of the heart are under the microscope ('I'm not taking his calls. He can stew for a bit. Contemplate his dickhead ways').

At Davenport, sixth-formers released from their studies for an early Friday finish join the carriage and start planning their weekends. Two lads – pierced ears, hair tumbling into their eyes – discuss which boardgames to take round to Jack's house tonight. It's all rather sweet and innocent, unless 'Scrabble' is code for cider, and 'Cluedo' a euphemism for crack cocaine.

A blind man gets on at Disley, but strangely refuses several offers to sit down, electing to stand all the way to Buxton. A very friendly fox-red Labrador is led through the carriage, his nose raised to the air, taking note of everyone's lunch. His owner keeps him on a short lead, continually apologising.

The first half of the hour-long ride has been pleasant if unremarkable. The second half will offer much more. After Disley, suburbia slows and the peaks that give the area its name announce themselves in the middle distance. After a few days of train travel across northern Britain, they look an attractive proposition to this carriage-bound rider of the rails, a chance to detour, to clear the mind and stretch the legs.

A sign at New Mills Newtown advises that this is the station at which to alight 'for the Millennium Walkway and the Sett Valley Trail'. I'm tempted to get off and try either. Or both. The next stop – Furness Vale – dangles even further temptation, being the station that serves 'the Peak Forest Canal and the Midshires Way'. Walkers around these parts are clearly spoiled for choice.

At Whaley Bridge, the sixth-formers largely depart, including the two lads for whom a night of boardgames/hedonism (delete as appropriate) is on the cards. A flock of birdwatchers also leaves here, all binoculars and sensible footwear.

The train presses on and the peaks continue to rise, some pointed, others more rounded. Every time the carriage clips a trackside bush, a confetti flurry of leaves flutters through the open windows. Some land on the fine grey hair of a snoozing senior citizen. He doesn't wake up.

As well as tourist signs explaining this is where passengers for Eccles Pike or Combs Reservoir need to leave the train, the platform at Chapel-en-le-Frith station also features another sign of interest. Certain small towns in the US like to boast, on 'Welcome to' signs on their outskirts, their connection to a particular industry or company. Bentonville, Arkansas is the unlikely host of the headquarters of Walmart, the planet's largest retailer, for instance, while Battle Creek, Michigan is the base of the Kellogg empire. The sign on the platform at Chapel-en-le-Frith announces the town to be 'Home of Ferodo'. The brake manufacturer has been here since 1902, a major employer across the intervening years.

There's a horrible irony here. For also on the platform is a plaque, a memorial to two railwaymen 'who gave their lives in the line of duty at this station'. On 9 February 1957, John Axon was driving a freight train towards Chapel-en-le-Frith from Buxton when he realised the brakes had failed. Rather than leave his post, he remained in position as the runaway train accelerated down the hill towards the town, in an attempt to minimise the extent of the potential carnage. At the station, the locomotive smashed into the rear of another freight train, killing both Axon and the other train's guard, John Creamer. Axon was posthumously awarded the George Cross for his efforts to keep the loss of life as low as possible.

It's a chastening story that I reflect on as today's train climbs that hill towards Buxton. We're high above the valley now, the terrain rockier once we reach the tops, a landscape presumably on the dark side of inhospitable on days less balmy and benign than today. And then, suddenly, we're here, at journey's end. Buxton – nestled high in the hills, high up at the end of the line.

I know three things about Buxton. And they're all music related.

1. It has an opera house.
2. Echo and the Bunnymen played live in a venue in the town's Pavilion Gardens for the central element of their 1981 film *Shine So Hard*.
3. It is the birthplace of Lloyd Cole.

Oh, I lied. There's a fourth thing I know. It's a spa town, its waters drunk the world over.

Indeed, Buxtonians – like the residents of other spa towns – are pioneers of sustainability, leading the campaign against single-use plastic many generations before plastic was even invented. Buxton's waters pour from St Ann's Well, a continually flowing fountain in the centre of town, from which local residents are invited to fill whatever receptacle they wish. This afternoon, one resident has half a dozen of the largest water bottles imaginable lined up on the pavement, ready to be filled. She needs to use both hands when carrying each one back to the open boot of her car. However, strangely, the free availability of the freshest, cleanest water doesn't stop visitors electing to pop into the visitor centre to pay for a bottle of the stuff instead.

Free water is far from Buxton's only attraction. It boasts a cultural life far deeper and richer than towns twice, three, four times its size, including a disproportionate number of festivals, chief of which is the Buxton International Festival. This runs throughout July, offering the cream of opera, classical, jazz, dance and author talks. There's also a parallel fringe festival, along with the annual Gilbert & Sullivan Festival, the Well Dressing Festival (an event where the town's wells are imaginatively decorated, rather than a fashion parade) and numerous food festivals.

The town's social diary is always full, chiefly thanks to the Opera House offering high-calibre culture throughout the calendar. Forthcoming attractions include Swan Lake, Elvis Costello, Dawn French and In the Night Garden Live. The Pavilion Arts Centre next door is home to both a cinema and a comedy club.

If Buxton offers plenty to the culture vulture, those who appreciate fine architecture have much to feast on too. Of primary interest is surely The Crescent, a single semi-circular Georgian building designed and built for the fifth Duke of Devonshire in the late eighteenth century in order to entice visitors of renown and regard to sample the town's delights. It's been immaculately restored in recent times and now, as per this afternoon, entices wedding parties of renown and regard to sample the town's delights. Every other car parked in front is a Range Rover.

The Opera House is just as striking. Built in 1903, it's a terrific example of Edwardian baroque and is believed by many to be the masterpiece of the celebrated theatre architect Frank Matcham. Restored just before its centenary, outside its handsome twin domes dominate; inside, the detailing is both ornate and fun, with mischievous plaster cherubs a popular motif. The dome of the Octagon concert hall in the Pavilion Gardens, where Echo and the Bunnymen played back in 1981, is on a large scale, sitting above the hall's plentiful glass and cast-iron frames.

The Octagon's dome might be impressive, but it's not the largest one in town. That honour belongs to the Devonshire Dome, to the north of Pavilion Gardens. Another building commissioned by the fifth Duke of Devonshire, for many years it was the largest unsupported dome in Europe, its diameter greater than that of the domes of both the Pantheon and St Peter's

Basilica in Rome, and of our own St Paul's Cathedral. Remarkably, the visiting pedestrian can easily miss it, out of view behind a tall hedge. Even more remarkably, the duke commissioned its construction as a mere stable block for the horses of well-to-do visitors taking the waters. It seems just a touch extravagant for that use; I suspect the duke was a bit of a show-off. Later used as a hospital, the Devonshire Dome now houses the Buxton campus of the University of Derby.

Buxton boasts some handsome old homes too, especially on and around Park Road, a looping avenue just west of the Devonshire Dome and with a picturesque cricket ground at its centre. Between 1907 and 1914, number 151 Park Road was the residence of the town's most famous daughter, the feminist writer Vera Brittain, during her adolescence and early womanhood. She recounted her time in her classic World War I memoir *Testament of Youth*, in which she was far from kind about the town.

'I hated Buxton,' she wrote, 'with a detestation that I have never felt since for any set of circumstances.' Bearing in mind that, by 1918, Brittain's circumstances would include the deaths of her fiancé, her brother and her two best male friends, this is quite a statement. But her resentment is more aimed at the stifling middle-class environment of the time, one that didn't actively encourage the easy advancement of ambitious young women. It wasn't Buxton, per se. If she were living in Brighton, Bath or Bristol, she may well have felt the exact same way. Era rather than location.

I'm certainly not feeling the snobbishness and petty values that Brittain felt more than a century ago. Buxton is smart, yes, but seemingly devoid of an excess of airs and graces and narrow-mindedness. It's broad, it's open.

I spend a further hour or two wandering around town, admiring more handsome buildings, browsing its dusty bookshops, sampling the wares of its tea rooms. Not that Buxton's stiff topography is made for idle wandering. The clue is in the place names. Not only is there a Higher Buxton and a Lower Buxton, but one of the town centre's parks is called The Slopes. Buxtonians must have the biggest calf muscles in the county.

While I've been wandering, I've also been considering my options for this evening. It's entirely appropriate that I spend my one night in Buxton absorbing some culture, ideally at the Opera House. However, tonight's turn – Tiny Dancer: The Music of Elton John – far from grabs me. This being Buxton, though, means other options are available. I head to the nearest bus stop to catch the next Transpeak service, which deposits me at the High Peak Bookstore and Café on the very far edge of town. Tonight marks the first night of the fourth and final weekend of Bookstock, a month-long music festival held here in the shop's café.

It's a curious spot for a bookshop, on the site of a decommissioned petrol station on a speedy A-road and surrounded by countryside. But the store has been open, and has been a roaring success, for the past 23 years. 'I've driven past this a hundred times,' one of its first-time customers tells one of the staff at the till. 'I didn't know it was so big.'

I collar the owner, Louisa McPhie, to find out more.

'My mum and dad have always been in books and bookshops – although they had a record shop to start. When they split up, she became a publisher and he opened this place. It was just books for fifteen years and then, eight years ago, my dad wanted to retire because he was seventy-five by then. He asked me if I wanted it. I was a teacher at that point. "Can I do what I want with it? Can I put a café in?" He said yes. "OK, then..." So I came here eight years ago and changed a lot of things. I'm always changing things, trying to improve it.'

The shop's success is not despite its location, but quite possibly partly because of it.

'My dad likes to have out-of-town places. It's definitely more of a destination now that the café's in. People will come and spend hours and hours here. In fact, they sometimes stay all day. Literally all day. And when the festival's on, they can stay all evening too. One chap does. He comes in, sits there, has a coffee, brings a book with him, then has his lunch, then has a little wander around, then has another coffee in the afternoon. I think he's stayed on for three of the music events now.'

Across the café, Louisa's daughter Freya reels off that particular customer's sandwich of choice and favoured coffee. He's a creature of habit and the Bookstore is clearly a sanctuary of sorts for him. 'We have a lot of regulars here,' says Louisa, 'and Freya clearly knows what they all have.'

The location is a clear USP. 'We're a bookshop in the middle of nowhere. I don't wish we were down in the town centre at all. I've got a little shop in the middle of Matlock and it's nowhere near as busy as this place. The quietest days here are the sunny days. On rainy days, though, we are absolutely packed. Because it's the Peak District, there are plenty of people on holiday in the caravan parks and B&Bs and hotels needing somewhere to go. People seem to love it here. It's quirky. It's definitely quirky.'

Behind us, a guitar is plugged into the mains and its tuning checked. Louisa's dad, David, wanders in, looking for a mic stand. 'I think I might have left it at home. Oh well...'

Louisa then reveals the shop's other USP. 'Apart from the local author and local interest sections, and the Taschen books, all of our books are less than half price. But it doesn't look like a cheap bookshop. It doesn't look like the books are going to be cheap. It's not like The Works where it's plastered on all the covers. But people pick them up and say "£2.99? Is that right?" "Yes, it is." "I'll have two then."

'People ask if it's the café that makes the money, but it's actually the books. It's like vinyl. Book-buying is a massive thing again, especially when the books are less than half price. It's a bit like Ikea here. You come in thinking you want one thing and come out with a basket-load. We literally have trolleys at the entrance. People fill them with books.'

This is the second year of Bookstock, adding another chapter to the shop's success story. 'Last year, it was mostly local bands that we had on. And we did it, stupidly, every single night for a whole month. So this year we decided to do four weekends – Friday, Saturday, Sunday, Monday. It's going really well, especially the folk nights and the jazz nights. One of the jazz performers said, "It's like playing at Ronnie Scott's in here. You can hear a pin drop." It is lovely when the lights are off.'

The festival is another string to the Bookstore's bow, to add to Louisa's packed monthly quiz nights ('the best quiz ever') and to the shop's presence as a venue on Buxton's fringe festival. With the town already punching above its weight culturally, Bookstock adds further red-letter dates to the calendar. And it's all done for the right reasons.

'One hundred per cent of the ticket sales go to the performers. We just keep what we take on the bar. And that's fine. We're supporting musicians and giving local people some lovely live music.' It's an admirable attitude.

Louisa's warm welcome extends across the generations. I share a long conversation with David, her octogenarian father, about the glories of non-league football. Then law-student Freya makes me a mug of tea in exchange for me proofreading her latest assignment, which needs to be submitted by midnight. The finishing touches are being made, here in the café, as tonight's musicians run through their soundcheck. Who needs the hush of a university library?

Over the next couple of hours, a trio of singer-songwriters will pay tribute to the late English folk guitarist and singer Michael Chapman, immaculately played songs under the twinkling lights of the café. I'm in no doubt that, in sidestepping an Elton John tribute act, I've made the right decision. I'm sat here with a bottle of an excellent local-ish brew, Chatsworth Gold, and munching on humous-dipped breadsticks, while the dextrous musician Henry Parker shows he's pretty much the equal of legendary folk guitarists like Bert Jansch and Davey Graham (and Michael Chapman himself), masters from a generation or two before. Outside, in the blackness of the A-road, the tail-lights of passing cars are red shooting stars, disappearing in a flash. These drivers don't know what they're missing.

When it's all over, when the last song's been sung, I say my goodbyes and, with next to no effort, blag a lift back down into the town from a kindly soul. I'm deposited right outside the door of my hotel, the end of an agreeable evening populated by agreeable people.

The hotel is most agreeable too. Even though the floor of my room boasts a gradient not dissimilar to that of the railway line up from Chapel-en-le-Frith, it's an infinite improvement on last night's B&B in Morecambe. The character of the place comes with its age. The Old Hall's main point of attraction is that it claims to be the oldest hotel in all England, dating back to the sixteenth century when Mary, Queen of Scots stayed here to take in Buxton's rejuvenating waters to cure her debili-tating rheumatism. Indeed, the windowpane of room 26 is inscribed with words that Mary allegedly scratched onto it using her diamond ring. 'Buxton, whose warm waters have made thy name famous, perchance I shall visit thee no more – Farewell.'

Daniel Defoe visited the hotel around 150 years later, describ-ing it as 'a special place with its own special feeling'. That special feeling pervades today, prompting regular ghost hunts to be hosted in its corridors and corners.

The following morning, after an undisturbed, unhaunted sleep, I take a pre-breakfast stroll in the Pavilion Gardens across the road. Bill Bryson once described them as constituting 'the most delightful town park in the country' and I'm inclined to agree. Today is a gloriously sun-kissed Saturday and I wander around accompanied by a dual soundtrack of the famous waters gushing over a large weir and the happy songs of the Gardens' chirping avian population.

It's only eight in the morning, but the park is busy. A man places a remote-controlled miniature fishing trawler on the broad stream that cuts through the park and steers it back and forth, upstream and downstream, much to the indifference of the local wildfowl. Then he retrieves his vessel and strides with purpose towards the boating lake. That was just a soundcheck ahead of the main performance.

Over near the Octagon, an orderly queue is forming. But, unlike in 1981, this isn't a gaggle of pre-gig, long-coated Echo and the Bunnymen fans. This weekend's event is the Wool Gathering, 'a festival dedicated to the best of yarn, knitting and crochet'. It's possibly uncharitable to note that one attendee in the queue, a spinning wheel sat on the ground before her, has a definite resemblance to Wendolene Ramsbottom, the wool shop owner in Wallace & Gromit's *A Close Shave*.

There's another event happening, down in the centre of the Gardens, just beyond the bandstand. And it seems a more popular draw than the Wool Gathering. Here, dozens of runners are limbering up, stretching those hamstrings and calves, ahead of this morning's parkrun.

New Order's 'World in Motion' cranks into action over the PA to gee up the runners. A couple of pink-bibbed marshals jog and jiggle on the spot. Nobody seems concerned that this is a football song. The sub-pedestrian *Chariots of Fire* theme remains unplayed. One runner, tying and retying his laces, is word-perfect on John Barnes's rap.

Parkruns are famously intended to be non-competitive, but that doesn't stop the more serious runners, wearing compression socks and with heart-rate monitors strapped to their arms, ensuring – ever so casually, feigning nonchalance – that they're at the very front of the start line. Over the PA, there are a few pre-run shout-outs to certain participants. The biggest applause, accompanied by a few whoops for good measure, is reserved for a runner called Mark who's travelled the 120 miles from Middlesbrough to take part in his 600th parkrun.

And they're off, three laps of the Gardens, up and over its gradients, around its waterways, over its bridges. No dogs are permitted on the run, but the marshals are happy to dog-sit while their owners complete their laps. A collie, her lead wrapped around the wrist of a marshal, yelps every time she spies her owner running past.

'Our record number of runners is two hundred and eighty six,' the race director tells me between issuing personalised encouragement over the PA ('Keep going, Will!', 'One more lap, John!').

'I think we might break three hundred today.' She waves an arm to the blue skies. 'Thanks to the weather…'

The whole spectacle is a heart-warming tableau, a sign of bonhomie and fraternity much missing from an increasingly fractured society, even if the elbows-out sprint finish between two runners battling it out for a placing outside the top 10 is a little undignified. The collie barks her approval, at least.

I head back to the hotel for breakfast, on the way spying a poster for yet another cultural happening: a two-day food and music festival being held here in the Pavilion Gardens come August. Strangely, another – different – Elton John tribute act is headlining. Buxton must like the man. I've always been appreciative of a clever name for a tribute act (Earth, Wind for Hire is undeniably the greatest), but Young Elton isn't one. Further down the bill, Noel Gallagher's High-Flying Carpets is a new one on me.

After checking out of the supposedly haunted hotel, and with another hour or two before the train back down the hill to Manchester Piccadilly leaves, I keep on sauntering, guided by no map, just unconscious urge. I could saunter all day.

In certain parts of some of the destinations I've visited so far, the word 'moribund' could justifiably be bandied about. Desolate seafronts, no-hope shopping centres. Buxton could never be described as such. Not a jot, not an ounce, not an iota.

It's well-heeled and sure of itself without being remotely stuffy or toffee-nosed. It's Harrogate without the snootiness and the endless kitchen design shops. And more hills, of course. Definitely more hills.

Aside from a year in landlocked Minnesota, I've always lived within comparatively easy reach of the coast. Most of my childhood years were spent within 200 yards of the high-tide mark. Living inland, with perhaps a half-day journey to the sea, has never appealed. Like many, I've always needed the coastline as a definition, a context, a margin. Being somewhere in the middle, floating, surrounded by great swathes of land on all sides, was never a pipe dream.

But a place like Buxton could make me reconsider. Perhaps it's an altitude thing; being high up in the hills means the sky would be the new definition, the new context, the new margin. Or maybe it's just the great architecture, the rich cultural offerings, the restaurants, the cafés, the parks, the bookshops, the warm welcomes…

That Colorblind James Experience song 'Considering a Move to Memphis' is back playing in my head, in particular the line where the narrator explains that he likes the way that Memphis 'sits there on the map'.

I like the way Buxton sits there on the map too. And, unlike Mary, Queen of Scots, I have no need to scratch a final farewell on a windowpane. I'll be back.

— 8 —

THE LAST RESORT

Birmingham New Street–Pwllheli

Navigating Birmingham New Street station is a complicated enough exercise at the best of times, a Kafka-esque, nine-circles-of-hell kind of place. At first light, though, an hour at which the brain remains foggy and untrustworthy, it's even worse.

We're six hours beyond the midnight hour, but tell that to the gaggle of post-concert Take That fans who, unable to find a room in the fully subscribed hotels of downtown Birmingham, have been rendered homeless for the night. Once the last bar shut in the wee small hours, they've been aimlessly wandering the streets of the city's Chinatown, a journey without maps – or even a sense of direction. All the while, they've been serenading themselves with a medley of their favourite group's greatest hits. And they're doing so much to the annoyance of those who did plan ahead, who did book a hotel room when some were still available. It's a broken night's sleep for us. And it's no sleep at all for the wandering singers.

The streets finally fell silent at 4.30 a.m. This is the hour at which Birmingham New Street opens for business, a mere two and a half hours after it locked its doors last night. Now part of the larger Grand Central complex that houses numerous eateries and a colossal mechanical bull that, partly constructed using materials from local factories, represents the region's heavy-industry past, the station boasts one of the UK rail network's most impressive concourses, one that's on a proper scale. In fact, it calls its concourse an atrium.

New Street station clearly fancies itself as the departure lounge of an international airport. It's actually swankier than most of those. The ultra-contemporary atrium roof, featuring a series of translucent 'bubbles', sets the ambitious tone.

The permanently homeless are already here. The concourse offers shelter for the 21½ hours of the day that the station is open. They shuffle from commuter to commuter, fruitlessly looking for financial assistance in a near-cashless society.

Anyway, enough praise for its looks: back to New Street being one of the most baffling, most infuriating stations around. For no apparent reason, it's divided into three colour-coded zones – red, green and blue – each of which is protected by separate ticket barriers. This often means that passengers changing trains here have to change zone too. And, nearly as often, their ticket won't allow them entry into the next zone.

But the real madness is that the same train can sometimes straddle two different colour-coded zones. If your seat is in a carriage in the front portion of the train, you're instructed to head to the blue zone. But if your carriage is in the rear half, the yellow zone is the one you must stumble confusingly towards.

Furthermore, announcements are only made for delays, cancellations or platform changes, not to announce scheduled departures, which only heightens the sense of confusion. Lost souls wander around, unknowing, asking anyone for the secret code that will unlock onward travel.

Thankfully, my train this morning isn't of a sufficient length to straddle zones. Just two carriages will take me and the other early risers through the Black Country, before bearing due west all the way to the mid-Wales coast, at which point our train will head northwards while largely hugging the Cambrian foreshore. We'll finally come to a stop, just in time for elevenses, at Pwllheli on the Llŷn Peninsula. Four hours, fifty-one minutes and a possible thirty-five station stops lie between me and there.

With a beep, the ticket barrier allows me entrance to the sainted red zone. In the past, decades ago, Birmingham New Street was the crucible for a guerrilla-style photoshoot for the original, pre-dungarees iteration of Dexys Midnight Runners. This musical gang developed a reputation for bunking the train, for leaping over the New Street barriers without paying in order to travel down to London and harangue their record company. They even still did this after they'd had their first number-one single.

This was a generation or so before New Street got all tarted up. The band wouldn't recognise the place now; indeed, they'd surely get confused about which barrier into which zone they needed to vault over, thus increasing their chances of being apprehended by British Transport Police. However, if they did manage to evade the long arm of the law, those eight young men would certainly recognise the platforms underneath the concourse. It seems all the money got spent upstairs. The New Street platforms still inhabit the dark, no-frills subterrania they always did.

The 06.22 leaves on time, moving underneath Birmingham and out into the murk of its suburbs. Then it curls around the outskirts towards the Black Country, underneath motorways and alongside black-water canals that carry little, if any, human traffic now. Rendered impotent by the coming of the railways in the nineteenth century, they were once the arteries that pumped the lifeblood into the region, that fed the dirty industries which gave the Black Country its name. They're now merely the playground of the odd swan, the king of the canal.

At Sandwell & Dudley, two rail employees hold clipboards and jot down the number of passengers getting on and getting off, a rare analogue exercise in a digital world. The train presses on, gliding with a swan's effortlessness over more canals, past golden-minareted mosques and above road junctions already clogged up at this early hour. Let the train take the strain.

On a large patch of waste ground coming into Wolverhampton, early-morning graffiti artists set about a brick wall with brush and spray-can, a billboard on which to exhibit their craft to a couple of dozen passing trains each hour.

Once beyond Wolverhampton's clutches, as the crumbling concrete of the Black Country starts to surrender to the green fields of Shropshire, the music in my head changes. It moves from the uptight urgency of Dexys Midnight Runners and their singer Kevin Rowland to the sturdy, stately melodies of another Wolves fan: Edward Elgar.

Strictly speaking, Elgar was a man of Worcestershire, born and raised there. But the iron-clad swell of his most famous creation, the Adagio of the Enigma Variations – otherwise and probably better known as 'Nimrod' – are perfectly transferable to other, equally green parts of the English countryside.

Despite the clock yet to strike seven, one passenger is receiving an inordinate number of phone calls. And he is not a quiet man. The rest of the carriage is treated to updates of his prodigious vomiting on the holiday he's just returned from. 'I was just dry-retching at the end' is the tasteful denouement of the story he repeats to several callers. His purple suitcase lies on its side, taking up both seats opposite. The luggage rack is empty.

Plenty of commuters get on at Telford Central for their daily short(ish) sprint into Shrewsbury. I play a solo game of Guess the Profession. The likelihood of the guy with the neat beard and mountain bike being a graphic designer is quite high. The young woman in the 13-hole Dr Martens is definitely a student. And the NHS laminate around the neck of the woman who's chosen to stand next to the door is too generous a clue.

I'm already ticked off by the way that the voice of the recorded announcement goes up in intonation when announcing each destination, as if she's unsure of where we're heading – 'The next station is ... Shrewsbury?' – but these commuters have to hear them twice a day, every day. No wonder everyone's got headphones on.

At Shrewsbury, a spaghetti junction of tracks leads in various directions, overseen by a large red-brick signal box that was served its redundancy papers some time ago. Many of the commuters leave here, replaced by optimistic, rucksack-carrying daytrippers in shorts heading across the border into Wales. There is also the welcome sight of a man pushing a refreshments trolley on board.

Three rail workers in Belisha-orange Transport for Wales tabards also get on. Despite their branded hi-vis workwear, the ticket inspector insists on seeing their free-travel passes.

'I've still got to scan them,' he says, attempting a smile. He's greeted by the shaking of heads.

'Thanks, fellas,' he offers by way of appeasement. 'Have a good day.' He's offered nothing in return. Instead, the three of them embark on an appraisal of what's likely to happen this weekend, the final day of the Premier League season.

'Luton are gone. They've got to win ten–nil, I think, and Forest have to lose.'

'United might not make Europe now.'

'What about Villa? Amazing. Ollie Watkins has got to go to the Euros.'

One of the three doesn't join in the discussion. He clearly knows not of what his colleagues speak so passionately and sits there in bemused silence, his eyes doing all his talking, back and forth. Only when the conversation switches to a comparison of the relative merits of a half-board holiday vs all-inclusive does he take part. Rather enthusiastically, too. 'Every cocktail, every night.'

The rolling hills of Shropshire give way to the rolling hills of Powys when we cross the border. A succession of mid-Wales towns come and go – Welshpool, Newtown, Caersws – each separated by stretches of boundless natural beauty. At each, more daytripping walkers in shorts get on, several with dogs.

There are plentiful wooded valleys as we approach Machynlleth, studded by the occasional cottage or wooden lodge – enviable boltholes largely out of sight, out of scrutiny from the rest of the world. Mountains begin to rise in the distance too.

A different guard, one sunnier in disposition than the last, checks my ticket after Machynlleth.

'Pwllheli? That's a long way.'

I know, pal. Twenty-six more stations to go (I'm counting). And another 35 in the opposite direction this evening. Marathon man, me.

At Dovey Junction, a skinny man with tattooed knuckles and a *Taxi Driver* mohawk gets on with a pink-haired woman and a whippet. By the time we reach the coast a short while later, the sunny guard is back on his rounds.

'I've got my old person's railcard here,' says the pink-haired woman, reaching into her bag.

'OK, great.'

'This is the point at which you're supposed to say, "How on earth are you in possession of such a thing?"'

'That's taken as read, madam.'

The wise passengers have taken up positions on the left-hand side of the carriage, bagging those front-row views as we head up the coast, over sands, over estuaries. The water shines blue.

Another Transport for Wales employee, quite possibly an off-duty driver, is one of the few passengers sitting on the right-hand side, leaving the plum seats to the tourists. He's seen it all before. Instead, he's getting lost in the pages of John Connolly's *The Wolf in Winter*, a crime thriller set in a distant, provincial town that guards itself against outsiders. Hmmm…

Aberdovey means sand dunes, cabins on the beach and a golf course. More walkers get on here, ready to tackle another stretch of the coastal path. Yet more of this tribe climb on board at Tywyn. Most are of retirement age. Martin, who perches on the seat next to me, is one of these. He's travelling up to Llwyngwril, before walking back along the shoreline to Tonfanau station, from where he'll catch the train back to Tywyn and his campsite. He's restless to get out there, his leg vibrating. 'Best weather of the week.' He smiles, leaning across me to take in the view. The aqua sea looks properly Mediterranean today. He hopes to have walked 40 or so miles of the coastline before the weekend. It's an admirable – and enviable – hobby.

Static caravans pepper the coastline, while cormorants perch on rocks, drying their oily-looking wings. Before Fairbourne, the train rides right on the edge of a sheer face of cliff, the rocks a couple of hundred feet below. Those passengers whose eyes haven't instinctively shut can watch the gulls below, launching themselves off and out. Our eyes ride on their wings. Across the

Afon Mawddach in Barmouth, empty fairground waltzers await the busy days of high season.

A German man in his sixties gets on here with a couple of friends and retrieves a book from his bag, a guide to wild Wales. He takes alternating glances at its pages and out of the window, his keen blue eyes picking out the local geography. He's a clear Wales-ophile, his pronunciation of certain consonant-heavy Welsh place names more faithful than the feeble efforts of one particular Brummie man who's been on board since New Street. 'We will shortly be arriving at Aberdovey,' said an announcement earlier. 'Abu Dhabi?' was his witless response. Meanwhile, our German friend is syllable-perfect on 'Ffestiniog'. He even gets the joke when the guard wanders back through the carriage. 'Any tickets from the Costa del Harlech?'

There are plenty of canine passengers on this stretch of the journey. Along with Mohawk Man's whippet, there's also a pair of dachshunds, as well as a long-haired, nervous-as-hell German shepherd. 'His first train ride!' his owner explains, trying to placate and appease the carriage for her dog's slightly frantic behaviour.

Before us, the brooding peaks of the Llŷn Peninsula rise from the earth like upturned fangs, drawing ever closer, ever bigger. Once we're beyond Tygwyn, a westward glance gives a middle-distance glimpse of the Italianate follies of Portmeirion village.

As the train approaches Porthmadog, Mohawk Man doesn't let his sleeping dog lie, summoning him awake. He's also anxiously fingering his vape. It's been two hours since Dovey Junction, two hours without a puff. He'll be first off the train. Most of the carriage evacuates at Porthmadog too. A lad in a Wales football shirt, who shares a remarkable resemblance to a young Gareth Bale, gets on, sitting where the whippet has been snoozing for the last hour. 'Are these seats heated?' he asks his girlfriend. 'This one's really warm...'

Transport for Wales's plans to halve the four-times-a-day service between Machynlleth and Pwllheli have recently drawn ire from the county councillors of Gwynedd – and are at direct odds with the fact that today's train was full coming into Porthmadog. There are still plenty of us riding all the way to the buffers at Pwllheli too. Several councillors have indicated how TfW's decision seems in direct opposition to the company's own campaign to reduce car usage and increase passenger numbers on public transport. As one of them, Councillor Gwynfor Owen, points out, 'the way to improve train use is by increasing the number of trains and definitely not cutting them'. This seems irrefutably obvious.

For now, at least, the service is intact. A few miles shy of Pwllheli itself, the railway bisects Hafan y Môr, the holiday camp formerly known as Butlins Pwllheli. The line goes right down the middle of the site, the two halves connected by a road bridge. It became a holiday camp a couple of years after the guns of World War II fell silent; during wartime, it had served as the Navy training base HMS *Glendower*. The first Butlins site in Wales, it offered attractions that at the time would have been regarded as impossibly glamorous: *two* big wheels, water-skiing, go-kart racing and – most cosmopolitan of them all – a cable car.

The camp was a magnet for Merseysiders, who made a great exodus there during the summer months. Liverpudlian stand-ups Jimmy Tarbuck and Stan Boardman were both Redcoats there in their early careers, while Ringo Starr played a three-month residency as the drummer of Rory Storm and the Hurricanes. Even fictional Scousers were drawn to its delights; in 1993, *Brookside* made a rare three-episode excursion beyond Liverpool's city limits, which saw middle-aged shopkeeper Ron Dixon eloping there with his younger paramour Bev. Ron tries desperately to convince her he's brought the couple to some kind of heaven on earth. 'We're staying in a palace, here,' he protests. Beauty is in the eye of the beholder of the credit card.

Many of those Merseyside punters during the glory years of Butlins Pwllheli will have arrived there by train at the dedicated station at Penychain, just west of the camp. To do so nowadays – and, indeed, to board – passengers have to request it stops there. No one does so today. We just breeze on by, with Pwllheli very much in our sights. The final straight.

Eight minutes later, we pull into town. One of the remaining dogs on board seems to realise he's home and lets out a little howl of delight. After nearly five hours' travel, he's speaking for us all.

I'm on a couple of clear missions now I've reached Pwllheli, the first of which is to seek out some decent food after so long with only the refreshments trolley at my disposal. My friend Nigel has issued me with a culinary recommendation: 'the Sparta café by the roundabout in the centre of town, where I had the greatest apple pie and custard of my life'. The trouble is, that was in the early 1970s. 'I imagine it's no longer there.' Nigel's not wrong, although enquiries on the ground reveal the Sparta only closed within the last five years. In its place is a chocolatier.

Nigel also remembers – or thinks he does – that the upstairs rooms of the Sparta, or those of a neighbouring building, used to host clandestine meetings of Mudiad Amddiffyn Cymru, aka MAC, the Welsh paramilitary group once engaged in terrorist acts in the name of Welsh independence. They were led by John

Jenkins, a former British Army officer who was involved in the procurement and planting of bombs to disrupt the then Prince of Wales's investiture in Caernavon in 1969.

Clandestine meetings are quite tricky to Google with any success, so I can't confirm Nigel's vague recollections, but what's not in doubt is the fact that, a hundred or so yards past the roundabout, a significant moment in Welsh political history definitely did occur in the summer of 1925. In a building here on Y Maes, a meeting of six men saw the merging of two Welsh nationalist groups into a new separatist entity, the political party Plaid Cymru. After initially rejecting the idea of standing in elections to Westminster, Plaid put up a single parliamentary candidate in the 1929 general election. It would be 37 more years before the party boasted its first MP. By the time of the first election to the new National Assembly for Wales in 1999, Plaid took nearly a third of the seats in the Senedd.

There is a discreet plaque on the outside wall of the building in question that commemorates that initial meeting in 1925. But that's it. It's now occupied by a shop selling vapes, crystals and tarot cards. The street is far from a hotbed of insurrection today.

I've deliberately made this journey on a Wednesday as this is market day in Pwllheli, and the market sets its stalls out just across the road from Plaid Cymru's birthplace. It is, I have to announce with disappointment, hugely underwhelming. An endless Marrakech souk of winding alleys and haggling hawkers it is not. There are only around a dozen stalls here, generously spaced out in the sizeable car park. Aside from a couple of stall-holders selling clothes, the goods on offer are decidedly random: cheap (but rubbish) paperbacks, plants, toys, chutneys and jams, eggs, garden furniture… One stall exclusively sells Hoover parts; unsurprisingly, business is slow. Another trades in nothing but liquorice laces. A third hedges its bets by offering two distinct and unconnected product lines: carved wooden nick-nacks and Foster Grant sunglasses.

The town suddenly freezes – pedestrians and motor traffic alike – as a tandem of police cars fly through its centre, a double dose of the screaming blues and twos. A spaniel good-naturedly howls along to the sirens, while a young girl in a pushchair fires a water pistol at the speeding patrol cars.

I'm still yet to find suitable sustenance, but the disappointing market is now off my to-do list. The other main item on my itinerary (save for 'wander round aimlessly') is a visit to Capel Salem, the derelict chapel currently being renovated for the delight of Channel 4's viewers.

Our Welsh Chapel Dream chronicles the trials and tribulations of its new owners – Keith Brymer Jones, the eternally damp-eyed judge on *The Great Pottery Throw Down*, and his wife, the actor/bag-maker Marj Hogarth – as they grapple with rotting timbers and rising damp. The programme also examines how they attempt to reassure the residents of a very different community than that of their previous home on the north Kent coast. I'm hopeful that Keith and Marj are home today as I want to hear their thoughts on Pwllheli and its people. If I need to graft a little in the service of the couple – take out some timbers, perhaps, or shift some rubble – in exchange for hearing their views on their new home, I'm more than up for that. I just need to refuel first.

I wander in the chapel's direction via a Welsh-language record/bookshop where I pick up the one solo record by former Gorky's Zygotic Mynci frontman Euros Childs that's missing from the collection back home. I also pay a visit to the bakers a few doors down, which serves the most perfect egg mayonnaise sandwich that I've ever tasted, its vinegary filling so fresh that it could only have been made within the last hour. It instantly joins Nigel's apple-pie-and-custard in the pantheon of immortal Pwllheli dining experiences.

Capel Salem can't be missed, a hulking great building in the centre of town that once offered sanctity and salvation. Every inch of its renovation, its rebirth, is being captured by the Channel 4 cameras – cameras that the neighbours in the houses across the road aren't necessarily always pleased to see.

'I'm scared to open the door to the postman in case I'm filmed in my pyjamas!' laughs one of them as she sits outside the front of her house, enjoying the spring sunshine. 'But it's great that something's happening with that building. It's been empty and deteriorating for years. I've been here fifteen years and it's been derelict in all that time. It's going to be a long project, though. The best thing so far is that they've got rid of all the pigeons that used to live in the roof. My neighbour counted them one day. There were ninety-six. Ninety-six! But now, instead, they scare the smaller birds off the feeders in my back garden…'

A couple are walking up the hill, stopping every few steps to take photos of the chapel, now afforded celebrity status after decades of neglect. 'I've been loving the series,' says the woman. 'Have you come here just to see the chapel? We have.' There's undeniably a sad note in her voice; Keith and Marj aren't on site today. No one is. Fencing remains intact and impenetrable around the building's perimeter. I'm a little sad too.

'It's a great thing for Pwllheli,' the woman's husband announces. 'It'll really bring people into the town. The local economy will really benefit.' The presence of this particular couple is small, but real, proof of this hypothesis. At the very least, today the local economy will be richer to the price of a couple of lunches, courtesy of this pair of pilgrimage-making *Our Welsh Chapel Dream* fans.

I catch up with Keith and Marj a couple of weeks later, eager to get a sense of Pwllheli from a pair of incomers keen to not be outsiders. Why was the pin inserted right here on their map?

'Marj and I were starting again,' says Keith, 'and we were looking for somewhere to live. We didn't want to live in Kent. We were looking at old petrol stations, cinemas, libraries... It could have been anything, as long as it was big enough to have a studio, predominantly for me. And it had to be really cheap. We didn't have much money.'

'We had nothing to sell,' confirms Marj. 'We didn't have property in Kent. The preference was always for a seaside town, because I've lived in a few and Keith had lived in Whitstable. And we lived in Margate for nine years. Once you've lived by the sea, it's very difficult to not live by the sea.

'Plus, I like to know where I am on the map. I know that sounds a bit insane, but I really loved it when we moved to Margate because I could picture the map and I knew where I was. I'm from Leicestershire, right in the middle.

'We fell in love with the building, and the building could have been anywhere. It just happened to be in this funny little town that time forgot.'

The building, with the main chapel and the old Sunday school out the back, ticked all their boxes: for a studio, for living quarters, for a community space. It just so happened that it was located in a beautiful corner of the country. Neither of them knew Pwllheli before they jumped in the car to come and look at the chapel, although Keith, the son of South Walian parents, thinks he probably came here as a kid on holiday.

'We didn't realise that the Llŷn Peninsula is so beautiful,' he says. 'We've really fallen in love with the area. The coastline is incredible. There are extraordinary beaches all the way around the Llŷn. I'm a keen sea swimmer, so I'll be swimming every day.'

The geography made an instant connection with Marj, too. 'It's very like Scotland, where I lived for a very long time. My mother's side of the family are all from the Isle of Bute on the west coast, and when you're on the Llŷn, it feels like you're on an island. It's long and thin and there's water on both sides.'

Keith goes further. 'People say to us, "Pwllheli? Oh God, that's a long way. Do you know anyone there?" We reply, "No! And that's great." At the end of the day, as long as there's decent wi-fi, you can do and be anything anywhere now.

'There's a wonderful wood sculptor called David Nash who lives on the Llŷn. He was once asked, in one of those broadsheet interviews, about what the worst thing was about living on the Llŷn. He said, "Leaving". I'm with him on that. Going by the latest figures, Pwllheli has three thousand six hundred inhabitants. Whitstable has thirty-three thousand. On the whole of the Llŷn, there's fifteen thousand. I rest my case.'

'Even without the TV series about the chapel,' says Marj, 'we're still in a really specific position where Keith's visibility has gone off the scale. So why would we not want to move far, far away?' The pair dissolve into laughter.

While the area, the town and the chapel made an instant impression on the couple, what about their new neighbours? Was there an automatic connection there too?

'One of the incredible things about Pwllheli is the sense of community,' says Marj, who has previously described it as 'a culture of kindness'. 'It's extraordinary, it really is. They look out for each other. When you have a scaffolder who jumps down from the scaffolding on the top of the building to say hello to an old lady who's walking up the hill and whom he's known all his life, that's brilliant. That's what you want. That's what people should be like.

'People here have eyes on each other all the time, whereas in Whitstable, they won't make eye contact with you. I've lived in a lot of places, but I've never lived in a place like Kent, where people just don't engage. That does mess with your well-being. We're animals and we're designed to signal to each other. The fact that people have learnt, for whatever reason, not to signal is just bizarre.'

That said, the connection with the locals in Pwllheli wasn't necessarily immediate.

'They were very accepting of us, but we've worked hard at it. We don't want to be outsiders. We don't want to appear to be the people who are loaded.' A pause. 'We're not anyway.'

'When we bought the building,' explains Keith, 'we were in the local paper every week. "Pottery Celebrity Moves to Pwllheli". Oh, and apparently we "snapped the building up". It had been on the market for twelve years…'

Marj soon understood that patience would be required. 'There's a lovely woman who has a brilliant business on the Llŷn and she moved from further east. She said, "When I first moved here, a local person said to me, 'The people here are slow to warm to you, but they're also slow to judge you.'" And I think that's quite marvellous. They're slow to open up and you have to meet them halfway. And you have to do that in a really careful, non-patronising way. We're really lucky that we work with a series producer on the show who's Welsh. He knew that they needed to visit a few times before they took cameras. People are not desperate to be on the telly. On the whole, I'd say that they're quite shy. But they're not embarrassed by silence. There's no awkwardness.'

'They talk quite slowly and quite definitely,' says Keith. 'Some of them are trying to figure out the English from the Welsh, their first language.'

Marj offers an update. 'There has been a gear shift since the first four episodes aired. People are a little more forthcoming, a little bit warmer. They've been able to see, from a distance, what we actually want to do. Not rumour, but what we're actually talking about, what we're hoping to achieve.'

What the couple are hoping to achieve will undeniably benefit Pwllheli. Although he won't be hosting pottery classes in his workshops, Keith will be taking on some local apprentices once the renovation is complete. Plus, the main chapel hall will be available – free of charge – for certain community events, be those art exhibitions or performances or a farmers' market or even bingo nights.

'Ultimately,' cautions Marj, 'it's not a community asset because it's our home. But we have to be able to share it with people. They have a sense of ownership already.'

Keith nods. 'The building is so central to the town. Everyone has a story about it. Everyone has a connection. Our solicitor, who did our conveyancing, took his piano lessons in the Sunday school when he was a child. He's seventy now.'

Once it's fully renovated, nothing would please the couple more than to disappear into the general way of life in Pwllheli, to become less visible. There is, after all, the danger that their presence overshadows what they'll achieve with the building, that they'll become the attraction, that they'll become public property. It turns out that the couple I met on a day trip to see the chapel – and hopeful to have some kind of interaction with the show's stars – were far from an anomaly. There have been plenty of unannounced visitors.

'We are a bit concerned about it,' admits Keith. 'When I'm in the studio or when Marj is making bags, we have to be on it. We're working. We have to earn some money. We can't just stop for everyone to say hello. Nothing would ever get done.'

A final smile from Marj. 'People say "We've come from Yorkshire."'

'Why...?'

Whether or not their celebrity will fade over time, Keith and Marj's presence will undeniably add to the cultural scene of the town. The current main hub of this is the Neuadd Dwyfor Arts Centre, which consists of a well-stocked library and cinema/performance space. Forthcoming attractions include the Welsh harpist Catrin Finch, formerly harpist to the now-king Charles. Not all the art is high in nature. *Kung Fu Panda 4* is also on the way.

I take a wander out of town, down towards the beach, breathing in lungfuls of that clean Llŷn air. I walk past Victorian terraces, through a council estate and down a sand-dusted lane lined with land-locked yachts. I kick my way across the sands and climb onto Gimblet Rock.

A couple of locals are already perched here. A couple of holidaymakers too. The enormous expanse of Cardigan Bay stretches out before us. Sea and sky, sky and sea. The brain empties. And whatever's left has been cleansed. Marj would agree.

'There's a purity here. A purity to the environment. A purity to the people. They feel such a connection to the land. I call it old magic.'

The chaos and confusion of Birmingham New Street seems – and is – far, far away.

9

INTO THE VALLEY

Cardiff Central–Ebbw Vale Town

It doesn't quite emit the same depth of puzzlement that Birmingham New Street station dishes out, but Cardiff Central is not without its brain-troubling curiosities.

For starters, there's a Platform 4A, a Platform 4B and a Platform 6, but there's no Platform 5.

Even more bafflingly, there is a Platform 0. Yes, *zero*.

And it's Platform 0 you need to locate if you're riding the rails to Ebbw Vale. Its location, though, is as mysterious as that of Platform 9¾ in the *Harry Potter* books.

It turns out that passengers for stations to Ebbw Vale Town shouldn't make the schoolboy/schoolgirl error of actually passing through the main barriers into the station itself. Oh no. Instead, they should fight their way across the tidal flow of laminate-wearing commuters heading for the offices of BBC Cymru across the square and aim for the entrance of the station's branch of M&S Simply Food, before making a quick diversion up the steps to the car park. Unlikely as it sounds, this is indeed where the mythical Platform 0 can be found – along with the 9.02 service to Ebbw Vale Town, two carriages patiently awaiting their modest cargo of passengers.

And modest it definitely is at this hour, as it probably is most days. The direction of morning travel on this line is almost exclusively into Cardiff, not out of. Just eight of us get on.

With no sudden last-minute surge of passengers, we leave on time to the second, heading east on the mainline between Cardiff and Paddington, past the former's changing skyline, one now dominated and defined by high-rise student living. High-speed trains, shuttling between the two capitals, whoosh past in an instant. As with that long pull up to Buxton, we're happy to take our own sweet time. Once out of town, the view from the window comprises flatlands of nothingness, of marshy, unused fields dotted with pylons. The horizon to the south is defined by cranes and chimneys. As we reach the outskirts of Newport, our train peels off northwards. Our constant companion will now be the River Ebbw, the watercourse that gives both the valley and our end destination its name.

The eight becomes nine when a young man gets on at Pye Corner. He's swiftly interrogated by the guard as to why he's got on the train without a ticket. His explanation is unconvincing.

'I've been trying to buy one online but my phone's low on battery.'

The guard has heard all of the excuses before. This one frequently recurs, a perennial favourite in the age of the smartphone. He gives an instant response.

'Well, I'll sell you an actual paper ticket. It won't ever run out of battery power.'

While it's not officially designated as such, this is undeniably a quiet carriage, its half-dozen occupants all studying their phones. Except me. I'm studying *them*. The only sound comes from the man sat in front of me, who is gently chuckling away to himself. I sneak a glance at his phone to find the source of his amusement.

There's a picture of Fred and Rose West on his screen. I slink back into my seat, beating a hasty retreat. I consider switching carriages, just as a precaution.

Beyond the joint station of Risca & Pontymister with its pleasing pararhyme, the hills begin to emerge, the gradients reducing the train's speed as it continues its passage up the valley floor. On either side, the hills start to graduate to mountains. I ponder the height at which a hill is still a hill, but a mountain is a mountain. There was a Hugh Grant film with this very dilemma at its core: the functionally titled *The Englishman Who Went Up a Hill But Came Down a Mountain*. Grant plays a cartographer charged with measuring a Welsh hill to see if it actually qualifies to be a mountain. It needs to reach at least 1,000 feet to be classified as such. Even a foot or two shorter and a hill remains a hill. There's my answer.

Rugby clubs and chapels are fixtures out of the window as we climb through the villages, the tracks parallel to each high street. The strong Italian–Welsh connection is apparent too, confirmed by the likes of Tony's Pizzeria in Crosskeys and the Conti fish bar in Newbridge – although the former's pizza oven has fallen into disuse, permanently cold after 25 years of trading, presumably unable to compete with the ubiquity of Domino's, the nearest branch of which is less than a mile and a half away in Risca.

This is not the south Wales of rugged coastlines and romantic castles and endless beaches. This is the south Wales that doesn't make it into any tourist brochures. Old workers' cottages cling to the hillside, while miners' institutes and labour clubs sit empty, redundant. Their fading signage are symbols of the heavy industry that once defined the area, as is the odd burnt-out factory. The premises are charred, blackened, cremated.

Crumlin Navigation Colliery hasn't suffered a cremation, but nature is wrapping itself around its striking brick buildings, performing a slow strangulation. It closed down in 1967 and ever since has occupied a state of purgatory – its Grade II-listed historical importance as one of Wales' first brick-built collieries making it immune to the wrecking ball. But the cash of a sympathetic property developer has yet to appear. It's been in limbo for more than half a century, vacant and unloved – unloved by anyone other than the volunteer Friends of the Navigation, that is.

A couple of miles outside Ebbw Vale stands Marine Colliery in the village of Cwm. Dilwyn Williams used to work here, but his son didn't follow in his bootsteps. He stayed above ground instead and now lives in a big house on the hillside that looks over the old colliery. He is Ebbw Vale's most famous resident: the three-time world snooker champion Mark Williams.

By all accounts, Williams' achievements haven't turned him into someone who swanks around town, someone who needs lungfuls of the oxygen of recognition. Far from it. Often wearing a tracksuit, he tends to merge into the background, unstarry and anonymous. 'You see him walking around Cwm or Ebbw Vale,' Dilwyn explained to the *Telegraph*, 'and you wouldn't think he was a professional snooker player.' In fact, as unlikely as it sounds, Williams has his own fashion range on his website – hoodies and gilets and bobble hats branded with his initials.

Dilwyn was instrumental in his son's passage to sporting superstardom, secretly taking him to the snooker hall rather than dropping him off at school. One day in particular was responsible for making the teenager resolute in chasing his dream: it was the day that Dilwyn introduced young Mark to life down the pit.

'I got snuck in with these ten or fifteen men, snuck in the middle, and down in the lift,' the younger Williams revealed in that same *Telegraph* feature. 'It was horrific. The battery pack with a light on was nearly as heavy as me. Awful.

'I was glad to get back up. But I said to myself, "If I don't make it in snooker, this is where I'm going for twelve hours a day."'

Over the next few hours, I'll be keeping my eye out for Mark Williams. Perhaps I'll engage him in chat and he'll invite me up to his big house for a frame or three of snooker. Perhaps. I later find that there are plenty of men wearing tracksuits in Ebbw Vale today, just like any other day. The ones outside Wetherspoons uniformly wear their tracksuit bottoms halfway down their arses. But none of them are him. A glance at the calendar of the World Snooker Tour, the body that organises all of the sport's main tournaments across the globe, confirms that, unlike Tyson Fury when I visited Morecambe, Williams isn't away, competing somewhere exotic. He's probably just over the hill in Tredegar, practising the art of potting at the snooker club he owns there. It goes by the imaginative name of the Mark Williams Snooker Club.

Only three of us are still on the train when it reaches the buffers at Ebbw Vale Town. But the platform is busy, with a few dozen waiting to take the return journey back down the valley.

'Rhys! Show some manners and let the man off first!'

The impatience is understandable. It's half term, and buckets and spades are being enthusiastically carried by excitable children. We've headed inland, but they're all bound for Barry Island.

There are also plenty of Ebbw Vale's kids not heading to the seaside. It being half term, they hang about, kicking their heels, letting the hours slip by in unimaginative fashion. The station is on the low-lying site of the town's former steelworks and a free, self-operated funicular railway takes people up to the town centre. It's a low-thrill journey that takes precisely 36 seconds, but this doesn't stop the local teenagers riding it up and down an interminable number of times – until, that is, their enjoyment is curtailed by the intervention of a security guard. Instead, one of the teens finds a shopping trolley to climb into, his friends more than willing to spin him round and round in tight circles until he begs for mercy.

Ebbw Vale's most impressive historical building can be found still standing on the old steelworks site: the General Offices. Where you'd expect its interior to be largely functional, it's surprisingly grand and ornate, designed in the Dutch baroque style. Built between 1915 and 1916, it is therefore possibly indicative of the prosperity of the Ebbw Vale Steel, Iron and Coal Company in the early years of the twentieth century, despite the turbulence that World War I was placing on the world's economies. Actually, scrap 'despite'. The prosperity is more likely to be *because of* the war, because of the gargantuan requirements of the war effort and the contracts issued.

That such effort and expense was invested in the construction of the General Offices is surely what has secured its survival, its listed status beating off any approaches from the bulldozer. These days, it's home to a range of bookable meeting rooms, along with a 4D cinema, a 360-degree projection room and something called the Sandpit interactive system. Much can change in a hundred years. As it goes about its twenty-first-century business, the building will be a much quieter, calmer environment than it was in the works' heyday, when it was the administrative epicentre of an enterprise that, at its height, employed as many as 34,000 men.

The General Offices also house both the Ebbw Vale Works Museum and, in a modern extension out the back, the Gwent

Archives. Volunteer-run, the museum doesn't open every day. It's open on Wednesdays and Fridays, but not on Thursdays. Today is a Thursday. The international conspiracy to keep me locked out of the nation's museums and heritage centres continues.

I go off in search of an overdue breakfast instead.

That overdue breakfast is found in Caffe Lina on Bethcar Street, the main drag through the centre of Ebbw Vale. Two orange-bibbed workmen employed in the remediation trade, the profession that makes contaminated land suitable for use again, are at the front of the queue. I daresay the waitress could guess what they're about to order.

'Mega-breakfast please, my lovely,' says the first.

'Beans or tomato?'

'Both please. And a caramel latte.'

His colleague also plumps for a mega-breakfast. And a cappuccino.

A paint-flecked decorator is next. He orders a bacon baguette.

'Do you want salad on the side?'

His answer is just a chuckle. The chuckle makes his rounded cheeks wobble.

I place my order for scrambled eggs on toast and take the table behind the pair of remediation workers. They're chatting about last night's telly.

'Did you see *Race Across the World*?'

'The final? Don't tell me. Haven't seen it yet.'

'All I'll say is that the winners deserved it.'

A third man, also wearing an orange bib, joins them at their table and dives straight into the conversation.

'That pair did well, didn't they? They—'

'Stop! Now!'

The third man reluctantly halts mid-stream.

'Well, all I'll say is that I fancy going to Java now. All those volcanoes…'

The travel agent across the road could help him get there, its window offering escapes to faraway destinations – Caribbean cruises and all-inclusive packages to Mexico. The bossa nova currently playing in the café offers further teases of warmer climes.

Their breakfasts demolished before mine even arrives, the men get up to settle their bill.

'It's cold today, isn't it?' says the waitress. 'Can you believe it's June in a couple of days' time?'

'I'm normally in shorts by April,' says the man whose turn it is today to pay for the breakfasts.

They leave to return to their remediation work, but talk of the inclement weather leads the staff to discuss overseas holidays, the highlight of which is the story of someone they know who once went to Egypt.

'He took one of those George Foreman grills with him. Had bacon, sausages and beans in his suitcase. Fussy eater. Didn't trust the food.'

Outside in the comparative chill, Ebbw Vale can't exactly be described as buzzy. The busiest place seems to be the local branch of Heron Foods, the value frozen food specialists, although there is also a steady stream of pensioners heading for the library to warm their bones and read today's paper, or maybe undertake some light local history research. Perhaps even a mid-morning snooze.

I climb the hill above the town centre to get the lie of the land, to see how the town fits into the landscape. This grid of terraced streets is even quieter, save for a Jack Russell yapping at me from his perch on the windowsill of a front room, his claws performing an excited tap dance. A roofer, leaning against the chimney of the house he's working on, looks up at the darkening sky over towards the Brecon Beacons and then down at the untiled roof. 'Better get a wriggle on, boys!'

Over there, in the direction of that darkening sky, things might not have been so quiet had a certain commercial proposal, a certain ambitious dream, have come to fruition. It would have brought the noise. It would have helped reshape the town too.

In late 2011, plans were unveiled for a sizeable development on the northern edge of town, next to the Heads of the Valleys trunk road. The proposal was for the construction of a motor-racing circuit capable of hosting races in both the World Touring Car Championship and motorbike racing's MotoGP series. The developers' announcement was an excited one, proclaiming that the Circuit of Wales 'would be of international importance [and] would transform the region and bring thousands of new jobs'.

The Circuit of Wales was to be an innovative partnership between private investors and the Welsh government. It turned out to be a long and protracted process that didn't get very far. In 2016, the project's insurers announced that they'd be unable to underwrite even a fifth of its reported £357 million price tag; the following year, the government confirmed that it couldn't shoulder such a large proportion of the outlay. The risk to the public finances was too great and the dream of high-level motorsport coming to south Wales was forced into the pits, its race over.

The promise of those mooted thousands of jobs disappeared with it. And doesn't Ebbw Vale need jobs. For at least a generation, the county of Blaenau Gwent has been consistently in the top 6 per cent in the UK when it comes to unemployment. In not unconnected news, in 2013 it was revealed that one in every six adults in the borough was being prescribed anti-depressants, the highest ratio in the entire country. For all the ills affecting the economy since then – Brexit and the pandemic being the most conspicuous – it's not exactly unlikely that that figure has risen during the last decade. Unless, of course, those prescriptions are less easy to come by because of the subsequent disappearance of reliable access to GPs.

  It's not just the closure of the works that still affects the town. That was back in 2002, after all. Automation has also reduced the need for human hands in the light industries that sprung up in the wake of the area's heavy industry collapsing.

  I wander down to the job centre to see what vacancies are currently available. It's not found in the middle of town but is set in an otherwise abandoned industrial estate. It's not a hive of activity; there are just a couple of cars in the car park. Pedestrians access the centre via an underpass underneath a busy A-road. There are some jobs available – children's support worker, specialist teacher – but these are highly skilled positions requiring people of long experience. Bearing in mind those anti-depressant figures, I shouldn't be surprised that there are multiple vacancies for mental health nurses.

  There's just one job which doesn't require a precise qualification: that of a delivery driver for Evri, the company formerly known as Hermes. 'Join our team this summer!' the advert chirps. In possibly contradictory fashion, it bigs up the position's hourly rate of pay while making a virtue of how few hours the successful candidate would have to work, 'giving you plenty of time to enjoy the summer sun'. An escape route from poverty this is unlikely to be.

  Back on the other side of the underpass, there's a slow-walking guy in front of me who's just dropped a piece of paper. I pick it up.

'Excuse me…'

'Oh, thanks. That's my shopping list. Would be lost without it.'

There are no more than five items on the list.

'Going to Tesco's is one of the highlights of my day,' he sighs.

He's in, I guess, his early sixties, with lacquered black hair and dark, sad eyes. He looks like he might be called Ray. And he's keen to talk, to tell me his not-so-potted life story.

For years, Ray was a bar steward on the Fishguard–Rosslare ferry before he developed an inner-ear problem, his diminished sense of balance incompatible with life on the churning Irish Sea. At that point, he moved back to Ebbw Vale, encouraged by the prospect of the proposed development up the road.

'You know about the motor-racing circuit that was going to be built, yeah? That would have been great if it had gone ahead. Not so great for the traffic round here, but there would have been plenty of bar work. There was talk of it having a dozen bars open on race days. But it turned out to just be a pipe dream. Reality took over. They couldn't find the money.'

There's been the odd bit of casual bar work since ('It's the only thing I know'), but now it's largely a case of Ray running down the clock until he reaches state pension age. 'I've only got a couple of years to go. Even back in my late fifties, it was too late for me to retrain for anything else. Everything seemed to be related to IT and I haven't got a clue where that's concerned. I was too much of an old dog to learn new tricks.'

Or perhaps not. Ray tells me that baking is now a great hobby of his, something productive that fills the hours, the days. 'Yeah, it turns out I'm half-decent at it. That's where I'm off to now, to get more ingredients.' He waves his shopping list. 'It's coffee and walnut today and I'm out of both walnuts and eggs. And don't get me started on the price of butter.'

157

We go our separate ways. 'Will see you again,' he says, unaware that I'll be leaving town later, unlikely to return. 'I'm Michael, by the way...'

I turn back towards the town centre, which is a little livelier now that it's closer to lunchtime. Those Wetherspoons patrons, with their half-mast tracksuit bottoms, are another pint or two in, another pint or two louder.

I'm on the hunt for an imprint left by the person, other than Mark Williams, who's synonymous with Ebbw Vale. His name was Aneurin Bevan.

Today marks 95 years to the day that Bevan was elected as the town's MP for the first time. He wasn't a man content to simply serve his constituents. He served the entire country. And, nearly 65 years after his death, his mark on people's lives today remains indelible. Indeed, so significant has his effect been on the nation that his name won't be erased for another generation or two. He was an agitator, a firebrand and a visionary. And Aneurin Bevan was, of course, the father of the NHS.

Prime minister-in-waiting Keir Starmer is on the election trail in south Wales today, but none of his advisers appears wise to the anniversary. An hour or so in Ebbw Vale, saluting one of the most impactful Labour ministers ever, would have been a neat fit, a happy coincidence, and a chance for the party's current leader to vocally rail against the treatment of the NHS in Conservative hands over the last 14 years.

No one else appears to have clocked the anniversary either. Perhaps they will in five years' time when the century gets chalked up. In fact, there is little visible trace of Bevan's existence and achievements around the town centre. No plaques, no statues. Just the odd biography in the local history section of the library.

Beyond the town centre, on the old steelworks site, Ebbw Vale's hospital is at least named after him: Ysbyty Aneurin Bevan. There's a modest tribute to the man in a display cabinet in its reception area – a portrait in watercolour, a commemorative dinner plate – but nothing more. You suspect this would be a state of affairs that he'd have been comfortable with. Spend the money on healthcare instead.

(The hospital shares that Bevanian sense of innovation, of progress. Opened in 2010, it was the first publicly funded hospital in the UK to be exclusively fitted with single rooms, all with their own en-suite facilities.)

Besides the hospital, the rest of the steelworks site has been both reclaimed by nature and renewed by civic planning. A school, a college and a leisure centre – all impressively state of the art – also occupy the site, as does Central Valley, a large and sprawling nature reserve.

The reserve blooms with the yellows of buttercups and dandelions, and the purples of common knapweed and tufted vetch. Butterflies flutter by, while magpies hop, skip and jump about the place. Oil beetles scuttle across the path, the metallic gold of their abdomens flickering in the sunlight. A young couple take pictures of each other on a wooden bridge. It's all rather idyllic and peaceful.

Comparatively so, at least. Traffic still zooms past on the main road out of town and there's the twice-hourly diesel charge of the train on the adjacent tracks. But measured against the sound of 34,000 men banging and clanging, it's an absolute sanctuary of peace and escapism.

Another couple, of retirement age rather than in the first flush of youthful love, are also taking in the reserve's flora and fauna. They slow for a chat as I approach.

'Scarcely recognisable, isn't it?' offers the husband. 'I used to work here in the Seventies, when it became a tinplate works. What a difference this place is now. It's beautiful. Except it means all those jobs are gone, of course. That's the downside. We live in Portugal now. First time we've been back in years. We're visiting nieces and nephews. They all have to commute to Cardiff for work.'

A bee buzzes past, a yellow-and-black ball of humming contentment.

'I'm glad it wasn't just left to rot. Nature's been given this land back. She always wins. She'll be here when we're all gone.'

'Our dog back in Portugal would love this,' says his wife. 'He'd get rid of that bunch of crows over there for starters.'

'Murder,' says the husband.

'No, he'd only chase them.'

He shakes his head.

'A murder of crows. That's what a group of them are called. It came up in the quiz the other week.'

He turns back to me, turning back the years as he does so.

'It was hot and dirty and noisy here. I won't romanticise it. But it was work. You didn't have to worry about money. But I had enough of it after a while and retrained as an HGV driver. Those were long hours though. Not sure if it was better. Away from home a lot, sleeping in the cab. That's when I first went to Portugal.'

'Seems so long ago now,' says his wife. 'Don't the days just zoom by...?'

Her thought is left wistfully hanging on the warm air, but only for a moment. Possibly spooked by this reminder of mortality, of the speed with which time slips by imperceptibly, the husband abruptly turns on his heels. 'Be seeing you...'

I must be saying my goodbyes too. The next train into town roars past me up the valley; I need to be on board for the return journey back to Cardiff, for my search for the legacy of Ebbw Vale's most famous politician isn't yet over. I'm off to the Wales Millennium Centre this evening for the next performance of *Nye*, the theatrical production dedicated to Bevan's life and times, with Michael Sheen – who else? – in the lead role.

A couple of hours later, after a train ride made a few minutes quicker than the outward journey thanks to the laws of gravity, I'm sat in the Centre's glorious main auditorium, dazzled and dizzied by what's unfolding on stage. This is no standard, cradle-to-grave telling of a man's life story. It's one broadly told in flash-backs from the hospital bed of the older, ailing Bevan, and is a whirling, brilliantly choreographed fantasia, an impressionistic, often surreal tour de force. Sheen remains in Bevan's pyjamas throughout.

It pulls the audience to its feet in salute as the curtain falls, shining the sunlight of optimism down hard on them in the murky half-light of these otherwise troubled times. It is simply the most imaginative, most original play I've ever seen. The fact that its subject is one of the greatest Britons of the twentieth century (when it comes to public service, that is, if not in his private life; in the play, his first wife refers to him as a 'rutting stag') simply doubles the achievement.

The *Observer*'s reviewer praised Sheen's capture of 'the power of the man, the motor of his conviction'. In the absence of a statue in Ebbw Vale, it's a fine way to acknowledge that 95th anniversary.

10

LAST MAN SITTING

Bristol Temple Meads–Severn Beach

Daybreak over Temple Meads. The early trains.

Don't turn right after the ticket barrier. Don't follow the thrusting executives down the stairs and through the underpass as they confidently stride for the 10-carriage London train waiting for them all the way over on Platform 15. Don't stand behind them as they place their orders for artisan coffees and reassuringly expensive pastries. Don't slide into the seat next to them as they hurtle, in expenses-paid comfort, towards the dark heart of the capital.

Instead turn left after the ticket barrier. Follow the lone worker in his late fifties, shuffling without energy or excitement, a slight limp detectable and his orange protective wear smudged black by toil over the days and the weeks, the months and the years. Follow him around the corner to Platform 1, the hidden departure point unknown to almost all of the station's passengers. Climb aboard the three-carriage service sat there. Trundling at its own pace, it will take you somewhere and possibly nowhere at the same time. Pick whichever seat you want. There are plenty spare. Only four other passengers are along for the ride.

But don't follow the orange-clad workman when, 45 minutes later, he leaves the train for a shift of drudgery and dirt in the oil refineries of Avonmouth, his shuffle even less purposeful than before.

Stay on the train for four more miles, until it trundles no more. Stay on until the end of the line. Stay on until Severn Beach.

I haven't ridden the Severn Beach Line in more than 30 years. And I've only ridden it once before. Newly arrived in Bristol in the early 1990s, we headed out on a weekend day trip to the nearest place with 'Beach' in its name. I thought Severn Beach might be a resort of faded glamour and peeling paint that still gave off a frisson of cool. Or, at least, we might encounter something approaching Clacton-on-Severn. We got neither that day. And I've never been back since.

Back then, it was a single-carriage affair that carried us curious newcomers north-westwards. These were the days of train travel before patchy onboard wi-fi, scrolling digital displays and endless recorded announcements.

No 'This is a Great Western Railway service to…'.

No 'We will be calling at…'.

No 'The next station is…'.

Over the next 51 minutes today, this train will stop at 11 stations. The announcements will come thick and fast. I prefer the silence of times past. Everybody does.

I do, though, appreciate the early-Nineties feel of the fare. It's just two quid from Temple Meads to Severn Beach at any time of day. And an extra quid if you want to come back again. Other than that £2.90 fare between Middlesbrough and Whitby, it must represent the best minutes-to-money value on the entire rail network. Today I'll ride these rails, there and back again, for 94 minutes. Rudimentary maths tells me that works out at little more than three pence a minute.

There's a thin smile of sun on the horizon to the east as we roll out of Temple Meads, but it'll be the only glimpse of sunshine seen today. As the train moves through the eastern reaches of the city centre, the shapes of Bristol begin to reveal themselves, silhouettes of tower blocks and church spires against the grey-blue early-morning gloom. The red lights of cranes blink in the middle distance.

Of the five passengers on this dawn departure, I'm the only one not wearing at least one item of protective, reflective workwear. There are, however, two ticket inspectors on board. They're not overworked. By the time we've reached Stapleton Road, five minutes and two stations into our journey, my ticket has already been checked twice.

A few others get on at Stapleton Road. Although travelling separately, their ticket requests are uniform. 'Return to Avonmouth.' One passenger doesn't bother sticking his bike in the rack provided. He leans it in the aisle, as he presumably does every morning. Then he attempts to grab some shut-eye, as he presumably does every morning. He's pulled his woolly hat down over his ears to blank out the fast-flowing stream of announcements.

This line to the coast was completed in the first year of the twentieth century and managed to dodge the swiping machete that British Railways chairman Dr Richard Beeching took to the rail network in the early 1960s. It's survived occasional threats to its existence since but, despite the low numbers on this first-light service, seems in comparatively rude health. It's now home to the newest station on the national network – Portway Park & Ride – suggesting its future is secure for some time to come.

As it cuts across the suburbs east and north of the city centre, the line traces an upwardly mobile route, rolling past the tower blocks of Lawrence Hill and tightly packed terraced housing of Easton, before arcing and climbing, past allotments and through trees, as it slices its way across the bohemian slopes of Montpelier towards Redland's leafy avenues and Clifton's imposing Georgian townhouses.

Montpelier station has always been a prime spot for the spray-can gang, an unofficial gallery for the city's street artists. That tradition hasn't diminished over the decades. On its walls and fences, painted faces and figures in blues and purples stare ominously at the train and its passengers through the gloom. Nobody gets on.

The train then passes over the Arches, the viaduct straddling Cheltenham Road and the most prominent landmark in this part of town. This used to be my playground, my home patch – first working in a second-hand bookshop south of the Arches, then as a magazine editor a couple of hundred yards to the north on the other side of the tracks. The fast-food outlets underneath the viaduct's span may come and go – and, indeed, large parts of the city centre have been radically reconfigured in recent years – but the Arches pleasingly remain a symbol of permanence in a shifting landscape.

After pulling out of Redland station (nobody gets on), the train passes the bottom of our old street as it heads through the cutting towards Clifton. Other than those brief seconds traversing the Arches, the line is largely out of view as it passes through these northern suburbs, through tunnels and wooded cuttings, behind thick, overgrown hedges. It's almost an invisible line. Out of sight. And certainly out of mind of the residents of Clifton. Nobody gets on here either.

Before it reaches the largest, poshest homes in the grandest part of town, up near the Downs and the Suspension Bridge, the line disappears even further from view, burrowing its way through the limestone and mudstone on which Clifton proprietorially sits. When it emerges into what passes for daylight today, the train is now parallel to the River Avon. The tide is high, the water inching close to the lip of the muddy bank.

The travel agents Thomas Cook once anointed the Severn Beach Line as 'one of Europe's top scenic routes'. Bearing in mind the line's shyness up until now, its willingness to stay largely under cover (not to mention the industrial zone it's shortly going to dissect), it can only have been garlanded for this particular river-adjacent stretch. Even so, both the highly photogenic cliffs of the Avon Gorge and Isambard Kingdom Brunel's famous bridge are behind us, further upstream, round a couple of bends in the river. And it's not as if there's much view of the slow old Avon itself these days either, it being largely obscured by trackside bramble, 20 feet high in most places. How and why Thomas Cook gave the line such a billing is anybody's guess.

As we leave Sea Mills station and glide over the creek at the mouth of the River Trym, the recorded announcement hits a glitch.

'The next station is Shirehampton. The next station is Shire-hampton. The next station is Shirehampton.'

The repetition acts as an alarm clock for our man with the bike. He jerks awake, pulling off his hat but leaving his earphones in, some tinny hip hop leaking from them.

After heading slightly inland to the thrice-announced suburb, our next stop is that new one, Portway Park & Ride. Trains stopped here for the first time exactly four weeks ago. The station, Bristol's first new one in 96 years, is still immaculate. Stick your nose up to its signs and you can probably still smell the paint. So far, it's eluded the spray can too.

Nobody gets on.

The towering Avonmouth Bridge, carrying the M5 high over the river, is the next landmark. A cradle, awaiting this morning's maintenance crew, hangs over the side. I think – as I always do whenever I'm driving across the bridge – of the awful accident almost 25 years ago when four steelworkers dropped out of the sky to their deaths after the cradle they were working in became unhitched. There are few more horrific ways to die than that.

The bridge marks the border between suburbia and the industry-heavy port of Avonmouth. We slide into the town's station and Bike Boy gets off, along with most people in the carriage. His phone is now on speaker, revealing that, to everyone's surprise, he's swapped tinny hip hop for the *Today* programme.

Although far from a new station, there's no street art here either. Instead, charming paintings of lapwings and curlews adorn the station's wall, a display of nature's beauty to offset the industrial – some might say post-apocalyptic – landscape we're just about to enter.

The platform is damp. The forecast rain has arrived. The early-morning blue-grey tinge is now strictly grey. We sit here for a few minutes, awaiting the arrival of the next train out of Severn Beach in the opposite direction so that ours can take possession of the single track to the end of the line. I don't mind the wait. While we're stationary, the announcements fall silent.

For the next few miles, once we're past the town's cramped terraced housing, we slide through the kingdom of the iron giants – the pylons, the cranes, the turbines. Behind cherry-red fencing, diggers and trucks sprint back and forth, a frenzy of flashing lights and roaring engines. Huge silos overlook vast yards where hundreds of new cars just off the boat from Korea and Japan await their onward passage. Wind turbines grind, while heaps of indeterminate industrial waste continue to grow. The representative from Thomas Cook surely didn't stay on the train this far.

The last orange-clad worker gets off at the penultimate stop, St Andrews Road. I'm the only passenger on board now, the last man sitting. Here the tracks in the lesser-used rail sidings have been embroidered by weeds and wildflowers, by thistle and thorn, while the enormous circular tanks of the refinery rise out of the ground like cathedral basilicas. A petrochemical stink leaks in through the carriage's ventilation system.

The last pylon, the last crane, the last turbine are all eventually behind us. There's nothing left to interrupt the view across the marshy banks and the salty estuary towards the Second Severn Crossing. The view remains limited though. South Wales, just a couple of miles to the west, is barely visible in the gloom.

The train slows, the buffers await. 'The next station is Severn Beach.'

All change, all change.

I'm in no hurry to leave the station. The rain is steadier now and, at this time of the morning, there won't be many places open yet in the village in which to take cover. Instead, I linger, taking refuge in the platform's steel shelter, the rainfall rattling its roof. Severn Beach is a place that's slow to wake up but, over the next 10 minutes, 20 or so of its villagers roll up to take the waiting train back towards Bristol. A couple with small suitcases but no coats are clearly heading for warmer climes for a few days, but the remainder are largely commuters off to their desks in the city. A couple of them carry fold-up bikes, but one passenger, attempting to lift an electric scooter on board, is denied entry by the guard. He wheels his steed back out of the station, towards the bus stop. The train leaves without him.

It's only once the platform falls silent that I realise I'm not alone in the shelter. Head down and making some notes, the odd raindrop managing to penetrate the roof and blot the page, I haven't noticed the short, older man sat at the other end. After he coughs, we catch each other's eye. I keep scribbling things down. Without invitation, he moves closer, plonking himself down right next to me.

'Trainspotter, eh?'

I smile politely. It's easier to smile politely than to explain to someone that what you're actually doing is jotting down observations about them. I turn the page in my notebook so he doesn't see the words 'nosy parker'.

'It's not exactly Clapham Junction or Crewe here, you know.'

His accent has plenty of this corner of the West Country about it, but it also carries a strong whiff of Yorkshire. It's a lesser-heard combination. He wears a cream-coloured mac, under which a white shirt and dark tie are partially visible. His silver hair has been recently trimmed.

'Not really,' I finally answer, before turning nosy parker myself. 'Why are you here at this time in the morning? Did you miss the train?'

'Oh no. I never ride it. I'm a terrible back-seat driver. I have to be in the cab or nothing.'

'Train driver?'

'Used to be, lad. But I'll take the compliment. I'm eighty-two now. No, I often wander down here when I can't sleep. There's another funeral today. Can't sleep the night before one of those. Gets me thinking too much.

'Coming here takes me back. Back to the best days. Makes me happier. I used to drive trains all over – Cardiff, Gloucester, Birmingham, Weston. But this line was my favourite. Coming out of the tunnel from Clifton alongside the river. Wonderful. And that view across the estuary. Bridge or no bridge, that's one of the great views. Never got bored of it.

'You can call me Sid, by the way,' he says, a little mysteriously. It's as if Sid isn't actually his name. A woolly-gloved handshake is more genuine.

Sid tells me a potted version of his life story – although, clearly not in a hurry, it's not as potted as it might be. He was stationed near Cardiff in the last year of national service in the late Fifties, where he met a girl from Bristol. Once demobbed, he was lured by her charms down to the West Country from his native Featherstone. He's been here ever since. It's where a *Boy's Own* dream of becoming a train driver gave him several decades of job satisfaction.

'God, I missed it when I retired. This is as close as I get now, sitting here watching the trains roll in and then roll out again. It's like that Otis Redding song. You know it?'

Sid replicates the whistling that draws 'Sittin' on the Dock of the Bay' to a close. He is a fine whistler. The rain on the roof acts as his accompanying percussion.

'But I can't say I'm not jealous every time a train comes in. God I'd love to still be one of those drivers, leaving their cab, having a crafty smoke and then walking down the platform to the other end of the train for the return journey. Some drivers didn't like this line. They couldn't get the train up to a decent lick, what with all the stops. Preferred the main line, so they did. But I adored coming out here. Wasn't bothered about it being a slow train. It was all about the view. Loved it so much we moved here when I retired. We came all the way from Southmead. Seven whole miles away…

'Peace was what we wanted. But we didn't come here just to see our time out. Though I do seem to be outlasting everyone…'

He reaches up to straighten his tie, which was showing no sign of being out of place, and clears his throat.

'So *are you* a trainspotter then? There's no shame in it.'

I think quickly. 'No, just doing a shopping list.'

'Ah, there's a decent shop here,' Sid says proudly, not pausing to consider why I might have ventured all the way out to Severn Beach just to visit a convenience store. 'Bit pricey, mind. But what isn't these days?'

I'm about to tell Sid that a return ticket from Temple Meads certainly isn't when his ears prick up and he leans beyond me to look down the track. Despite his age, he appears to have the hearing of a dog.

'Here we go. She's a couple of minutes away. Right on time, though.'

The next train comes into view and slows to a halt. Sid's eyes trace the passage of the driver striding down the platform towards what will now be the front of the train. Those eyes are sad, that smile is thin. He's lost in his memories, tangled up in a past that can't be retrieved. I decide to let him be. He doesn't even notice my hand on his shoulder as I rise to leave.

Severn Beach station is just a couple of hundred yards from the waterfront, where the estuary makes landfall. Below the sea wall, water the colour of day-old tea laps at the boulders forming part of the defences. The tide here is a busy one. The Severn Estuary has the second-highest tidal range on the entire planet, beaten only by the Bay of Fundy in Nova Scotia.

That hasn't changed since I was last here, but plenty else has. And those changes are very audible. The Second Severn Crossing, on the northern edge of the village, didn't exist back then, nor did the M49, to the east of the village, built to feed northbound M5 traffic to the bridge and to south Wales. Already hemmed in by the estuary, the village is now hemmed in on two other sides. To my mind, this is inescapably claustrophobic. To those who've chosen to move here since, though, it presumably feels like a cocoon, like some kind of security, of protection.

I pull my hood up and head along the sea wall towards the bridge. There are few souls about and the prom has an optimistic number of benches which have surely never all been occupied at any one moment. There are no legions of happy-go-lucky roller-bladers and joggers and speed-walkers using the prom. It's only me and the odd dog-walker. And this is not the weather for conversation. Just a nod of the head as we pass, owners and dogs conspiring to get back indoors as quickly as possible. A black lab called Eric comes up to me, nuzzling my leg to dry his wet snout on my trousers.

Severn Beach may appear as sleepy as it did to me all those decades back, but it can't be described as a quiet place. The stereo sound of those adjacent motorways is loud and relentless. I pass a park homes estate tucked into the neck of the bridge and wonder who has opted to spend their retirement in such an unpeaceful environment. Perhaps the incessant sound of traffic works as white noise for late-in-their-lives insomniacs. Horlicks for the ears. The clack-clack of the next near-empty train arriving from Bristol adds to the volume, as does the belch of a ship's horn leaving Avonmouth.

The blues and reds and oranges of lorries above me on the bridge cut through the gloom. I shelter beneath its hulking concrete mass to avoid the incessant rain. Surprisingly, it's the quietest place in Severn Beach, the otherwise ever-present roar of road noise reduced to a low, bass rumble. I sit on a pillar and stare at the water lapping below me, watching the eddies forming that indicate the turning of the tide.

A cyclist approaches, peroxide curls spilling out from beneath an orange baseball cap as he nods a greeting.

'Alright?'

A squeal of brakes.

'I mean, are you *alright*?'

It takes a moment or two for me to register how I must appear – this non-dog-walking man with no discernible reason to be out in miserable weather at this ungodly hour, staring intently at the sea. His concern is that I might be considering divesting myself of my worldly possessions (and clothes) and striding, Reggie Perrin-like, into the unforgiving depths. After all, the original Severn Bridge, a couple of miles up the estuary, is a notorious suicide spot. It's where Richey Edwards from Manic Street Preachers left his silver Vauxhall Cavalier in 1995 before vanishing off the face of the earth. Pedestrians are denied access to the newer bridge, presumably to deter those wishing to surrender themselves to the tides.

I give out an embarrassed laugh. 'Yes, yes, yes. I'm fine.' He rides off. 'But thanks.'

I decide to walk back towards the village so as not to alarm any more passers-by. I gaze out further, past Avonmouth and Portishead, out to where the Severn Estuary becomes the Bristol

Channel. Murky sky, murky sea. No dividing line between the two. No horizon. Only a distant container ship offers scale and context.

The waters start to recede, to embark on their return journey, revealing the tiramisu of mud that passes for sand round these parts. One morning eight years ago, the outgoing tide uncovered a six-foot swordfish flailing around in the shallows before coming to the end of its days on the low-tide pebbles. Believed to have chased mackerel all the way from the Mediterranean, the swordfish resisted the locals' attempts to get him back into the water. It was the last – *only?* – time that little Severn Beach made the national news.

I head down a ramp to the water's edge, but the shingle is swordfish-free today. A flock of dunlins flit about and then take to the wing en masse, a shape-shifting cloud drawing huge arcs over the estuary before heading inland, up above the streets and houses. I'm so lost watching them that I don't notice a young man under the sea wall, his black hood up. It's now my turn to ask someone about their welfare. The binoculars around his neck, and the takeaway cup of coffee at his side, tell me he is OK. Just an early-morning birdwatcher taking shelter and refreshment. He was watching the dunlins' show too.

It's still not sitting-down weather and all those benches up on the prom remain unoccupied. Many have small metal plaques on which are inscribed dedications to former residents no longer with us. One is in memory of two sisters.

Phyllis Humphries (later Anderson)
1.4.1930–27.12.2016
Margaret Humphries (later Gormley)
28.9.1932–2.8.2009

Sisters who grew up here and made many
treasured friends and memories

Another is a little more esoterically worded.

Mary Lily Thurza Ogborn (née Sheppard)
1st September 1926–4th June 2020
Moon daisies and her sweet memories

These aren't simply memorials to passed-over former residents. These are also memorials to another life that's gone – and an unlikely one, one that occurred right where I'm standing. It was a time and a place that provided many with, as the dedications suggest, memories to last a lifetime.

For Severn Beach wasn't always the sleepy place it may seem today. From the 1920s onwards, it was known as – more than a little optimistically, it has to be said – the 'Blackpool of the West'. Some top spin-doctoring from the PR department there. It didn't have a pier. It didn't have a tower. And it certainly didn't have miles of golden sands. Yet folks fled here, mainly from Bristol but also by ferry from south Wales, in search of good clean fun and innocent amusement. They found plenty.

There's now a heritage trail pinpointing the locations of all that brought the crowds here. The boating lake. The miniature railway. The paddling pool. The fairground. The putting green. The numerous tea rooms dotted along the waterfront. The decommissioned double-decker buses offering overnight sleeping accommodation. And the centrepiece – the Blue Lagoon, a long open-air swimming pool filled with water pumped from the Severn.

The most alluring of the attractions was arguably the cinema owned and run by the implausibly named Mr Shufflebottom.

Largely dedicated to the showing of Westerns, the cinema was rough and ready, constructed from corrugated iron. It had a great nickname: the Galvanised Gaumont.

To create a seaside resort in a location not blessed by golden sands and next to a dangerous old body of water took some vision. Severn Beach was the brainchild of Robert Stride, a former World War I ambulance driver and a member of the family which, a couple of generations earlier, had founded and developed Avonmouth Docks. Stride moved here from Shirehampton, building roads, shops and houses on the farmland, before effectively turning the village into one medium-sized amusement park. There's no statue commemorating his achievements. There's no figure cast in bronze or granite, looking out over the estuary or welcoming arrivals at the station. The only salute is in the naming of Stride Close, a nondescript cul-de-sac of Eighties housing and garages that runs parallel to the train tracks.

Stride's vision lasted a generation or two until accelerating car ownership took people further afield for their thrills, mainly to places with sand and piers and safer waters.

There are few, if any, remnants of these pre-war halcyon days. The infrastructure of the attractions was demolished when the sea defences were upgraded and new housing built. The resort was extinguished. And while the heritage trail has plenty of stopping-off points, Severn Beach of the 1920s and Severn Beach of the 2020s bear only a passing resemblance. The heritage trail demands a fair amount of imagination. Without visual proof before our eyes, without hard evidence sticking out of the ground, we have to trust that the Blue Lagoon was right here, that the boating lake was just over there, that the putting green was inland a little towards the parade of shops. The information boards tell us so. We just have to believe.

One information board, entitled 'An Estuary of Passage', describes the vista that can be taken in on days when the visibility is much sharper. Certainly, being able to see the merest smudge of the north Devon coast today is the stuff of the wildest dreams. 'The estuary is a thoroughfare for all types of creatures,' the board announces rather sweetly, 'including tiny eel, flocks of wildfowl and ourselves.'

There's a similar theme elsewhere on the prom. What I initially thought to be a couple of blocks of stone left over from times past turn out, on closer inspection, to be a sculpture. The top block has been carved into the shape of a suitcase. 'Over the centuries,' its legend reads, 'so many people have passed through here on their journeys as traders, migrants and holidaymakers.' Add nosy authors to that list now.

While other, more picturesque locations have had the full National Trust treatment, their histories frozen in time, pickled and preserved and protected from the ingress of modern life, Severn Beach has seen the world change around it. The world has tightened and squeezed and flattened its history. A new identity has been forced upon the place. What is it now? And who lives here?

Tracey over in the estate agents will know. Her doors have just opened for business. I tell her that, when I was last here those 30 years ago, the place felt like a final destination for those in the early evening of their lives. I expected the place to have shrunk and shrivelled over the intervening years, but the number of 'Sold Subject to Contract' properties in her window suggests otherwise.

Tracey explains that, despite the current spiralling mortgage rates, demand for properties in Severn Beach comfortably outstrips supply. It makes her job easier. And, certainly, the queue in the baker's just a few doors down shows a clientele that's anything but retirement age. It seems that, a century after the delights of Severn Beach thrilled daytrippers by the thousands, the popularity of the place is on the climb again.

The ready availability of jobs within a mile's radius has made this happen. The corridor between the village and the M49 is now home to a multitude of warehouses and distribution hubs – and quite understandably so. There are four motorways in the vicinity heading in all four directions of the compass. Amazon has an enormous warehouse here and is a major employer. Tracey explains that, on moving to the village into rental properties, Amazon employees find they enjoy the bracing sea air and the unstressed nature of the place, and decide to stay here and buy. There are two park home estates in Severn Beach and, contrary to my preconception, these are not the preserve of retirees. Instead, they represent the easiest way for first-time buyers to put their excited feet on the first rung of property ownership. Those regular trains to Bristol, plus the close proximity of the retail paradise that is The Mall at Cribbs Causeway, also help to exert a magnetic pull.

Despite the influx and demand, though, Severn Beach isn't overwhelmed with facilities. Surprisingly for a community originally created for the purposes of leisure, there's neither a pub nor a chippy (although those with a hankering for fried and/or greasy fare can later pay a visit to the kebab van permanently parked outside the village hall). The lack of a pub is surely down to Robert Stride's Methodist tendencies. Instead, the centre of the village, the meridian point, appears to be the shop, as praised by Sid on the station platform. Open from early until late, and incorporating the local post office, it seems to know its importance to the residents. If you have a late-night need for colouring pencils, a

4.2-metre extension cable or even kitten milk (milk for kittens, that is), you won't be disappointed.

I continue to head away from the sea, eastwards towards the M49, to see what this latest incarnation, this reinvention, of Severn Beach – more accurately, the hinterland just beyond the village limits – looks like.

On my way there, I pass a very well-stocked children's playground and the bunting-clad village hall. If the number of classes offered therein is a barometer reading of civic pride, then the villagers of Severn Beach must be proud as Punch. It's a handsome hall, with its domed roof and parquet flooring, and hosts a community library, four-days-a-week Zumba sessions, dog training, yoga, badminton, bingo and the karate-based martial art tang soo du. All that's missing are Mr Shufflebottom's Westerns.

There's also a range of other courses through which to better yourself. Refresh your maths? Cooking on a budget? Art for self-expression? Allotment theory for beginners? Step through the doors and enlightenment shall be yours.

Beyond the busy A-road that separates the village from the industrial park, it's a battleground between nature and 'development'. There are multiple signs advertising box-fresh 'distribution units' of varying size, from comparatively modest 20,000-square-feet affairs to mammoth hangars with a footprint of nearly half a million square feet. The more combative, well-armoured plants – bramble, holly, nettle – do their best to swallow and strangle these signs and what they're advertising, to create a force field that repels these interlopers. But the invasion of this breathing space between village and motorway is without pause or hesitation. Nature is largely helpless against diggers that can remove and erase forever in a blink.

Before it's all filled in, this hinterland has yet to be defined, resembling what the writers Paul Farley and Michael Symmons Roberts dubbed 'edgelands' in their book of the same name. To them, edgelands are 'a complex landscape, a debateable zone' that can take all manner of shapes and forms: 'the wooded perimeter of a golf course, an old path leading through scratchy shrubland, the course of a drainage ditch...'

At the perimeter of the industrial park, beyond the endless roundabouts and high-security gates and cameras and watchmen, beyond the lorries squatting in lay-bys while their drivers settle their tachograph debts, these are Severn Beach's edgelands, the fragile territory soon to be reclaimed.

Keep out.

Authorisation only.

Here, behind the link roads, behind the trees, are hidden cycle paths, pristine and unused. I walk down them, uneasy at their haunting silence, their emptiness. I come out at a busy junction where a fury of deadline-meeting lorries and vans jostle and compete for road space. Logistics is the new religion, the boom trade servicing a world of ever-increasing conspicuous consumption, of easy ordering and easy delivery. Get it there fast, faster than the rest. The lorries compete, and so do the company mottos on their trailers. 'Excellence. Simply delivered' say the DHL trucks. Gregory's fleet returns fire with 'Delivering winners'.

This is no place for pedestrians. I push the button at the crossing and the air brakes of half a dozen lorries sigh deeply. I suspect I may be the only person to use this crossing today. Possibly this week. But then I see a young couple approaching on the other side. He's carrying two bouquets of flowers. There's no obvious place they're heading; there are no houses in that direction, no birthday parties, no celebrations of any kind. And it's a Thursday, so definitely not Mother's Day. They avoid eye contact as we cross, their expressions solemn. A cold thought shivers through me: the flowers may well be the latest contribution to a roadside memorial. A death perhaps deliberate, or perhaps unplanned. No place for pedestrians.

The vast warehouses, these cathedrals to mass consumerism, have redrawn the horizon: Amazon, Lidl, Warburtons, Currys, Boots, Next, Farmfoods and the rest. But these link roads heading back towards Severn Beach should be much quieter. Four years ago, a new junction was built on the M49, a portal which would get these lorries onto the motorway network in seconds. But the junction has never opened, embroiled in a dispute over land ownership. Its blue motorway signs have been blacked out ever since. Here, near the end of the line, is a road to nowhere.

I loop back to the village in search of sustenance, a late breakfast. For the Amazon workers being dropped off after their night shifts, it's actually dinner time. Inexplicably, neither of Severn Beach's two cafés – the Just As You Are 'tea cottage' and the long-established, more traditional Shirley's Café – open before 10 in the morning. But thanks to a lengthy, map-less saunter around the recesses of the industrial park, it's almost that hour now. I plump for Shirley's. Not only am I a sucker for an old-style caff, it's also a scone's throw from the station.

'Do you want to sit inside or out?' asks the teenage girl behind the counter as I place my order. I don't answer. I turn to the window, letting the noise of the rain lashing the pane talk for me.

Behind me in the queue, a quintet of paint-flecked decorators deliver precise breakfast orders that they've probably been hungrily rehearsing over the past couple of hours of paintwork. The fifth and final decorator orders a 10 a.m. plate of sausage and chips, and a can of apple Tango.

Shirley's Café has been here since 1940, making it one of the few existing relics of the village's golden years, and it remains a favourite of many, from fair-weather scooter enthusiasts to all-weather birdwatchers. The Space Race-themed pinball machine and the handsome Seeburg jukebox have been in situ since the 1960s. Neither work any more – and possibly haven't for some time. The jukebox's most recent 45 is Toni Basil's 'Mickey', a hit from 1982.

This is a shame. I quite fancy demolishing my hash browns and double egg to a soundtrack of Jonathan Richman's 'Egyptian Reggae' or OMD's 'Maid of Orleans'. The latter would be quite fitting. The discordant industrial sounds in its intro could be field recordings made down the road in Avonmouth.

Although I'm the first customer of the day, the café fills quickly; there are more people in here than I've seen in several hours of wandering the streets and footpaths of Severn Beach. So, in lieu of musical accompaniment to my breakfast, there are plenty of conversations to tune into instead.

The decorators' chat isn't worth tuning into: a discussion of the relative merits of various online banks. A couple of flooring contractors sit across from them. They too favour fizzy drinks with their breakfasts. One has also ordered a teetering slice of the triple-decker Victoria sponge. Their Lancastrian accents suggest they're working away from home, presumably lining the floor of one of those mammoth hangars. 'I like working with Dean,' the cake-eater announces, 'but he's only got one speed.'

Behind me sit a mother and daughter running through a job application. 'It's only an entry-level position,' advises the mother between bites of her bacon and mushroom sandwich. 'It's well within your skill set.' The daughter stays silent, nervous.

Their breakfasts demolished, the decorators' chat has reached a juicier subject: an upcoming stag do/golf weekend near Brighton.

'Strip club!' yells the oldest decorator. 'We've got to go to a strip club!'

'You can go if you want,' says his bearded, bespectacled colleague, the one who knew most about online banks. 'I'll be sat outside in the minibus.'

The rest of the clientele are also precise with their orders. The widower who polishes off his cappuccino and shortbread seemingly before he's begun it. The older couple (two flat whites) and their pre-school grandson (strawberry milkshake). And the twitcher with his head in a book on seabird identification (mug of tea and a veggie breakfast). More than 80 years on, Shirley's Café is busier than ever. Half an hour after opening, there's only one spare table. Unless, of course, you're happy to take up the teenager's offer of alfresco dining.

All around Shirley's walls are postcards of Severn Beach's past. There are shots of beaming children in the Blue Lagoon, shots of beaming children on swings, shots of beaming children in front of the dodgems. There's also a photograph of the station from nearly a century ago, the platform teeming with dressed-to-the-nines daytrippers. The steam train that's brought them here puffs away in the background. These are phantoms from the past and this is their ghost train.

I zip up my jacket and head round the corner to the station. Sid has abandoned his sentry post in exchange for the funeral service and the platform is empty. The next train rolls into the terminus. For half of the journey back to Temple Meads – through the industrial zone of Avonmouth, under the M5 bridge, into the tunnels of Clifton – I have the entire carriage to myself.

My own personal ghost train.

— 11 —
THE VIKINGS ARE COMING!

Norwich–Sheringham

'Go to London. I guarantee you'll either be mugged or not appreciated.'

The concourse of Norwich station, modest in size and scale, is possibly best known for a scene in the second series of *I'm Alan Partridge*. It's where the hapless Radio Norwich presenter has been reduced to hawking unsold copies of his autobiography in the manner of a meat-market auctioneer.

Business is slow – non-existent, actually – so Alan, complete with headset, resorts to haranguing passengers more interested in not missing their train.

'Catch the train to London,' he calls out, 'stopping at Rejection, Disappointment, Backstabbing Central and Shattered Dreams Parkway.'

These days – or, more precisely, *in reality* – there's a flower stall in the spot where Alan set up shop. It's been there for 14 years now, serving the last-minute, gift-buying needs of the station's ill-organised patrons. Here's one of them now, a gangly, bookish man in a tweed jacket making an urgent purchase.

'Can you do a thirty-quid bouquet?' he asks, anxiously looking over his shoulder towards Platform 3, where the London train is just pulling in. 'Or maybe just that one there?' he says, pointing at a ready-made arrangement.

The reason for his anxiety will be made clear in around a minute's time; his girlfriend is just getting off the train. All that's between her seeing his desperate purchase is a gaggle of Ipswich Town fans waiting to take that same train back south for their side's home game this afternoon. Their number – presumably swollen of late thanks to the club's rapid rise to the threshold of the Premier League, form that has given them the confidence to walk around Norwich in Ipswich blue – does the trick for the flower buyer, obscuring his girlfriend's view of his panicked purchase. By the time she reaches the ticket barrier, the transaction has gone through. And here he is, welcoming her with a broad smile and an armful of blooms. It's the thought that counts – even if that thought only occurred at half-past the eleventh hour.

On the next platform, my train awaits, the 10.45 to Sheringham on the north Norfolk coast. The line from here to there has been known as the Bittern Line since 1997, the name having been chosen in a newspaper competition. The bittern is a member of the heron family, one whose secret ways see it usually operating out of view, down at the water's edge among screen-providing reeds. If it's something of a hidden gem for a birdwatcher to spot, the name is appropriate. The Bittern Line is something of a hidden gem too, angling north-eastwards from Norwich and flirting with the fringes of the Norfolk Broads before straightening up towards the county's north coast and the seaside towns of Cromer and Sheringham.

It originally ran beyond Sheringham to the inland village of Melton Constable, but the stretch between these two points died a bloody death in the early Sixties at the hands of Dr Beeching and his infamous report, 'The Reshaping of British Railways' – as did much of Norfolk's railway network. With the 12-mile stretch to Melton Constable out of commission, Sheringham became the terminus to those north-bound trains from Norwich.

Not that British Rail had too much faith in the town – or in those along the line. At the beginning of 1967, it shut the old railway station in Sheringham, opening up a new platform a hundred yards or so to the east, across the high street. This new station was now an unmanned halt, nothing more than a wooden platform and with no shelter to protect waiting passengers from inclement weather.

If this new, basic platform looked for all the world like a temporary measure, that may well have been what was intended. Later that year, British Rail signalled its determination to close the entire Norwich–Sheringham line. Fortunately, that was successfully resisted and, nearly 60 years on, the line is thriving.

For a rural service, the Bittern Line's timetable is extremely comprehensive. The first train out of Norwich for the north Norfolk coast leaves at twelve minutes past five in the morning. The last one out of Sheringham departs at seven minutes past midnight. Such a full service suggests that passenger numbers are strong enough to warrant it.

Numbers are certainly strong on this morning's 10.45. After we leave the station, gliding eastwards out of the city, the train briefly accompanies canoes, pleasure-craft and swans on the adjacent River Yare. The weather is warm and it's a fine day for messing about in boats. It's also a fine day for messing around at the seaside, a sentiment confirmed by all aboard this three-carriage service.

It's a rural route, taken leisurely, of unmanned level crossings and unmanned village stations. Crop-sprayers with enormous arms are on patrol beyond the train windows, quenching the thirst of the dusty fields. Other meadows worship the sun, filled with row after row after row of solar panels.

Lonesome farmhouses slide by, the kind that newspapers would invariably describe as 'remote' when reporting on a dark deed done within its walls, as if it's an adjective that could also be applied to the character of the perpetrator.

On-board conversation is chilled and chipper. Kids sing and parents laugh. One man has a loud and jovial conversation on the phone in Polish, but nobody's concerned. (It turns out that Partridge's catchphrase survives translation. 'A-ha,' says the Pole, as he repeatedly agrees to the points being made at the other end of the phone line. 'A-ha … A-ha … A-ha.') There's a rather more academic conversation about bacteria going on behind me. My lack of Polish and my ignorance of the finer points of microbiology means both are difficult to understand.

Pleasingly, there are also a few – which translates, in the smartphone era, as a disproportionately high amount of – passengers reading good old-fashioned paperbacks. Curiously enough, two passengers sitting half a carriage apart – a young lad with curly ginger hair, possibly an English student, and a guy in his late fifties, possibly an English teacher – are both reading novels from the backlist of Howard Jacobson. The student seems to be particularly enjoying what he's reading. His leg vibrates with pleasure.

Across the aisle from me, a pair of women, in matching supermarket uniforms, embark on a conversation with a friend that's surely too personal to be put on speakerphone for the ears of the rest of the carriage. I suspect their friend on the other end of the line has no idea her words are available for public consumption. 'I can't do the job if it's detrimental to my mental health … Her behaviour is completely out of order … All the power's gone to her head … This just can't go on. I'm barely eating and sleeping.'

Once the phone call is finished, the pair lower their voices to little more than a whisper. This is, weirdly, just as distracting as their loud, three-way conversation. I look across to their table. A deck of cards has been produced, but one of the women has also laid out a black rectangle of fabric with a silver design on it. This is no normal deck of cards. Either on the way to or from work, the older woman is giving her friend a tarot reading.

Their voices continue at a whisper, so I not-so-subtly inch across my double seat to catch what's being said. The hushed tones are all part of the ceremony and I can make out nothing until the final card is turned. 'So this is saying you need to be careful with money.' It's a far-from-revelatory block-busting climax. I'm not sure you need a tarot set and a public reading to be handed this particular piece of advice.

At North Walsham, a quartet of pleasure-seekers – three men, one woman – get on. They're already on the beer. The guard comes along to ask to see their tickets.

'How about a beer in return for a ticket?' one of them jokily ventures.

The guard demurs. 'I suspect the beer's cheaper. I'd be losing on the deal…'

The closer to the coast, the slower the trundle as the train rises up a rare Norfolk gradient, followed by the first glimpse of the North Sea, today reflecting back the sky's cloudless, spotless blue. We descend into Cromer.

While Sheringham owes its existence as a bustling seaside resort to the coming of the railway in 1887, Cromer was already established as a retreat for the wealthy members of Norfolk society well before the first toot of a locomotive's whistle was heard here. The Hotel de Paris, a grand-looking establishment set up above the esplanade and pier, had introduced the town's belle époque several decades earlier. And before that, in 1816 Cromer was namechecked in Jane Austen's *Emma* as a place of recreation worth travelling to, praised for being 'the best of all the seabathing places'. For its deeper history, as well as for receiving the railway 10 years before Sheringham, Cromer has always felt like the more senior of the two resorts, even though at the last census their respective populations were near-identical.

We reverse out of the station, tracking the coast westwards. It's less than four miles until Sheringham. On an adjacent golf course, a golfer delays his tee shot, presumably with one eye on the safety of the train and its passengers. Past the caravans and lodges of a campsite, the train slides into the one-track terminus. It's good timing. The student has just finished his novel.

As our train arrives, another departs, but not down the track we've just travelled along. Instead, across the high street, is another railway line: the heritage railway known as the Poppy Line. A steam locomotive toots and shuffles out of Sheringham's original station, off towards the market town of Holt, five miles away to the south-west.

We'll pay the old station a visit later. For now, though, I want to take Sheringham in, to get the lie of the land. And to do this, I need to climb up one of the highest points in all Norfolk – the steep, sharp hill known as Beeston Bump.

Never mind the end of the line. When you're at the summit, this could be the edge of the world.

Thanks to the direction its beaches face, looking out into the abyss of the North Sea, Sheringham has always been susceptible to the angriest weather that various points north can throw at it. This, of course, takes its toll on the coastline. It's in the line of fire. But global warming is accelerating the process, with rising sea levels foreshortening beaches and stripping them of their shingle, a natural protection for sea cliffs.

North Norfolk District Council indicated in 2023 that erosion threatens Sheringham's coastal path and golf course, along with an 'iconic geomorphological feature to the east'. By this, they mean Beeston Bump, the land currently beneath my feet. These warnings are delivered in good faith. There are plenty of examples of how north Norfolk has been affected in this way over the years.

'Before' and 'after' photos of caravan parks along the coast from Sheringham show the dramatic ingress of the erosion, with landslips removing portions of land forever. Campsites are lost to the sea and footpaths are forcibly rerouted – in that they're now part of the landslip down below. In the words of the nature writer Robert Macfarlane, 'coastlines have become ghostlines'. The land is haunted by the spectre of global warming. An exorcism of sorts – in the shape of improved sea defences all along this stretch of Norfolk – needs to happen quickly.

Beeston Bump is no remote hill standing alone in splendid isolation. There are now a number of houses up here near to its crest, perched along unmade, sandy lanes. The house names are soft-sounding – Dayspring, Meadow View, Sunnyside – and give no sense of the inherent fragility and danger up here. The house nearest the cliff edge is a relatively recent new-build, suggesting more than a degree of optimism from the local planning office. Barely 30 yards of potentially crumbling clay cliff lie between its back garden and the beach far below.

I gaze over Sheringham, over its handsome orange roofs. Robert Louis Stevenson, the man who railed against the greyness of the slates in Wick, would surely approve, his heart gladdened by the warmer tones. The town is fine-looking but remains modest about its charms. The local tourist board has tried hard to market the place, listing '23 Amazing Things to Do in Sheringham' on its website. 'Amazing' is doing some seriously heavy lifting here. One suggestion is 'Explore the town centre'. Sure, will do. Another is 'Spend a day at the beach'. Erm, OK. 'Eat some fish and chips.' Hmmm, you can do that almost anywhere in the country.

Remarkably, in an effort to draw people to Sheringham, another suggestion is 'Take a day trip to Cromer'...

(This isn't completely fair on Sheringham. There's a full programme of weekend festivities over the coming months in the town, among them a commemoration of the 80th anniversary of D-Day, two classic car shows, a folk festival, carnival week and something called the Gansey of Inclusivity Display – plenty to add to those 23 suggestions.)

Today, though, as evidenced by the grunts and the groans, the shouting and the cheers rising from the common far below, Sheringham boasts one reason in particular to pay it a visit. Today, the town is hosting its annual Viking festival.

Everyone in Sheringham gets into the spirit for the one-day event. A post box wears a crocheted cover with a pair of Viking horns, while the bakery's window has given pride of place to specially baked Viking biscuits – gingerbread faces of Scandinavian interlopers with beards of pink icing.

Down on the common, there's no sign of the attractions that usually grace outdoor community gatherings. There's no tombola, there's no coconut shy. The stalls here are altogether more niche, more Viking-specific. Metalsmiths show off their creations while local producers of mead, that potent honey wine so beloved by our ancestors, offer a free taste with no obligation to buy. Festival-goers can also strike their own Viking coin, feel the weight of an iron tunic, or get their picture taken with a Viking helmet or shield or blade. Or all three.

You can also tune into ancient times by buying some Viking jewellery or investing in a sheepskin jerkin. And there's a burger van too. Apparently, the Vikings loved their burgers.

The action in the main arena is provided by Wuffa, a Viking and Saxon re-enactment society named after an early East Anglian king, which 'recreates life and war from the ninth century'. For the men, the requirements for membership appear to be having the physique of a front-row forward and ownership of a fulsome beard. Sturdy, meat-chomping types with bloodlust in their eyes need only apply.

To the untrained eye, the battles look full-blooded and authentic. It's not restrained nor seemingly over-choreographed. A roped-off, baying crowd, four- or five-deep in places, roars its approval, relishing every blow, every crunch, every groan. Beyond the arena, a small gang of pre-pubescent boys are staging their own battle (a re-enactment of a re-enactment?) with makeshift weaponry, their parents turning a blind eye. The take-home message? That, for one day only, it's perfectly acceptable for kids to recreate the violence of what they've just seen, to forcibly poke each other with sharpened sticks. All bets are off when the Vikings are in town.

Entire families take their place as members of the re-enactment society. Some of the teenagers don't appear to be quite as fundamentalist as their parents. As with that goth family on the first train of the day to Whitby, their demeanours seem to confirm they're here under sufferance, that they'd prefer to be arsing around with people their own age, and not indulging their parents' attraction to sword-based combat and blackened carcasses roasting over an open fire.

'This is probably my favourite day of the year,' a burly re-enactor tells me between battles. I don't catch his Viking name – it's a tangle of consonants that don't belong next to each other – but he looks like an Adrian or a Simon to me. 'We train every week for events like this. I'm as fit as I ever was when I played rugby. But rugby doesn't speak to my love of history in this way.'

There is history and heritage at play, plus an eagerness to show others how we used to live. But, being so many centuries later, it obviously can't be defined as anything approaching nostalgia. It is also, as Adrian/Simon has indicated, a good old workout. The re-enactment society runs three weekly training sessions across East Anglia – in Ipswich, Norwich and Beccles – to keep those combat skills as sharp as their spears.

Another warrior – possibly Grimnir or Ivan the Bowless – is red-faced from his exertions, the veins in his temples positively pulsing. He sips from a historically inaccurate can of Red Bull. Meanwhile, with his shaven head, the Viking known as Völundr – 'the Berserker of Wuffa' – looks like an executioner straight out of Central Casting, his authority further enhanced by him brandishing a fearsome bladed weapon that could remove a limb in a single strike. A head too, possibly.

After the final battle is completed (spoiler alert: there are no killings, no deaths. The St John's Ambulance haven't had to get busy with a body bag), the decidedly un-Viking prospect of a stock inventory is underway.

'We're down a spear. Anyone seen a spear?'

Walking back into town after the final skirmish of the day, a woman, one of the spectators, wears a replica Viking helmet, complete with horns.

'Why the hell have I bought this?' she asks her friend. 'I knew I shouldn't have drunk that mead.'

Unsurprisingly, things are more genteel away from the battle-ground. With cute cottages and narrow back streets running down to the sea, Sheringham carries echoes of St Ives (Cornwall that is, not Cambridgeshire), albeit with fewer artists and more amusement arcades – all of two of them. It's neither above itself nor remotely tacky. It's just right.

The quietness of life in this corner of Norfolk doesn't mean it's a place out of step or out of time – even if the presence of the Vikings and the steam-train hobbyists might suggest otherwise. It's simply that the north Norfolk coast feels like a refuge, a distant shore away from a scorched world constantly in conflict with itself.

A few notable people from history have sought refuge here, with one particular residence proving most suitable for this purpose. A sizeable home called Martincross, west of the town centre, was rented in the summer of 1910 by the explorer Ernest Shackleton. It was a time for him to rest and recuperate, a fleeting refuel, a brief respite. But his adventures became becalmed while he awaited his next commission, the next berth on a forthcoming polar expedition. Shackleton's wife soon found they were marooned at the top of Norfolk.

'Emily at first thought it was a well-earned seaside holiday,' wrote Shackleton's biographer, Roland Huntford. 'Summer, however, turned to autumn, autumn to winter, and still there was no sign of a move. To Emily's distress, Sheringham had become a port of call while her husband waited for something to show up.' Bizarrely, after learning of Roald Amundsen's conquering of the South Pole, Shackleton appeared to regain his mojo and planned a transcontinental journey right across Antarctica via the Pole. The threshold of Martincross, a house that represented a period of inertia and stasis in Shackleton's life, was never graced by his shadow again.

Martincross is a spacious white house with pale-blue wood-work. A blue plaque is visible on one of its outer walls, but it doesn't mention Shackleton's enforced sojourn. Instead, it celebrates the time spent here by its next famous inhabitant, one who moved in less than a decade after the explorer. Ralph Vaughan Williams took occupation of the house in 1919, and it was while living there that he composed his London Symphony. You can imagine him taking the short stroll down from Martincross to a bench high above the beach, contemplating the endless grey ocean before him as the wind slightly ruffled his hair, before wandering home, resisting the allure of the penny arcade, to turn his thoughts into melody, and to turn that melody into a big, bold symphony.

This afternoon, a pair of French windows leading out to Martincross's garden are open to let the warm air inside, but no music can be heard. No symphonies are being penned today by whoever lives here now.

The playwright and novelist Patrick Hamilton also called it home, albeit after the house was carved up into flats. Hamilton was the author of the play *Rope*, later taken to the big screen by Alfred Hitchcock, but his dwindling success led to alcoholism and in 1962 he died from cirrhosis of the liver, here in his flat at the age of 58. J. B. Priestley once tartly observed that Hamilton was 'an unhappy man who needed whisky as a car needs petrol'.

The restorative qualities of Sheringham couldn't mend Hamilton, but others would confirm that the Norfolk coast retains the power to heal. Roger Deakin, the famous alfresco swimmer of East Anglia and author of the classic *Waterlog*, would take to the salty seawater of Norfolk whenever he was struggling mentally. It was a cleansing exercise: 'like the fox ridding himself of his fleas,' he explained, 'I leave my devils on the waves.'

The twin attractions of warm sunshine and a Viking festival mean that the streets of Sheringham are somewhat over-subscribed today. Its food outlets are struggling to keep up with demand. I head for the calm of the buffet of the old station instead.

I take a seat by the window, swirls of smoke and steam from the train currently sitting at the platform drifting past. The hot-water urn in the kitchen hisses in fraternity. In this era-faithful buffet, you half-expect Celia Johnson to wander through the door at any moment. She doesn't, though. Not even the briefest of encounters.

Here on the Poppy Line, nostalgia is definitely the opium of the people. All aboard to the 1940s.

Vintage props sit on the platform, unused signifiers of a life long gone – milk churns, old suitcases, vintage advertising hoard-ings – an era not sullied by unattended packages or shifty-looking passengers, a world before the mantra of the railways became 'See it. Say it. Sorted.'

One of the stokers – dark smudges on his overalls, mutton-chop sideburns – pops into the buffet to recharge his coffee mug. He looks the spit of Gaz Coombes from Supergrass. 'Gaz?' I half-heartedly venture. He doesn't turn around.

One of the stationmasters sticks his head round the door of the buffet. 'Any more for Holt? Last train of the day. Anyone else for Holt?' He pops back out, a green flag is raised, a whistle blown. And away.

Although mentioned in the Domesday Book as 'Siringeham', it wasn't until the railway reached the town that Sheringham's posi-tion as a seaside resort worth people's attention truly took hold.

Into the mid-twentieth century, those evocatively painted railway posters made the town look impossibly alluring, especially when accompanied by the tagline 'Twixt sea and pine', a reference to Sheringham's Latin motto, which translates as 'The sea enriches and the pine adorns'. Back then, the trains arrived here from both directions, up from London and across from Leicester, a pincer movement by tourists grabbing the town for their own for a week or two.

For these volunteers, it's the fulfilment of boyhood fantasies – the ultimate model railway. The last days of steam are given an extension by the love and obsession of these volunteers. They might remember these times from their youth. Or they might not. There's the odd teenager among the volunteers. They might as well be upholding the traditions of the dinosaurs.

Two of the more senior volunteers – silver whiskers, peaked caps, three-piece suits with pocket watches hanging from their waistcoats – await the arrival of the next train from Holt.

'Is your wife not interested in volunteering?' asks one.

'She hasn't the slightest interest in any of this stuff.'

'And she doesn't mind you spending all your time up here?'

A hollow laugh.

'She volunteered me to join…'

Despite its brigade of enthusiastic volunteers, the Poppy Line is no small, amateur enterprise. Signs appealing for donations explain that the railway costs £3.6 million a year to maintain. That's £10,000 a day.

That seems an astonishing amount. But Chris, one of the stationmasters, explains that this covers the specialist maintenance of all the stations and rolling stock, along with the purchase of new locomotives and carriages, along with whatever renovation of them is required.

And it does appear to be a lucrative endeavour. The station buffet here at Sheringham, and the one at Holt at the far end of the line, is apparently perfectly capable of taking a few thousand quid on a busy day.

'We've had five or six hundred passengers today,' Chris says. 'We're fortunate. We're in a tourist area, so we have a ready supply of visitors. Other heritage railways are suffering because they don't have that. I know of one that was running trains over Easter with only five or six passengers on board. We're not rolling in cash by any means, but we keep our heads above water.'

Certainly, there's a sharp entrepreneurial edge underscoring the nostalgia. These volunteers know their market. And they know their money-spinners.

A host of special excursions keep the money flowing in, whether that's 'gin trains' ('Sit back and savour a variety of premium gins') or 'comedy dining trains' where, in addition to a steam-pulled excursion, you'll be served your evening meal by lookalikes of characters from either *'Allo 'Allo* or *Fawlty Towers*. 'You can expect to be caught up in the immersive, hilarious adventure from the start,' explains the event's blurb. Thanks for the warning.

These railway folk can even turn bad news into a penny. They recently hosted a commemoration of the 60th anniversary of the Poppy Line's closure, as advocated by Beeching's report. The event's promotional material even made curious use of jovial exclamation marks. I suppose that a resurrected railway needs closure in order to rise up and exist again...

The volunteers – whether on board, on the platform, in the buffet or working anonymously in the train sheds – clearly love their vocation. They also clearly love the time travel.

They're not the only ones.

The last whistle of the day has been blown and the cos-players of the railway hand back to the cos-players of the Viking invasion. The faux Scandinavians have gathered next to the old level crossing, from where they will march down through the town before setting fire to a replica longship on the beach.

It's a genteel invasion, the politest of incursions, guided and guarded by a squadron of hi-vis volunteer marshals. Yes, there's fire. Yes, there's drumming. Yes, there's chanting. But pillaging is low on the ground. The Sheringham branch of Holland & Barrett remains un-looted. The windows of Costa Coffee stay intact. These Vikings come in peace.

Once they've marched past, the whole town moves en masse towards the beach. It's time for the ceremonial burning of the longship, which sits on the sands, awaiting its fate. It's a very credible-looking vessel, with a dragon figurehead, a beautifully shaped stern and intricate gold motifs painted on it. It's even got a sail. To a landlubber like me, it looks perfectly seaworthy. Many hands have spent the intervening year fashioning this boat, only for it to suffer a quick death. And while the ashes are still warm, thoughts will drift to making another for next year's burning.

Several thousand people look on as various members of the re-enactment society gingerly walk across the pebbles to toss naked flames into the boat, the hull of which is packed with fast-burning straw. The fire quickly takes hold, the longship's timbers crackling to throaty cheers from the packed prom and cliff.

It's not a slow, lingering process. The boat turns to ash within ten minutes. A voice in the crowd behind me laments 'all those months of work'. Another voice joins in. 'Well, I guess the moral is, fire spreads quickly.'

As the boat's corpse continues smouldering until the tide comes in to wash the remains out to sea, I complete my last lap of the town, heading down narrow streets of Edwardian terraces and pebble-clad cottages. It's time to do the Bittern Line in reverse, back to Norwich. At the old level crossing, the Vikings are saying farewell to the festival for another year. Adrian/Simon strides past me, proudly carrying the spoils of a successful hunting-and-gathering expedition: a selection of yellow-stickered markdowns from Tesco across the road.

The re-enactors are still in costume, but out of character. They hug the rest of their tribe with a tenderness that Vikings weren't known for. 'See you at training on Monday,' they tell each other before heading – in their jerkins and their helmets – towards the car park. It's a reminder that, when the Vikings next stage an invasion, it won't be in longships. It'll be in Ford Mondeos and Vauxhall Corsas.

EAST IS EAST

London Fenchurch Street–Shoeburyness

'This one looks like it's toppling down on top of us.'

In the small square outside Fenchurch Street station, a couple of workmen are on a mid-morning break. They're both lying back on a stone bench, passing a joint between each other as they gaze up at the heavens – or, rather, at the jungle of skyscrapers towering over them.

If the tower in question were to topple down on them, it would take the station with it. This would, of course, be a terrible thing, for Fenchurch Street is arguably one of London's cutest railway stations. From the outside, at least. It has the appearance of a small but perfectly formed Florentine opera house. John Betjeman once called it 'a delightful hidden old terminus', cocooned in a warren of history-drenched streets with names full of stories, full of legends. Seething Lane, Crutched Friars, Savage Gardens... It's even more hidden now than in his day, dwarfed by the anonymous, reaching-for-the-skies towers of steel and glass that are its twenty-first-century neighbours.

Until recently, just before you disappeared into the station's modest-sized bowels, you could look to your left and catch a partial glimpse of the curves of the Norman Foster-designed 30 St Mary Axe – or the Gherkin, as everyone knows it. Not any more.

Another anonymous tower – occupied by anonymous companies engaged in anonymous trades – has blocked the view. Nothing to see here, sonny.

Despite being one of the four sainted railway stations on the standard Monopoly board (as well as the only London terminus without a corresponding Tube station), Fenchurch is little more than a chapel compared to the great cathedrals of arrival and departure. Save the hosannas for the big guns: Paddington, St Pancras, the reconfigured King's Cross...

Instead, Fenchurch Street goes unheralded by fanfares. It's a discreet side entrance into the City, and thus also a discreet side exit. An invisible point of departure. A sidling-off, a slithering-away. A quick escape for those beating a hasty retreat. Up a short escalator, through the barrier, choose the first train to leave from its four platforms and you're away. Miscreants could be casually walking up Fenchurch Place one moment and then gone in 60 seconds.

The station has just four tracks with limited final destinations. Grays or Shoeburyness. Shoeburyness or Grays. Occasionally, the Shoeburyness train will terminate early at Southend Central. A rare note of jeopardy on an otherwise dependably limited line.

It's time for me to sidle off, to slither away, to escape. Grays or Shoeburyness. The decision is already made. Shoeburyness is at the end of a line. Grays isn't. I'm sidling off to the seaside.

Past the Tower of London and out of the reaches, out of the limited confinement of the tumbling, crumbling walls of the City, the Shoeburyness train rides along parallel lines to the ketchup-red driverless trains of the Docklands Light Railway, the service that the writer Iain Sinclair, the psychogeographer-general, calls 'the unmanned fairground ride'.

Beyond them, we also ride in further parallel with Cable Street, with its Jack the Ripper museum, its ancient music hall, its fascist-bashing heritage… A condensed history of the East End in a single thoroughfare.

East London speeds past the window, all cell-block housing and mosques, back-street garages and corner boozers, postage-stamp parks and boxing gyms. It's done a fair amount of time in the ring itself. Under this dark sky, it's battered and brooding, bloodshot and bruised. Swollen around the temples. The sun tries to squeeze through the clouds, keen to paint a smile on the East End's troubled face, keen to help it sparkle.

The DLR splits away at Limehouse, off to serve Canary Wharf, the peaks of which glower like distant monsters, or to head under the river to Woolwich, the ghost train below the water.

'The next station is West Ham.'

'Come on you Hammers!' squeals a pre-pubescent voice further down the carriage, the boy's faith undented by his team losing in a European tie last night.

Round the back of the East Ham train depot, the train traces a broad, sweeping right-hand curve before a re-tilting left at Barking, lining up this silent bullet of a train to fire arrow-straight into the heart of south Essex – out through the new towns, across the marshes, the main line to the sea.

By the time we get to Upminster, the cell-block housing is now distant. We've reached the suburban belt, the land of the semi-detached. Upminster is home to the eastern terminus of the District Line, that fern-green horizontal stripe cutting across the Tube map. It represents the last vestiges of London before Essex properly takes charge. Back gardens start to lengthen. Allotments start to appear. Fields too. Fields!

It's a fine day, warm and breezeless. The flag of St George, found on many a backyard shed, raises barely a flutter.

Upminster is the cradle of Ian Dury, a man who once put today's destination, Shoeburyness, into song, recalling 'a kindly, charming shag' who hailed from the town. The only other time Shoeburyness has been set to song was in Billy Bragg's Essex-isation of 'Route 66'. That version, 'A13 (Trunk Road to the Sea)', was gifted a series of rhyming place names: Pitsea, Thundersley, Hadleigh, Leigh-on-Sea... Bragg could have added Shoebury, as that's how everybody, bar this train's pre-recorded announcer, refers to the town.

Here at Upminster, an older West Indian woman gets on, taking the seat across the aisle. Fearing a penalty fare, she checks with me that she's not sat in first class. She's not, I tell her. There is no first-class carriage.

'One day I'll make it there,' she says, before almost instantly falling into a nap, fingers still wrapped around the handle of her suitcase. Her gentle snores are the purrs of a contented cat.

She's certainly not disturbed by a ponytailed man in double-denim, whose accent seems to vacillate between Canada, Dublin and north-east England. He's loudly delivering his verdict on the latest unpublished novel that a friend of his has asked him to read.

'This one is still too much "Oh woe is me",' he tells his travelling companion. 'But I can't tell her that. That's the job of the person writing the rejection letter.'

Nor is the West Indian woman's snooze affected by the two-year-old boy dancing on the seat in front of her, his blue sunglasses bouncing on his nose. His young mum puts out an arm to steady him.

'He loves trains,' she offers as a partial apology to those around them.

'Truck!' he shouts when he spots a lorry out of the window, proving he knows his onions when it comes to all manner of wheeled transport.

His mum strikes up a conversation with a woman in her seventies about the economics of parenthood. She gave birth to her second child three months ago; the younger son is with his grandfather further down the carriage.

'I'm on maternity leave at the moment,' she explains. 'I get a year, but the last three months are unpaid. I can't afford that with the cost of living, so I'll go back after nine months.'

'It's hard, isn't it?' offers the older woman. 'My mum had to work nights and then she looked after us during the day.'

No one on this train is working today. This is a Friday-in-half-term leisure ride. No one's face wears the stress of meetings, emails, deadlines. Kids read comics. Parents tackle crosswords. Daytrippers, yeah.

Once under and beyond the M25, housing estates nestle close to the tracks, the gentle curves of avenues and cul-de-sacs copying the gentle curves of the line.

Aside from Dury and Bragg, south Essex's other most notable musical sons are Dr Feelgood. When we reach Benfleet, the band's home turf of Canvey Island hoves into view, just the other side of Hadleigh Ray, the thick tongue of river poking inland from the Thames. Well, as much as a famously sub-sea-level island can hove into view – just the circular tanks of its oil refineries show on the horizon. Oil city, they call it.

The sun is properly out now, just as today's forecast predicted, and is on a mission to dry up the sodden pastures on both sides of the track. We hit the coast proper at Leigh-on-Sea, the cranes of the north Kent coast standing blue-grey across the sands and the estuary.

The carriage thins and quietens after Westcliff, and even more so at Southend Central, which is where the now-awake West Indian woman gets off. No penalty charge, as promised.

I can now hear Double-Denim Man again. He appears to be talking about a conceptual artist who substitutes toothpaste for paint. Forget Canada. Forget Dublin. Now that I can hear him clearly, his is definitely a north-east accent. Sunderland, to be more precise, as confirmed by the line 'I grew up in Roker'.

We slide into sun-soaked Shoeburyness, bang on time. It's getting properly, properly warm now. Coats are jettisoned; a further button or two undone on the next layer too. And a short-list of candidates for this afternoon's ice cream of choice is already being drawn up by the small gaggle of teens sauntering out of the exit. 'Mint choc chip?! Are you my grandma?'

We're at the seaside.

But, strangely, despite the front carriage of the eight-car train nudging the buffers, Shoeburyness station isn't technically the end of the line. There's another line on the other side of the narrow station car park. A secret line. A ghost line.

This single track crosses the high street, a high street in name more than anything, with just a smattering of shops, along with an Indian restaurant and a pub. For what I will find over the next few hours is that Shoeburyness doesn't have a discernible centre, one where a town hall, a post office, a police station and a doctor's surgery can be found in close proximity to each other. Instead, I discover a town bordered by fences and with no particular centre of gravity for everyday life.

I follow the ghost line as it carves through the town, towards the barracks. Technically, though, it's not carving through the town. The track was here well before the arrival of the 1970s housing stock that flanks it.

Near the high street's level crossing, there's plenty of detritus on this lost track, mainly discarded bottles and cans. Plants have taken over too, a rewilding of the line. It's just how you'd expect a disused railway to wear the passing of time.

But if you follow the track as it makes its way through the town, the closer it gets to the barracks, the better maintained it is. Pristine, in fact – its rails shiny, its gravel spotless, its sleepers devoid of any ingress from plant life, moss or otherwise. At this point, it shows all the signs of a railway line still in regular use.

A pair of postwomen are emptying the post box nearest to the entrance of the barracks. I ask them whether they know when a train last came through on this line. Their facial expressions – quizzical, stumped – offer no idea of timeframe.

'Well, I've never seen one,' says the first.

'Me neither,' says the other.

'Google will know,' says the first, fishing her phone out of her pocket. Her search reaches a local history site. 'Here we go. Looks like it stopped being used in 1959. So, sixty-five years ago.'

'Why are the tracks so pristine, then?' I ask. 'Why haven't they ripped them out and turned it into a cycle path or something?'

'There must be a reason,' says the second postwoman, picking up a half-empty sack of mail. 'Maybe they need it for another war...'

Later on, I will do my own digging. It's not that I don't believe the trustworthy employees of Royal Mail, but the condition of these tracks convinces me that they've not been out of use for six and a half decades.

My suspicions are proven to be well-founded. I find images online of a goods train crossing the high street that are clearly more recent than 1959. Much more recent. The cars shown waiting at the level crossing, obeying the commands of a couple of rail workers' manually operated stop/go signs, are definitely of twenty-first-century vintage. Indeed, it turns out this particular train made this particular journey in 2010.

I follow the ghost line as far as the fortified fences and gates of the barracks allow. Beyond these defences, there are allegedly six miles of track within the barracks' boundary. Apparently, this is where old railway stock was put out to pasture, a retirement home for slam-door carriages that were obsolete and unwanted, and that now required dismantling and disposal. Rumours circulate that this dismantling took the form of being used by the artillery for target practice. As one online commentator puts it, 'the sight of an old railway carriage on a low-loader heading through Southend was a sure-fire indication that we'd be hearing the big guns being fired in the next few days. Sometimes, living in the Southend/Thorpe Bay/Shoebury area was like living through the Battle of Borodino...'

All is quiet at the barracks today, though. There's no sign of movement, bar the security man in his hut at the barrier. This is prohibited land.

WARNING
AREA PATROLLED BY
SECURITY DOGS

This stretch of coastline, known as Pig Bay, is fenced off to civilians, thanks to the presence of firing ranges and ordnance disposal. (To iron out any confusion, Pig Bay is where a cadre of CIA-sponsored operatives did *not* launch an attempted overthrow of Fidel Castro's Cuban government in 1961.)

I've been told that a public footpath crosses the firing ranges and, if a flag denoting that shooting practice is in progress isn't flying, you can march – almost certainly at pace and with a tense sphincter – across this MoD land to Pig Bay. After a walk north out of Shoebury that's so long I'm now on the outskirts of the neighbouring village of Great Wakering, I eventually find the point at which admittance onto the firing ranges is possible. A lesser-used footpath disappears into the scrub. But the flag is flying today. Not that I've heard even the most modest boom, from either shelling practice or a training exercise in ordnance disposal, but the Admiral Nelson approach ('I hear no explosions' – or something similar) loses out. The path remains untrodden.

There's an even more dangerous footpath further beyond – the Broomway. Only accessible with a compliant tide, it heads two miles out to sea, taking intrepid souls past Wakering Stairs to a point close to the northern tip of Foulness Island. Unsurprisingly, the Broomway has gained the unofficial title of the deadliest footpath in Britain. Fast-recovering tides outpace any human-powered attempt to escape. The number of its victims over the years is a three-figure total.

The writer Robert Macfarlane is clearly a more intrepid soul than me. He's tackled this walk into the abyss. And he survived. 'If the Broomway hadn't existed,' he reported of his excursion, 'Wilkie Collins might have had to invent it. Edwardian newspapers, alert to its reputation, rechristened it "The Doomway".'

Macfarlane – who, for indistinct reasons, elected to walk the Broomway barefoot – bluntly outlines its quintessence. 'There is mud that can trap you,' he warns, 'and quicksand that can swallow you,' while also noting that the mortal danger on offer isn't just served up by nature's hand. The MoD signage team have been out there too.

WARNING: DO NOT APPROACH OR TOUCH ANY OBJECT AS IT MAY EXPLODE AND KILL YOU.

Back in Shoebury's northern reaches, here on East Beach, plenty is prohibited. As if all the MoD signage around the town didn't feel invasive enough, the local council has laid down the law, too.

No digging.

No metal detectors.

No horse riding.

No dogs.

No barbecues or fires.

And be aware of the unexpected.

A pair of pink-cheeked older men carry fold-up chairs onto the beach, but I can spot the contraband they've brought here. Secreted inside the folded-up chairs are modest-sized metal detectors. These are dissident detectorists.

Once the two of them are out of sight of the potentially prying eyes of the barracks, once they're hidden behind the bushes and dunes, they'll both turn their machines on and embark on their daily hunt for buried treasure. 'Mainly military ordnance,' whispers one of them to me. 'Although a Saxon burial ship would be nice.' They clamp their headphones on and begin their umpteenth sweep of this end of the beach.

Here, the posts of the Shoeburyness boom are visible, a sea defence that stretched out across the estuary for several miles to protect against incursions by submarines during both World War II and the Cold War. To the south of it, the beach is mainly the playground of kite surfers, sandcastle builders and over-enthusiastic dogs delighted to have the feel of sand under their paws, even if they're breaking a local by-law by doing so. Up on the substantial grassy area above the sands, impromptu kickabouts are breaking out. Essex boys in Man City tops? That's a practice that the local council need to get on top of.

Beyond the kite surfers, beyond the defence boom – several miles out to sea, in fact – the haunting shapes of the Shivering Sands fort can just about be made out on the horizon. Built to ward off enemy aerial raids, the fort comprises six towers; with their spindly legs, each resembles an outsized vintage box camera sat on a tripod. But much, much bigger.

South of East Beach, the old garrison land has been significantly repurposed in recent years, with a large-scale housing development fanning out across the site. But these aren't featureless, quick-cash-in homes being built. They're thoroughly in keeping, either built in the same, or similar, honey-coloured brick as the still-standing original buildings, or they're tasteful, low-level, half-timbered apartment blocks with balcony views across the estuary. Windows are wide open today. It's apparently obligatory to reach for Jamaican records when the sun is out, so a half-paced rocksteady tune spills from one apartment. Some light-as-a-breeze bossa nova can be heard from another. Less meteorologically appropriate, a stormy, thunderous version of 'Nessun Dorma' comes from a third.

Elsewhere, the original garrison buildings have been handed new lives. The former officers' mess has been repurposed as high-end accommodation; a fleet of similarly high-end cars are parked outside. The grandest of all the original buildings that's still lived in is the house that was once the garrison commandant's residence. While still a family home, it remains pretty much a mansion, one that could easily double as a generously proportioned country-house hotel.

The street names leave no one in any doubt about the area's history. Brigadier Way, Gunners Rise, Magazine Road... Artillery

Mews is a street currently being built. Heritage under construction.

The old garrison's cricket pitch, its wooden pavilion and the gorgeous Victorian houses on its boundary, with their immaculate hedging and blazer-stripe lawns, remind me of Barnes, my favourite part of west London. The new-build townhouses, distinctive in their shape and attractive in their butter-shade brickwork, carry echoes of Poundbury, the semi-urban experiment inspired by King Charles back when he was a mere prince, when his day-to-day duties allowed plenty of time to pontificate about architecture.

The old garrison's cart and wagon shed now houses the town's heritage centre, which holds a limited but still fascinating collection of old photographs, architects' plans, preserved uniforms and spent shells. There's also a quick-firing, 13-pounder field gun, which serves as a warning to anyone in the centre's café who's thinking of absconding without paying.

The most interesting exhibit tells the story of Godfrey Rampling. Godfrey was an officer with the Royal Artillery for almost 30 years, much of it spent here at Shoebury, where he also became the town's most notable sportsman. In 1932, he won silver at the Los Angeles Olympics as part of the British 4 x 400m relay squad. Four years later, at the Hitler-attended Berlin Olympics, he and his teammates converted it to gold. The leg that was run by Godfrey – which put Britain in front, a lead they didn't relinquish until the tape – relegated the home nation to bronze.

At this point, at the grand old age of 27, Godfrey hung up his spikes, ready to truly commit to his army career. He attributed his athletics success to 'running around the Shoebury Garrison cricket pitch a few times after working hours in my army boots'.

Oh, and he was also Charlotte Rampling's dad.

From the heritage centre, I continue wandering towards the coastline at Shoebury Common. Four twentysomethings – two couples – have liberated a shopping trolley from the Lidl down the road and are wheeling it towards the beach. I presumed it was full of booze, but its contents are a little more virtuous than that: multiple bottles of water, a range of salads, various meat products, some bread rolls and a single-use barbecue. The trolley is so laden that one of the lads is having difficulty steering it against the camber of the pavement. Its front two wheels dip over the kerb and he just about manages to wrestle control without all of the food pouring out into the path of a passing car. The other three carry on ahead, looking over their shoulders just to laugh at him.

Shoebury Common is where the coastline, having arced around the point, the ness, straightens up on its westerly approach to Thorpe Bay and, beyond it, Southend. It's where I aim to take refreshment at a local institution, Uncle Tom's Cabin. The café doesn't belong to anyone called Tom; the long-serving proprietor is a man called Peter Grubb. I've made it just before closing time and am served the last ice cream of the day as the waitresses shut up shop, cleaning the tables and stacking the chairs around me.

I expect Peter to be aglow with today's takings, it being the hottest day of the year so far, a day when the temperature has comfortably registered a higher reading than that forecast. Surely the drinks and ice creams have been flying off the shelves and out of the freezer.

'Not really,' he sighs. 'Just because the sun's shining, it doesn't mean that people automatically come out. The Golden Mile down the road will have been busy, with people going to Adventure Island.' The thrills and spills of Southend's eternally popular theme park are difficult to compete with.

'The weather's going to be the same tomorrow and it will be a Saturday, so here's hoping. When we're busy, this car park is full.' He extends his arm into a sweeping motion. 'And it's not been today. Far from it.'

Earlier on, I had a cup of tea at the café in the heritage centre. It was impossibly busy there, with all eight members of staff whizzing about like multi-tasking whirling dervishes. Perhaps Peter is a victim of the changing face of Shoebury. He's here on the common while the reconfigured buildings of the old garrison on the other side of town provide a more attractive place to hang out. And a new café soon to open at East Beach is unlikely to repel customers and send them Peter's way…

I wander back eastwards, the sun behind me starting to descend, setting the sea in silver. In an hour or so, as the sun closes in on the horizon – and just like Godfrey Rampling's Olympic career – that silver becomes gold. Nature's alchemy.

A flock of redshanks gathers on the pebbles below while, out at sea, a RIB flies across the waves to attend to a yacht that appears to be experiencing minor difficulty of an undiagnosed kind.

The combination of a hot day and a jetty will instantly make young men anywhere in the world strip to their underwear and hurl themselves into whatever body of water the jetty is serving. And so it is with Shoebury too – specifically the old barge pier, a long-decommissioned military jetty. Despite it being protected by a 12-foot fence topped with curls of barbed wire, a group of – mainly – lads (but a couple of young women too) have found a gap in the defences and are standing at the end of the jetty in their smalls, either considering whether they should take the plunge or shivering after having already done so.

Perhaps it's a Shoebury tradition to ignore all the signs that surround its citizens, limiting them, prohibiting them. Hidden metal detectors. Stolen shopping trolleys. And now trespassing that's ignored the decidedly unambiguous and plentiful signage.

DANGER
Unsafe structure
KEEP OFF
NO ACCESS PERMITTED

Then I spy the shopping trolley. The quartet I saw earlier are among the group on the jetty. The food – the salads and the meat and the bread rolls – remains untouched, unopened. The boys clearly just have to work up an appetite first.

Shoebury is a thoroughly dog-friendly place. Everyone seems to have one. The café in the heritage centre was thronging with them; it could have been a meeting of the Kennel Club. With the old garrison's extensive grounds reclaimed by its citizens, there's no shortage of wide-open green space. And, of course, the beaches when the town is out of season.

The playgrounds of the old garrison were once out of bounds to the Shoebury populace. Daryl Eastlea remembers those times well. A writer, DJ and music consultant, he grew up next door in Great Wakering during the 1970s and 80s and recalls the aura of the place just down the road.

'The garrison was simply off limits,' he tells me. 'The archway to the left of the Shoeburyness Hotel on the high street seemed to be a gateway to a world of war and danger. I remember a mate used to play cricket there against an army team and it just seemed so forbidden. Growing up in Wakering, you could hear the firing ranges every weekday and the windows of your house would rattle.'

Shoebury was where the young Daryl, aged 10 or 11, would cycle to buy singles and posters from P&P Records on West Road. His band rehearsed in the Thorpedene Community Centre, while he watched those of others play in the now-demolished Cambridge Hotel. Nonetheless, he never felt entirely comfortable when making the mile or two journey from his home.

'There was always a little tension – real or imagined – between us and Shoebury. It was our nearest train station, so you'd take a bus there and the adventures began. Shoebury always had a reputation for being rough and ready. East Beach felt pretty wild and absolutely enormous. Finding old bricks and glass in the sand was always fun. It also became the first place to drive to, after passing your test, for a snog.'

After initially commuting into London for work, Daryl left south-east Essex, decamping to north Wales and the Potteries for a number of years. But then, unlike Morecambe Liz, he came back to stay, back for good. 'While away, I idolised the train line in absentia and wrote a concept album called *Southend East*.' He offers up a sample rhyming couplet. 'On evenings your love for me / Will be a train ride down to Leigh-on-Sea.'

Shoebury is, in some ways, a different place now to the one Daryl knew as a kid. 'The population's been growing owing to all the building work. It still has something of a local rep, though. But the garrison has been giving people a sense of pride. They don't now try to cover living in Shoebury by fibbing that they live in Thorpe Bay.'

Absence appears to have made his heart grow fonder. As well as a deep admiration for the wares of the Khan Tandoori on the high street ('the proprietor calls me and my oldest pal Graham "the lovely gentlemen" and gives us complimentary Baileys'), the old place seems to be improving with age. 'From the end of Southend pier, looking back in bright sunshine, you could think Garrison Park resembles the Bahamas.'

While that's a comment shaped by the eye of the beholder, Daryl also offers firm confirmation that that postal worker's Google skills might be lacking. Born in the mid-Sixties, he can clearly remember trains using that lost line – 'our own sinister Chigley' he calls it. The notion of 1959 being the last time those rails felt wheels upon them is now thoroughly debunked.

It's time for me to head back to the tracks, but I take a long detour back to the station, off in search of this elusive town centre, the absence of which makes Shoebury feel a little unanchored. Further inland, with its innumerable food takeaways, Ness Road – the end point of Bragg's A13 – seems to be the closest thing that Shoebury has to a true centre-point.

I look in the window of an estate agents to get a sense of the kind of outlay necessary to become a resident of one of Shoebury's swankiest streets, but they've adopted the novel and far-sighted policy of not including the prices on any of the particulars of its properties. This deliberate action looks like the kind of fundamental error that Alan Sugar would rail against on *The Apprentice*, questioning the wannabes' commercial savviness. 'How do you expect people to buy the blessed thing,' I can hear him bark, 'if they don't know how much they'll be paying?'

These very streets used to actually resonate with Sugar's bark. Round the corner from the estate agents is the site of his old Amstrad factory, the production line of the company's computers in its 1980s/1990s heyday. I have to question Sugar's own commercial savviness here. The far corner of south Essex is perhaps not the wisest location for easy access to the motorway network, for efficiently reaching the rest of the country. But what do I know? He seems to have made a few bob, despite centring his business here in Shoebury.

Tragically, the old Amstrad site has another link to reality television. A few weeks ago, the former *Gogglebox* star George Gilbey – who, after also appearing on *Celebrity Big Brother*, had returned to life as a self-employed electrician – fell to his death while working at the factory, now occupied by a homecare company. Just awful. The floral tribute to George remains in position at the factory gates.

It's a sad note on which to leave Shoebury, and my pace is noticeably slower as I wander back to the station. There on the platform, waiting to be rushed back to the dark heart of the capital, to the concrete jungle, to metropolitan life, is Double-Denim Man and his travel companion. He's on the phone, his booming voice probably audible across the estuary in north Kent.

'No, no. I really enjoyed it. I really did ... Yeah, honestly.' Behind him, his companion is silently giggling. 'And I'm sure many publishers will too.'

While his nose doesn't grow from being economical with the truth, it does glow tomato-red. That's what a day in sunny Shoebury can do to you.

— 13 —

THE OUTER LIMITS

Aldgate–Chesham

I n 1972, the newly anointed Poet Laureate, John Betjeman, sat among the white tablecloths of the Chiltern Court restaurant on London's Marylebone Road, addressing a documentary crew from the BBC.

Fifty-two years later, I too am sat at a table in the same establishment. Now, though, it's called the Metropolitan Bar and isn't the haven of fine dining it was in Betjeman's day. It's now part of the Wetherspoons chain and today's diners are working their way through some of the capital's cheapest breakfasts. The high ceilings and claret walls remain, albeit now decorated by vintage-style posters on a railway theme.

Its early-morning clientele appears to be a combination of bike couriers fuelling up for a day of furious pedalling hither and thither around the capital, and those fresh off the earliest trains into Euston and King's Cross from points north. For the latter, it seems it's never too early for the first pint of the day. Nor is it too early for a flutter on the pub's huge Vegas-style fruit machines.

The Metropolitan sits above Baker Street station, the point which, for Betjeman at least, marks the gateway between the City and so-called Metroland, the suburbia which sprang up in the early twentieth century, following the London Underground's

Metropolitan Line as it forged its way through the pastures of Middlesex, Hertfordshire and Buckinghamshire.

Betjeman was here filming a documentary, *Metro-land*, which aired the following year and which examined the imposition of this massive programme of house-building upon the landscape, much of which was constructed at the bidding of Metropolitan Railway Country Estates Ltd. He started his north-west journey from here, from Baker Street. But the departure point for me this morning, once my breakfasting is done, will be at Aldgate, 16 minutes and 8 stations away, at the southernmost tip of the Tube map's famous magenta stripe. This magenta stripe represents the world's first underground railway, which opened to passengers back in 1863. The Metropolitan Line.

Aldgate station was built on the site of an old plague pit, where a four-figure number of bodies were buried, each of which had to be exhumed and removed before construction of the station could begin. The station opened in 1876.

It's nine in the morning, so Aldgate's exit barriers are swinging open much more often than the entrance ones, delivering commuters to the skyscrapers of the City of London. I'm heading for the suburbs and beyond, so I'm against the flow, against the shoals of commuters.

You can't help but think the engineers behind the world's first underground line were taking rather a gamble. The combination of smoke, wooden carriages and a limited oxygen supply sounds like a seriously dangerous mix. Aldgate did at least have fresh air. It remains unusual in this, one of those rare phenomena: a Tube station in the dark heart of central London that's open to daylight. (Farringdon, through which we'll pass in a few minutes, is another.) Accordingly, pigeons patrol the platforms, occasionally stepping through the open carriage doors to cadge a free ride to Liverpool Street.

Aldgate boasts another anomaly: it's a Tube station with buffers. It's both the start and the end of the line, as denoted by a red STOP sign and a red-and-white-striped barrier.

Do not pass. No entry.
Authorised personnel only beyond this point.

I'm almost certainly the only one of the two dozen people getting on board this train who'll be travelling all the way to the buffers at the far end of the line, all the way to the Buckinghamshire market town of Chesham. For the others, there's no care that this is the Chesham train. They're not bothered where it ultimately comes to a halt, where it will fall into silence, where the driver will be sprung from the cab. They're only concerned that it stops where they want it to stop: at the Barbican or Euston Square or Great Portland Street or wherever.

I've ignored all the other trains heading north-west on the Met Line and have waited it out for the twice-hourly service that will take me into Zone 9 on the Tube map, to the far side, to the outer limits.

The train makes quick progress through its early stations – bustling Liverpool Street, quiet Moorgate, sun-drenched Farring-don. Before you know it, we're beyond King's Cross and are tracing our way directly underneath the clogged A501, the thor-oughfare known at varying points as the Euston Road and the Marylebone Road.

Like the rest of the Tube network, this carriage is not the place for casual conversation, for idle chit-chat with fellow passengers.

This is an unwritten rule. Attempts to contravene this practice will cause hard stares and possible relocation to another part of the carriage. With chat, with friendliness, comes danger, apparently. Silence as defence. En garde.

Everyone is too engaged in other activities to be able to converse anyway, sending texts or emails while absorbing what's coming through their headphones or earbuds. Lost in music. Lost in podcasts.

Only a Spanish family – husband, wife and teenage daughter – talk and laugh as they and their suitcases navigate public transport to take them from King's Cross to Baker Street, where more sunshine welcomes them.

There's a long stretch without stopping between Baker Street and Finchley Road, with the Met allowing the Jubilee Line, which runs alongside on parallel lines, to stop at St John's Wood and Swiss Cottage.

The train bends westward at Finchley Road, taking it above the rooftops of Kilburn and through Willesden, where again the Jubilee Line stops at these intermediate stations while the Met maintains its pace. We burn straight past Neasden and its enormous depot, where the Tube's rolling stock comes to be cleaned and to spend the night.

In Betjeman's day, the Met Line did stop at Neasden. To him – the proto-Portillo, albeit more poetic in his commentary, of course – it's 'the suburb that's thought to be commonplace, home of the gnome and the average citizen'. Beyond its boundary, Betjeman notes, is 'an unimportant hamlet where, for years, the Metropolitan didn't bother to stop: Wembley'.

Out of the windows on the carriage's left-hand side, the arch of the new(er) Wembley Stadium demands attention. *Oi, look over here.* Without it, the stadium would be out of sight for Met Line passengers, hidden behind the growing towers of corporate hotels and high-rise apartments.

At Preston Road station, a squirrel runs along the parapet of a wall with the top half of a burger bun in its mouth. It renders him too wide to squeeze through the slats of the fencing on top of the wall, so our furry friend is forced to go up and over, in the process avoiding a fall onto the electrified track below.

A couple of outpatients, grasping their appointment letters, get off at Northwick Park for the nearby giant hospital of the same name. An elderly gent, his left eye patched and bandaged, presumably the recipient of an early-morning appointment, gingerly steps on board. A mile or so up the line, not a single straw-hatted public schoolboy gets on at Harrow-on-the-Hill.

A young woman walks through the carriage and silently places a packet of tissues on the seat next to me, along with a laminated card. The card explains that she has no job but does have a one-year-old brother to support and that any financial contribution will help – and that God will bless me for whatever help I can give. She walks on to the end of the carriage, where she takes a seat and waits.

A blessing from God seems good value in exchange for the 35 pence I have in my pocket (which is 35 pence more than my pocket usually contains in these cash-free times) and I place it on the seat next to me. She returns, I apologise that that's all the money I have on me and that she should save the tissues for a more generous customer. She gives me a tough little smile in return, perhaps offended that I made a handout, not a purchase.

She's not the only person walking up and down the carriage. A man in his early seventies – wearing shorts and multi-coloured compression socks – pushes his walker as he does multiple lengths of the train. 'I need the exercise,' he tells us. 'I can't sit down. I'd fall asleep. And then all hell would break loose.' Quite what form this hell would take is never disclosed.

When he arrived in Pinner, Betjeman described it as 'a parish of a thousand souls, 'til railways gave it many thousands more'. Indeed, Metroland saw Pinner's population grow eight-fold in the first three decades of the early twentieth century alone.

The architects of Metroland made impossible promises, contradictory reassurances. They neglected to mention that mass outward migration is just that: the large-scale relocation of people and all that entailed. Instead, as the brochure for homes on the Loudwater Estate in Chorleywood shows, the emphasis was diverted onto 'the trees, the fairy dingles, and a hundred and one things in which Dame Nature's fingers have lingered long in setting out this beautiful array of trout stream, wooded slope, meadow and hilltop sights'. The people were seduced, the downsides never investigated.

In fact, as Betjeman notes, much of this idyll was not just given up for but actually contributed to the building of suburbia; 'the landscape yields clay for warm brick, timber for post and rail'.

The writer Valerie Grove has observed that Metroland was 'a kinder word' than suburbia, one that offered more allure and attraction, mystery and mystique. Indeed, in his debut novel *Metroland*, Julian Barnes had his main character, the disillusioned suburbanite Chris, declare to none-the-wiser Parisians that he was a resident of Metroland, it sounding 'stranger than Middlesex'.

In *Tropic of Ruislip*, another novelist, Leslie Thomas, noted the illusion, how its residents were 'in the country but not of it. The fields seemed touchable but remote.' As the historian Dominic Sandbrook has said of the idyll disingenuously promised by the posters and the promotional literature, 'this was what people thought they were buying: their own little place in the lost English countryside, complete with a golf course, a cinema and a reliably fast connection to the capital'.

Metroland, green in its early days, has largely been filled in ever since, an endless belch of brick, concrete and tarmac, those breathing spaces suffocated. 'Semi-rural' is a term really only applicable once you're within earshot of the M25's 24-hour growl.

And we're there now, close to the orbital, moving into the territory of the well-heeled. Cricket clubs and golf courses and hockey pitches. We cross waterways with their time-oblivious narrowboat communities; we pass under the motorway, with its time-precious white van community. *Your package will be with you within the hour.*

There are sizeable homes in Chorleywood; Metroland's suburbs get smarter the further upcountry you go. Back in the early 1970s, Betjeman still regarded Chorleywood 'essential Metroland. Much trouble has been taken to preserve the country quality surviving here: oak, hazel, hawthorn, gorse and sandy tracks, better for sport than farming, I suspect. Common and cricket pitch, church school and church – all are reminders of a country past.'

This is what would invariably have been labelled the 'stockbroker belt' in days gone. Nowadays, those furiously working the financial markets are more likely to live in Docklands eyries, their time on the trading floor not compromised by lengthy train rides out to these parts.

Open farmland breaks out between Chorleywood and Chalfont & Latimer. We're reaching the tip of Metroland, speeding past cow parsley-tipped meadows. Beyond Chalfont & Latimer, we bear off to the right, avoiding the Amersham terminus and heading for Chesham's buffers instead. Unlike at Amersham, there's no onward travel on the national rail network from here. It is a true end of the line.

Chesham itself is closer to the original Metroland ideal that ultimately tainted itself, overpopulating the likes of North Harrow and Pinner. It's greener here, more rural. The railway helped Chesham's growth, but it has always remained a standalone market town, not a continuation of a conurbation. The spread outwards from the city had run out of gas before here.

It's a single track into Chesham, weaving and winding where previously we were taking the shortest distance possible. In these last couple of miles, hills make their first appearance on this morning's journey. These undulations represent the foothills of the northern half of the Chilterns. They don't remotely resemble the cloud-nudging peaks of the West Highland Line, but they're a welcome sight after all those suburban flatlands.

An hour and a quarter out of Aldgate, Chesham is undeniably one of the Underground's cutesiest stations. Every few yards along the platform, urns overflow with flowers of various shades of pink; one of its disused tracks is now an Italian sunken garden with a vintage bicycle as its centrepiece. Women in floral dresses wait to board the return service to London, standing in front of a notice advertising a forthcoming cream tea afternoon. A piano concerto plays over the station's speakers.

You could certainly imagine steam locomotives pulling in back in the day, greeted by a stationmaster stepping out of his office to welcome passengers to his town. It retains that branch line terminus feel, the calm ebb and flow of incoming and outgoing trains, leaving on time but never in a hurry.

Despite it being a Thursday morning, there's a cricket match in progress in Chesham. And despite it only being 11 a.m., one of the opening batsmen, a range of elegant shots at his disposal, has already notched up a half-century. Sat on a grass bank, it's a rather idyllic way for me to wait to meet a certain local resident to provide an overview of Chesham's virtues and delights. The knocking sound of leather repeatedly meeting willow is regular and frequent as the boundaries amass, accompanied by the clack-clack of the railway wafting across on a soft wind. The first leaves begin to tumble from the oak trees surrounding the pitch.

Across the car park from that grassy bank, a modest people-carrier with plenty of miles on the clock pulls up outside the gates of Chesham United FC. As a director of the club, the driver is well known around these parts. As a stand-up comedian, the leader of the comedy band The Horne Section and the presenter/creator of the televisual phenomenon *Taskmaster*, he's also now a house-hold name and face. He is Alex Horne.

We've arranged to meet so that Alex can help me get under the skin of the town that's been his home for nearly two decades. We head inside, but don't want to disturb the main activity in the clubhouse where the chairman has just signed another new player ahead of the start of the new season this weekend. And I mean, *just*. The contract and pen sit between the pair; run your finger over the signature and the ink would smudge.

Instead, we head back outside, taking seats in the directors' box in the stand and gazing out across a pitch that's currently being watered, despite rain being forecast for later today. After becom-ing a director two years ago, Alex can sit in these particular seats without fear of repercussions, although he is keen to tell me this isn't his favoured vantage point for matches, preferring to stand on the shallow terrace to our left, pint in hand and surrounded by family and friends.

But how did you get out here?

'We moved here about seventeen years ago. We lived in London, Kensal Green, and just couldn't quite afford it. And we didn't want to have kids there so we were persuaded out this way by my parents-in-law. They went to a wedding in the village of Chenies and told us it was a lovely area, so we had to come and see it to keep them happy. But they were completely right.

'We had a look in Amersham, which is next door, but again couldn't quite afford that. The estate agent told us to try Chesham instead. Seventeen years is a good long time, but we're definitely not locals.'

Alex grew up in Sussex, so somewhere south of London might have been a more obvious choice to put down new, if semi-familiar, roots, but back then the Chilterns made logistical sense for the couple.

'Rachel worked at the BBC at the time, so that's straight in on the A40 from here, and I was doing a lot of travelling as a stand-up. It was a practical solution. Someone in our band lives in Hastings and it's just a nightmare because from there everything is north. So going south would have been a disaster.

'We didn't know anyone here so we would spend most days on the Tube seeing friends in town. Or, getting them out here, because we were the first in our friendship group to move out of London. And we finally had a house, rather than a tiny London flat.

'I think I was aware of Chesham being at the end of the Met Line. Being a nerd, it's officially the furthest Tube station from Charing Cross. When we moved here, the Tube didn't actually come to Chesham. You had to get a shuttle bus from Chalfont. It always had a station, but it was a dotted line on the map. After reopening, it's a solid line again.

'Still, it's only two trains an hour, so you have to prepare a little more. I'm meeting friends in town tonight, so I need to be on the five o'clock. It's more of a train than the Tube. But I quite like that. You just have to plan your life a bit more.

'I don't use it for work though because we film *Taskmaster* in Chiswick and it's an absolute nightmare to get there on the Tube from here. It'd take about two and a half hours. If I am working in town though, I'll get the Met Line in and get lots of work done on the hour-long journey. Until Finchley Road, that is, where you go underground and lose the internet...'

For someone now on our television screens so frequently, being based in Chesham has placed a welcome buffer between Alex's work commitments and home life. Chesham cannot be described as showbizzy.

'No, it's not showbizzy, but it is very artsy round here. There are tons and tons of musicians and artists, because it's affordable. And there are quite a few stand-ups too. It's a good cultural place. It had its first fringe festival this year. Yes, it's not Chiswick media, but it's still artsy, which I prefer. Although Russell Grant does live here too, so it's a *little bit* showbizzy...

'I don't want to do Amersham down, as I do lots of things there, but that's more of a commuter town because it's always had the Tube. And it's got slightly bigger houses so it has more people who work in more impressive jobs in London. I'd say there's more of a community here.

'We don't think of ourselves as posh, which many other places in the area do. It feels fairly real with lots of very normal people. There's a bit of an underdog mentality, I think. It's quite a plucky town. We're clinging on to our high street like everybody else. There aren't too many empty buildings, but there are a lot of charity shops and tanning salons. But we've got some really great cafés and independent shops. We're clinging on to those – quite proudly, I think. Fingers crossed they survive.'

As he goes about his everyday life in Chesham, Alex doesn't insist on invisibility, on hiding out of view. He helps out with poetry competitions and school prize-giving ceremonies, and he turns on the Chesham Christmas lights ('if I wasn't here, it would be very dark'). Alex's most conspicuous contribution to the make-up of the town, though, is his directorship of the football club. He, Rachel and their three kids have been coming to matches regularly for five or so years; two years ago, he upped his involvement. How on earth does he fit being a director into such a crazily busy schedule?

'I'm not busy at the weekend. I used to be because of stand-up gigs, but now the weekends are protected. That's family time. We all come down here. It's such a sociable club. And you can drink at non-league football so we can have a beer.' The directorship isn't a bind, a chore. 'It's not "Oh, I've got to go and do that." It's more part of the weekend, part of the routine.

'I don't have any official duties, although there is a monthly board meeting, but I've only gone to a couple of them because they're on Mondays at five o'clock, when I tend to be filming. But they're very understanding.

'It's not a financial thing. Everyone talks about Ryan Reynolds and the other bloke at Wrexham. It's not chucking money at it. It's not that at all. I think it's my duty to attract more people through the gates by helping out with events, hosting them. It's just about being willing to say yes.'

Alex is a fine and willing ambassador for both the club and for Chesham itself. Despite the stellar success that's come his way since he and Rachel first moved here (at the last time of counting, *Taskmaster* has now been franchised in 13 countries), there are no plans to move anywhere more glamorous or more secluded. Or, indeed, into a bigger home.

'I like living in a normal house,' he concludes, rising out of his seat in the directors' box and heading back to his people-carrier. 'And Chesham is just a normal town.'

I return to the same bench on the grassy bank in time to see that opening batsman reach his century with a beautifully cut boundary. A few minutes later, he hits a six that causes a pair of spectators – desperate to avoid the ball, which is travelling like an Exocet in their direction – to fall out of their garden chairs and onto the grass. To a man, the fielders can't help but smirk.

A cricket match and a lovely chat with Alex Horne – and it's not even lunchtime. I wander back to the town centre to see if the rest of my time in Chesham will be as agreeable.

I opt for the scenic route along the Chess Valley Walk, a hidden, meandering footpath that follows the path of the River Chess. It is rather a modest, underwhelming body of water. The broad, majestic Shannon it is not. So modest is it, in fact – barely six feet across in places and only just covering your ankles should you fancy a paddle in its clear waters – that another conundrum has popped into my head, one on similar lines to that which engaged my brain on the way to Ebbw Vale. This time, instead of wondering at what height a hill becomes a mountain, I'm curious to know how shallow and narrow a river can get while still being deemed a river. To me, this particular stretch of the River Chess – which ultimately joins the River Colne down in Rickmansworth – is a stream and nothing more than a stream.

I cut back towards the town centre. Everything is all very pleasant and – bearing in mind that riots have hit the country over the past week – thankfully peaceful. There's a branch of

Waitrose, there's a grammar school, there's a twice-weekly market selling cheeses and jams. And the high street has been bricked over, in a neat herringbone design, to create a pedestrianised area.

Like the main shopping areas of so many towns and cities across the country, though, Chesham's high street has probably seen better days. Some of its independent shops seem to be doing well; the Chapter Two community bookshop is a more popular draw than the branch of Waterstones, while Pearces Hardware is a proper 'four candles' establishment, with hundreds of little drawers and boxes behind the counter containing nails, screws and bolts of every imaginable denomination. But there are a good few vacant units where other businesses have fallen by the wayside. Who knew that a town of this size couldn't sustain a shop devoted to boxing memorabilia? The dust gathers around its doorway.

In one of the high street's charity shops, I bump into another comedian, Robin Ince, who's donating a teetering pile of books from his ridiculously enormous collection. Robin was born, grew up and still lives locally – Chesham was where he used to go to the cinema as a kid – and he confirms that the high street definitely isn't what it once was. To prove his point, he had a choice of at least half a dozen charity shops to whom he could have donated those books.

I head round the corner to Chesham Museum to learn more about the town's pre-Met Line history, about its heritage in the brick, beer and boot industries. But no sooner am I through the open door than I'm evicted – apologetically so, granted, but evicted nonetheless. It only opens twice a week, I'm told, to which I question why a) a swinging metal sign has been placed outside the museum, suggesting it is indeed open today; and b) why the museum's door was wide open and looking like it was ready to welcome the historically curious. Still, at least I got over the threshold. That's more than I've managed at all those museums since Wick.

I cross the road to check out Lowndes Park, a vast expanse of open parkland that's home to a skate park, a bowls club and a duckpond. Half Man Half Biscuit songs are rarely far from the front of my brain, and my internal jukebox has just selected another one, the market-town ode 'For What Is Chatteris?'

> One way system, smooth and commendable,
> Go by bus, they're highly dependable,
> The swings in the park, for the kids, have won awards,
> The clean streets acknowledged in the Lords.

Chesham feels this calm and undramatic – at least it does until I circumnavigate the perimeter of the duckpond. A woman approaches me, a bag of bread in her hand which she's been feeding to the impossibly cute ducklings. But as she gets closer, making eye contact and smiling, she suddenly stumbles and it looks for all the world that she's heading for the drink. But then, in a feat of balance that suggests gymnastic training earlier in her life, she manages to shift her bodyweight and stay on terra firma. Her smile gets wider. It's a beam of relief.

A theme is emerging. Earlier on in the hardware store, the man behind the counter stumbled over a cardboard box and ended up on the floor, sending a container of hooks flying as he did so. 'I'm fine,' he announced to the customers, trying to cover his embarrassment. 'But I'm not sure who put that box there.' He appeared to be the only person working in the shop.

As I loop back towards the high street, I'm greeted by a sight from my youth. It's been quite some time since I've laid eyes on a proper-job mod – suede brogues, fishtail parka and a pair of Sta-Press ironed so sharply that you could slice a finger on them. He looks effortlessly immaculate, the best-dressed man in town. That said, his brogues won't do well with the drizzle that's starting to fall, drizzle that will soon graduate to fat raindrops.

The rain scatters most of those on the high street either into cafés or in the direction of home. I opt for the former, seeking shelter and solace in the form of a toasted teacake and a mug of tea. And more eavesdropping as entertainment.

A man with a Father Christmas beard orders an Americano and 'a Coca-Cola chaser'. Sitting alone, he dictates a shopping list to himself. 'Brown sauce … crackers … cling film …' Each time he announces an item and jots it down in a little notebook, he clears his throat at an unnecessary – and, frankly, ridiculous – volume.

A woman comes out of the rain and pretends to study a menu before dipping into the toilets. Two minutes later, she emerges, positively galloping towards the door, hopeful that no one's seen her. 'Thank you!' comes the call from behind the counter. 'Come again!'

A mobile phone rings in the far corner of the café. 'As long as it's a Transit van or smaller, I don't have to upgrade my insurance. If I do, I'll be getting the company to pay. And if they say no, I'll just have to go back to the taxis. Did okay out of them before. Had a few nice holidays, didn't we?'

A couple in their twenties take a window seat and order milkshakes. It's now the middle of the afternoon.

'Can I order a breakfast?' asks the woman.

'You can have anything on the menu,' says the waiter, 'whatever the time of day. Cake for breakfast. Breakfast at tea-time. Whatever. I won't judge.'

I'm not just eavesdropping on my fellow diners. The television in the corner is showing the Olympics. This afternoon it's the taekwondo and I've just heard a fine piece of commentary that no one else appears to have picked up on.

'Points-wise, it's now nine to five.' A beat. 'What a way to make a living.'

Outside the window, the rain doesn't seem to bother the clumps of mild-mannered teens in their light sportswear, striding up and down, doing lengths of the high street, just like the old man with the walker on the train. Up and down, back and forth. Even if the weather did remotely bother them, there's nowhere to run to, nowhere to hide.

I pretty much feel that I've got nowhere to run to either. With the cinema once frequented by the young Robin Ince having said a metaphorical 'Fin!' many moons ago, and with me unable to feign being the kind of man who can lose himself in a hardware store for hours on end, the rain is making me concede defeat. I head back up the high street one more time, heading for the station. The rain is putting a shine on that herringbone brickwork.

A tent that's been on display outside Millets all day is sodden and a little limp. With no member of staff realising what the weather forecast had in store, it's become a pointless promotion. No one buys tents in the rain. And now the staff have a sodden tent to deal with.

Chesham is a market town that could be anywhere in southern England – Hampshire, Suffolk, Oxfordshire – so turning back up the hill towards the station, it's something of a shock to see the large London Underground logo. It feels incongruous, out of place.

For Chesham is not just another Tube stop. It's a station cherished by the commuters beginning to arrive from all points between here and Aldgate. For them, the urns of flowers, the sunken Italian garden and the piped classical music all mean one thing: home.

John Betjeman would surely approve. The Metroland dream is still partially alive.

14

DESERT BLUES

Hythe–Dungeness

There are some residents of Hythe, the market town just south of Folkestone, who have long since dispensed with washing lines in their back gardens – unless, that is, they want their bright-white bedsheets to be coloured putty-grey or their freshly laundered smalls to come with the fragrance of coal smoke.

These are the residents whose rear gardens back on to the Romney, Hythe & Dymchurch Railway, the 15-inch-gauge steam railway that puffs its way back and forth along this portion of the Kent coast. It's been puffing its way back and forth for almost a hundred years.

Its unlikely existence is, at the outset at least, down to two charismatic, decidedly glamorous figures: Captain 'Jack' Howey and Count Louis Zborowski. While Howey had indeed been a captain in the Royal Flying Corps, the count wasn't actually a nobleman; a Londoner born to American parents, he inherited the fictitious title his father had given himself.

Zborowski was born into money, though, and able to indulge his passion for racing cars. This was how he befriended Howey, another millionaire racing driver. The two also shared a passion for trains and cooked up the idea of opening their own public railway, albeit at a smaller gauge than usual. It would be the smallest public railway in the world. Or, alternatively, the biggest miniature railway in the world.

Zborowski – also an automobile engineer, renowned for the 'Chitty Bang Bang' racing cars he designed and built, which would inspire the future author Ian Fleming – tragically took himself out of the project when he was killed while racing at the Italian Grand Prix in Monza in 1924. He was just 29. Howey retired from the sport and devoted himself to honouring his friend's memory by completing their dream railway. A year after the count's death, Howey settled on the Kent coast as its location.

Progress was swift and the line from Hythe to New Romney – constructed after compulsory purchases of land had been authorised by the government – opened little more than 18 months later. The line was extended to Dungeness by the following summer.

The intention wasn't to build a tourist line. The Romney, Hythe & Dymchurch Railway would be used for freight – mainly shingle, ballast and fish – as well as serving the local population as they went about their daily business. Indeed, for the best part of 40 years between 1977 and 2015, every day local schoolkids would ride dedicated services that delivered them to the local comprehensive in New Romney.

When World War II broke out, the line was used for reasons that the captain and the count couldn't have originally envisaged. It was utilised by the army, which installed a miniature armoured train upon its tracks to patrol the coastline in search of unwanted invaders. The railway also proved a useful way of transporting troops up and down the coast, the first line of defence against any cross-Channel incursion.

When the New Romney-to-Dungeness stretch reopened to passenger traffic in 1947, the ceremony was conducted by none other than Laurel and Hardy, the pair hamming it up for the huge crowds, especially when it came to squashing Oliver Hardy's bulky frame into one of the small carriages.

It might have had multiple uses over the decades, but that it's now largely a tourist attraction is fair to see from those arriving in the car park ahead of the 10.30 departure from Hythe, the line's northern terminus. It's largely a family affair, with multiple generations gathering for the ride to the southern terminus. There's also a group of 60- and 70-something female friends coming together for the day, arriving in a convoy of cars.

'You were speeding. We had trouble keeping up with you.'

'No, I wasn't.'

'You were. My speedo said seventy and you were going further away.'

'Well, that was on the motorway. It doesn't count.'

'It's still speeding.'

For this group of retirees, the next hour or so will be distinctly more sedate, and devoid of arguments, mild or otherwise. But it'll come without the home comforts of their outsized SUVs. Wooden benches, not leather seats.

The platform is filling up, but there'll be plenty of room for all. The engine will be pulling twelve carriages, a long, slow snake down the coast. A handful of passengers watch the engine rotate on a turntable and couple itself to the front carriage, overseen by a couple of members of staff. Those working on the line aren't quite the cos-players of Sheringham's steam railway, for this isn't a line reclaiming and reliving a past life. This is a continuum of the area's only public railway. It's just operating the way it always has.

We drift out of Hythe, past those empty washing lines, the air turning black with smoke. It'll take more than an hour to reach the far end of the line, 13½ miles away in Dungeness. This is no high-speed service. With our heads almost scraping the ceiling of the diminutive carriages, we get to watch the world go by in slow motion. Nothing is a blur.

We see parks of static caravans. We see flat, tinder-dry August fields; some have been shorn, others await the chop of the combine's blade. We see that it's feeding time at a llama farm that sits adjacent to the line.

The driver's whistle blasts every time we come to a pedestrian crossing across the narrow track. Poppies dot the side of the line. Bramble bushes are heavy and pregnant with blackberries. Sloes are ubiquitous too, full and purple and dusty.

We ride over moss-clogged drainage rhynes, past fields of sunflowers. A pair of flirting butterflies fly through the carriage's open window and out the other side. A squirrel, with the most acrobatic of leaps, narrowly avoids an unnecessarily premature death.

Just after the train glides over a level crossing, a black-granite memorial appears next to the line. This is to commemorate the life of Kevin Crouch, one of the RH&D's train drivers who lost his life here in 2003. The engine he was driving collided with a car, its driver having not noticed the crossing's warning lights. Kevin was just thirty-one. At the first station stop at Dymchurch, there's also a memorial garden in his honour.

His death wasn't the first on the line – there were fatal incidents in 1927, 1946 and 1973 – nor is it the most recent. Two years after the accident which claimed Kevin's life, another driver, Suzanne Martin, was killed near Dungeness when she became trapped under her engine after another collision with a car at a level crossing. Again, the car driver claimed not to have seen the warning lights.

These two most recent deaths prompted the railway – some might say belatedly – to install half-barriers at each of its 13 level crossings that involve public roads. Since these were introduced, there have been no collisions between trains and vehicles.

At the request stop at St Mary's Bay, a boy of around five in a Spiderman T-shirt, aided by his mum and his grandma, flags down the train. The three of them squeeze themselves into our carriage.

'I was your age when I first rode this train,' grandmother tells grandson.

'It must be a very old train, then,' he cheekily replies, running the risk of drawing short shrift from Granny in the gift shop later.

I was his age too – younger, even – when I first rode these particular rails. My grandparents lived within a whistle blow of the line as it cut through New Romney. It was a fixture of holidays in the Seventies, whether riding its small carriages or racing in parallel to the trains in my gran's Fiat 126, her at the wheel, trying to get to the next un-barriered level crossing first. She was something of a reckless woman. Not only did she not insist her grandsons used the seatbelt when sat in the front next to her, but she also encouraged us to stand on the handbrake mounting and poke our heads out of the sunroof as we buzzed along.

(Grandad was more cautious. Each time we rode the trains, he would tell us the tale of how one of his friends lost an arm when travelling on the railway, torn off when a train came by in the opposite direction. Whether true or apocryphal, the story made us keep our arms inside the carriage at all times. I'm guessing he never knew about the head-through-the-sunroof antics.)

We're coming into New Romney now and I try to spot their rambling old house on the edge of town. No chance. Giant leylandii, as tall as a Kent oast house, obscure the view.

Over there, across the same scorched field and behind the leylandii, is the location of my earliest memory. I'm in their back garden in the summer of 1972. The two family dogs – Sammy the labrador and Spike the collie – are studiously ignoring each other on the lawn. My dad's sitting on a bench, looking all the world like Elvis Costello a good few years before the singer-songwriter Declan MacManus invented the concept of Elvis Costello. And I'm gazing beyond the fence, across the road, across that field. I'm watching smoke and steam rise and move along the horizon. I'm hearing the toot of a steam train pulling into the station. I'm feeling nothing but joy and wonder.

These fields have seen more than 50 harvests since then, but a pang of nostalgia, of a past life, has made my heart skip a little. Time travel can do that.

Although not mathematically the halfway mark of the line, New Romney is certainly its psychological midpoint, as well as being its biggest station. Captain Howey had his ashes scattered here after his death in the 1960s and his name lives on as the name of the hotel just beyond. New Romney station is the railway's nerve centre, its headquarters, its base of operations. Here are the sheds where the locomotives sleep at night. There's also a café, heritage centre and model railway. But there's no time to hop off and have a nose. I'm saving all my exploring for Dungeness.

After New Romney, the line curves closer towards the coast-line, towards the village of Greatstone, with its sand dunes visible to the left.

There are more memories to be exhumed here. It was in one of Greatstone's beach shops, in the summer of 1979, that I bought my first album – a cassette, the most credible-looking one they had in the carousel on the counter. It was the Electric Light Orchestra's *A New World Record*. I was spending another summer week with my grandparents, who had by now moved out of the old house in New Romney into a smaller, more manageable, more modern home in neighbouring Littlestone. My gran was a little concerned that a 10-year-old was splurging his entire holiday spending money on a recording by a *light orchestra*. Half an hour later, she was reassured when we arrived back at her house and the heavy boogie of 'Rockaria!' roared out of my cassette player, sounding like no light orchestra she'd ever encountered. My grandad, a frail man within a year of his death, picked up his *Daily Telegraph* and left the room.

Greatstone is the crucible of another notable transaction, a more recent one that cost a little more than £2.99.

In the spring of 2023, Nigel Farage bought a beachfront property on Coast Drive, paying what appears to be the second-highest-ever amount for a house on this particular street. But he was clearly just paying for the location. Twelve months later, plans for the property were submitted to the local planning authority – less than two months before he was finally elected as an MP, at the eighth time of asking. His constituency of Clacton is a full 129 miles away by road from Greatstone.

The plans showed that the existing house was to be demolished and a new, swankier pad built in its place. This was despite Farage already being the owner of what the *Daily Mail* invariably described as 'a beachside love nest' that he shared with his French girlfriend in the neighbouring village of Lydd-on-Sea. Still, if approved, the three-storey new-build, leading straight onto the sand dunes, will give him unbroken views across the water, from which to spy refugees making Channel crossings, before welcoming them into his new house for tea and understanding.

This particular stretch of the Kent coast – the beaches of Greatstone, Lydd-on-Sea and Dungeness especially – has been the landing point for many migrant boats in recent years. The Dungeness lifeboat crew have sometimes faced vocal opposition on bringing rescued asylum seekers ashore (even being branded 'traitors' by a baying gallery), a scene fuelled by Farage denouncing the RNLI to be a 'taxi service for illegal immigration'.

In response, the then coxswain of the Dungeness vessel, a former fisherman called Stuart Adams, made a commendable declaration that went some way to neutralising the criticism. 'I joined the RNLI for one reason and that's to help people and save lives. Whatever the circumstances, whatever the nationality, it doesn't matter to me. We are there to save lives and that's what we do.'

The penultimate stop of the R,H&D serves a holiday park, Romney Sands. Only a couple of folk here want to take the train to Dungeness; most stay on the platform, waiting for the next service to take them to the sandier beaches in the opposite direction. Also on the platform is a grease monkey, a volunteer engineer working on the line. His face wears the mascara of oily toil. One or two of the younger kids look decidedly nervous when they catch sight of him. (In a few minutes' time, at journey's end, I'll similarly catch sight of our driver's face. It resembles that of an end-of-shift miner, its sooty black only parted by the whites of his wide eyes and a beaming, toothy smile.)

As the train heads off on its final stretch, a man watering his plants in his back garden meets my eye, smiles and nods. He's no more than six feet away. Having a steam train just over your back fence doesn't seem to lose its appeal, nor overly threaten your privacy, despite the number of services rattling by every day, every week, every month, every year.

The back gardens disappear once we reach the edge of the Dungeness Estate, a border effectively marked by the pub garden of the Pilot Inn. Houses are sparsely distributed now, randomly occupying the shingle-heavy landscape. There are no clearly defined boundaries or gardens. No walls, no fences.

These narrow rails have brought us to what's regarded as the UK's only desert. The Met Office disagrees with this categorisation, stating that the local levels of precipitation disqualify it. Well, it certainly looks like a desert – as long as you disregard the rather sizeable body of water that is the English Channel. Turn your back to it and we could be in New Mexico, if you take the clumps of bramble and gorse to be razor-sharp cactus.

The train comes to a halt in the shadow of the old disused lighthouse. As the engine noise quietens, the constant sound of Dungeness reveals itself: the unending hum of the nuclear station about 200 yards away. These days, it's the hum of a power station being turned down, being decommissioned. Its army of pylons, once charged with carrying electricity away from this barren peninsular and towards the homes of the nation, stand lifeless, retired, demobbed.

A nearby sign reassures people not to be distressed if they hear the sound of loud and furious alarms coming from the power station, as 'routine tests of emergency sirens and test of emergency arrangements regularly take place'. However, there is also a list of what to do in the 'unlikely' event of a scenario involving the release of radioactivity.

The first piece of advice is somewhat obvious. 'Leave the area immediately.'

As I make my way through the busy café at Dungeness station, my passage slow among all the other passengers who've just disembarked, a realisation hits me. I think I've come to Dungeness on the wrong day.

And I've almost certainly come at the wrong time of year.

Dungeness is undeniably the most end-of-the-line of all my end-of-the-line destinations. Arid landscapes and decommissioned nuclear power stations tend to give off that air. For maximum effect, I should be here in the depths of wind-blown winter. Dungeness should feel desolate, exposed, despondent. But in high summer, in bright sunshine, there are just too many people around for the place to feel that way. There's too much of a flip-flops-and-Calippo vibe. The air is pungent with the coconutty smell of sun cream being applied. The queue to climb up inside the old lighthouse is long.

I need to give the crowds the slip. But it's not just the train passengers. There's a steady stream of cars making their way up the single tarmac road, here for sun and cider and double-cooked chips. And now here comes a coach party...

Derek Jarman didn't come here for the crowds. The filmmaker retained a bolthole here, a hideaway from which to distance himself from the claustrophobia of London; it was 'the last of a long line of "escape houses" I started building as a child at the end of the garden', he once wrote in his diary. Jarman bought Prospect Cottage in 1987 for £32,000 and turned it into Dungeness's most distinctive and recognisable residence. He covered the wooden cottage's outer walls and corrugated-iron roof in tar-black paint (a move subsequently borrowed by other home-owners on the estate), softening it with mustard-yellow window frames. Inadvertently, this secret hideaway has become something of a totem for Dungeness and, since Jarman's death in 1994, a site of pilgrimage.

While Prospect Cottage's interior – its wood-panelled walls, its simplicity – is only open to a limited number of visitors at certain times of the year, its border-less, boundary-free garden has been greatly celebrated. Indeed, Jarman himself was rather pleased with the results of his hundreds of hours of careful tending. 'Paradise haunts gardens,' he declared, 'and some gardens are paradises. Mine is one of them. Others are like bad children, spoilt by their parents, over-watered and covered with noxious chemicals.'

Jarman planted marigolds and dog rose and orange Californian poppies among the wild, ubiquitous sea kelp. He created circles and patterns using flint stones. And he made arrangements of timbers recovered from the shoreline, smoothed by the ocean and gnawed by the winds. The result gave him much pleasure in his final years as he felt the toll of his illness. 'Every flower is a triumph,' he noted, alluding to the inhospitable environment. 'I've had more fun from this place than I've had with anything else in my life. I should have been a gardener.'

I'm the only one considering Jarman's legacy. Neither house nor garden (nor, you suspect, the man's filmography) piques the interest of the drivers of a string of high-performance cars rolling past towards the lighthouses. Down the road from Prospect Cottage, the Snack Shack, housed in a converted shipping container, is infinitely busier. It's not quite midday, but they're doing a roaring trade. 'Fish and potatoes' appears to be the most popular dish: three fillets of the catch of the day served with fried spuds, rather than chips.

'Jill!' commands one of the many diners sat on wooden benches. 'Just dip one of these potatoes in that tartare sauce and tell me it's not the best thing you've eaten this week.' Jill does as she's told and, mouth full, nods her agreement.

I wander in all directions with no destination in mind, just pulled by the nearest and next piece of above-ground archaeology. Abandoned sheds. Discarded tractors. Forgotten bicycles. The flotsam and jetsam of lives.

Outside one particular shed, and stuck to its exterior wall, is a collection of treasure left on the shingle or brought in by the sea. Plastic spades, plastic dinosaurs, plastic containers, plastic buoys, plastic sunglasses, a plastic Minnie Mouse figurine…

The 'decay as beauty' vibe is something of a cliché, but here it's unerringly attractive. The cramped accommodation of wonky cottages built out of old railway carriages wouldn't normally turn heads, but set here among the simplicity and bareness of the place, such dwellings carry some strange appeal. Life stripped back to the bone.

The lifeboat station, high up on the shingle, is ready for any eventuality. The Channel looks passive today, which makes it prime conditions for boats bringing refugees over, but none can be spotted aiming for the shores of Dungeness. There are only the pale silhouettes of a couple of oil tankers on the horizon. No protests today. And no tragedies either.

Near the entrance to the Dungeness Estate, a couple of hundred yards inside its white gates and butting up next to the railway line, is Ocean View, a pink cottage with an adjacent gallery and a caravan parked to the side of the house. This is the home of Helen Gillilan, an artist and long-term resident of Dungeness.

We meet in the gallery, leaving the house to her dog, Sam, who's recovering after an operation. The gallery showcases Helen's work in various media, whether paintings or etchings or fabrics. She's lived in Dungeness since the 1990s, after a colourful and peripatetic few decades. A spell as a shoeshine girl in San Diego airport is one of the more notable entries on her CV. 'One of the best jobs I ever had.' She smiles. 'It was wonderful.'

'I rolled up here because when I was at Rose Bruford College doing theatre design, I met a scenic painter called Paddy Hamilton. Shortly after we got together, he said he wanted to move down here. He was born in Africa and lived in the desert, and this place reminded him of that. I hadn't been here before, but I had knowledge – in a very detached way – about the Jarman thing. I'm not a Jarmanite. People literally worship at the Jarman shrine, which I find really weird.'

Initially living with Paddy at their open studios down near the lighthouses at the ness, the furthest point of the peninsula, in 2002 Helen moved to Ocean View, at the north end of the Estate, after her mother died and left her 'a little bit of money'.

Through the open door of the gallery comes a boom. Not of thunder, but of the next train heading back up the coast to Hythe.

'I hadn't necessarily planned to live here. I'd seen another house in St Mary's Bay, which would have been lovely, but someone else put an offer in on it, so I started looking elsewhere. I said to these estate agents, "If something comes up at Dungeness, let me know."

'I was on the M25, stuck in traffic, and got a call.

'"Ocean View has come up for sale."

'"Which one's that?"

'"The one on the corner."

'I just said, "I'll have it."

'I bought the house from the original fishing family. They were all lifeboat people and they'd all lived on the beach for much longer than this house had been around. This house was built in 1912. It was Doris Tart's house. She was an Oiller originally and married a Tart.'

The Oillers and the Tarts are true Dungeness families, the roots of whom go deep. But they are, ultimately, incomers too.

The Tarts are of Huguenot stock, while the Oillers are of Cornish descent.

'Everyone's done their houses up,' says Helen, 'but I've done mine down, really. I've brought it back. The inside was all covered with hardboard, so I took that out. Underneath was all this bead and butt. I've retained it how it was. And people get kind of emotional about it, even if they don't necessarily want to live like that themselves. When they see it, they well up. I've literally had people in tears when they come into the house. People don't realise they miss it. So many of the houses here are sterile.

'I'm not stuck in the past, but I do like to have a connection to it. There's a real connection to the past on this beach. You feel the presence of the people. And the house has a great vibe because of them. Wooden houses are just lovely. But the storms are frightening here.'

With Dungeness's houses scattered across the Estate, and thus most residents being a three- or four-minute walk away from their next-door neighbours' property, what is the sense of community?

'There are two communities,' explains Helen. 'One is what Paddy calls The Non-Residents' Committee. They're the people who go to all these effing meetings but don't actually live here. They're just here every now and again. They've got properties here but they don't live in them. Then there's the people who live here permanently.

'I've never worried about being part of a community because I was born in Cornwall but both my parents were Londoners. I was always a foreigner. So I've never pushed it here. I don't go to meetings or anything like that, and I don't seek people out necessarily. But I am definitely part of the community. People know who I am and are glad I've kept the house as it is. All of that matters to people. It's very deep for those who still have their family roots here, even if some don't have houses these days. Jerry Oiller has a boat, but doesn't live on the beach any more. But all his family lived in these houses. In fact, his family lived in the Jarman house. There are very deep attachments to the place.'

The sound of the level crossing's siren again pierces the air. A pair of motorbikes, over the track before the barrier comes down, growl past.

'Dungeness does attract artists, but they can't afford to live here. I was the last one to squeak in. Even then, I could only raise a third of the value of the house and had to get a mortgage. I had to grow up – at the age of forty-something.'

The cars going past Helen's house are certainly beyond the financial grasp of most artists or writers, whether struggling or otherwise. If I was expecting an artistic enclave of dreamers, a raggle-taggle bunch of creative folk, that's not exactly what I've found. 'It's very different now,' confirms Helen. 'It's trendier types.'

At one time, only a single house – a green house called Fulmar, over the road from Helen's home – was let out to tourists. Now, there are around fifteen rentable properties – the likes of The Cabin, Shingle House and Garage Cottage. The old coastguard lookout, a squat, unhandsome brick tower, is rentable too. Offering just two bedrooms and a single bathroom, it's nonetheless one of those properties that commands a four-figure price for a weekend's stay.

'I let my house out too,' admits Helen, 'but because I needed a new roof. For three years, I stayed in the caravan during the summer season. This is the first summer I'm back in the house.

'The beach does generally give people a living. There's still a reasonable fishing community here. There are still a few fishing families. It's really important that the place retains its personality.

It's such a loss otherwise. That's why people love it here. They go fantasy house-hunting because they think the houses are charming.'

While some properties have been reconfigured for contemporary tastes (the *Grand Designs* cameras have been visitors to Dungeness), the brakes have been applied on further gentrification, much to Helen's relief. 'If there was any more,' she says, raising an arm to point to the road behind her, 'particularly on this drag, it wouldn't be the same place. It would just become Millionaire's Row.'

Having grown up in Cornwall, she didn't feel any psychological or cultural shock about being at the end, at being on the edge of things. 'I had to take the little fella to the vets in Rye yesterday to get him checked out. It was hectic out there. But then we got back here and it was...' Helen lets out a relaxing exhalation. 'It was the same when I was in Cornwall. Our house had a walled garden and when you got home and went in there, it was...' She lets out another exhalation.

'The world was away. And Dungeness is like that. I'm happy that I live in an unusual situation.'

Helen locks up the gallery and retrieves Sam from the house. It's time for his constitutional.

'What time's your train?'

'About half an hour.'

'OK, we'll walk with you across The Badlands.'

Rather than following the tarmac in the direction of the ness, we head behind the house and over the tracks, into an inland area more barren than the rest of Dungeness. There are no cottages dotted around here, no abandoned machinery, no stranded boats. And no people – unless the area's nickname holds true and there are bandits and robbers hiding behind the next bramble patch.

We walk for about 10 minutes. 'OK, that's far enough for him.' A post-op dog can't overdo it.

Helen gives me a hug and issues instructions before she turns back to her pink cottage.

'Head along this path here.'

I look down. There is no discernible path, just shingle and scrub dotted with sea kelp and gorse.

'Follow it to that shingle bank over there. Once you're on top of that, you'll see another path. Take that to the next shingle bank and then you'll see the station. Have fun!'

Fortunately, I don't need the eye of a local to discern a seemingly non-existent path. Dungeness has plenty of waymarkers on its skyline. Two lighthouses and a bloody great power station for starters. I know my direction of travel.

It's probably impossible to get lost in Dungeness. But it's highly possible to lose yourself.

A young man of 19 sits next to me on my return journey as we shake, rattle and roll back towards Hythe. He lost himself over the past few hours, crunching his way over the Dungeness shingle, zigzagging and looping and double-backing his way across the stony tundra. It was his first time here. He loved the place, just as much as I did when I first came here at a quarter of his age. A camera has been around his neck all day (it still is), capturing the Estate in all its salty, wind-shaped quintessence.

He shows me what he's captured. The 50 shades of mono-chrome do the place justice, creating the isolation otherwise missing with today's visitor numbers. The monolithic lines of the power station, its cubes and cuboids. The loneliness and the fragility of the railway-carriage homes. The rotting hulls of boats left high and dry on shingle banks. The rust-rashed bull-dozers here to push and pull, to pull and push, to reshape the shingle after tides shift it into different patterns. The sky. The enormous sky.

By the time the train reaches New Romney, he's snoozing. I won't wake him, even though I want to point out where my grandparents' old house is, across that scorched field and behind those leylandii. I want him to have a taste of the time travel. After all, it was his great-grandparents' house. He is my son.

15

THE SANDS OF TIME

Ryde Pier Head–Shanklin

On this coin-bright morning, as on any and every coin-bright morning, the Solent – that channel of water created when the Isle of Wight slipped anchor from the mainland sometime around the last interglacial period 125,000 years ago – is a busy old thoroughfare.

There are scores of yachts on the water, bobbing this way and that without any overriding purpose, without any particular agenda. More determined is one of the Southsea–Ryde hover-crafts, scooting along at some speed. More lethargic is a container ship the size of a Hebridean island, its cargo piled high, making slow progress towards Southampton Docks.

This is the scene from the mid-morning ferry I'm aboard, a vessel that's barely a quarter full as it moves through the emerald waters of the Solent bound for the diamond-shaped Isle of Wight. Rather like the Pwllheli train up the Cambrian coast, where the daytrippers piled into the seats with the view and the local passengers didn't care where they were sitting, the tourists have positioned themselves at the windows of the ferry while the regulars stay in the seats in the middle. The locals don't need to keep a check on the view to see when we're nearing the jetty. The sound of a lowering throttle tells them it's time to gather their possessions and be first in line at the exit. The rest of us though, the irregulars, are gazing out the window where an offshore railway station is looming into view.

This is Ryde Pier Head, a station found, as its name suggests, all at sea. Terra firma, in the shape of the town of Ryde that's currently beaming in the sunshine, is half a mile away at the other end of the pier.

It's actually three separate piers: one for road, one for rail and one for feet. As we cross the ferry's gangway, about a third of the disembarking passengers are being picked up by cars or taxi here at the end of the pier. A third are heading to the station platform and the next service on the Island Line, which runs along two-thirds of the island's east coast. The remaining third can't be bothered to wait for the train, opting instead to walk down the pier into Ryde.

There's plenty to observe while standing on the platform. The hovercraft that earlier zoomed past us splashes out of Ryde and back towards the mainland. Along the pier road goes a quintessential 1950s American coupé – all tail fins and white-wall tyres, and in an eye-catching turquoise and white two-tone colour scheme – which has either dropped off or picked up some ferry passengers in style.

'What *is* that car?' an Asian-American woman on the platform asks her two male companions, both English. They shrug and apologise. They didn't see the car at all, two piers across.

She turns to me. 'Did you see it?'

'I did, but I've got no idea what it is. And if *you* don't know…'

(The car is later identified, by a friend of mine in the know to whom I supplied a hazy, distant picture of it, as a 1958 two-door Dodge Custom Royale.)

As the car disappears towards Ryde town, travelling in the opposite direction is the 11.30 service from Shanklin, which will, in just a minute or two's time, become the 12.03 *to* Shanklin. The Island Line is not a complicated one. There and back, there and back. And just six stops – although, excitingly, that six is sometimes seven. More about that later.

Opened in 1864, the island's railway was a steam service for the first hundred years of its existence, after which it was electrified. At this point, decommissioned London Underground rolling stock took over its rails, providing a somewhat surreal travelling experience as it chugged through the island's countryside.

More memories. I rode this line several times as a kid, one of the highlights of a series of daytrips from the mainland, along with a round of crazy golf in Shanklin. My abiding memory was the low-tech nature of the ride there. It was basic and it was bone-shaking, with the added joy of decades of cigarette smoke having been absorbed by the carriage seats. The train still smelt how London smelt, even though the capital was many miles, and a sea passage, away.

This was the late 1970s and early 80s, but those carriages stayed in service for decades after then. In 2018, the comic Mark Steel travelled to the island for an episode in his Radio 4 series *Mark Steel's in Town*. What he encountered, having disembarked at Ryde, was, to his irony-heavy eyes, 'the most luxurious railway network in the world, a beautiful, vast system of interconnected lines hurtling through the countryside at speeds that can reach up to three miles per hour'. He saved special praise for the service's 'wonderfully crafted seats that are so well designed they even manage to bounce up and down when the train is stood still'.

Built in 1938, these trains were finally withdrawn from service in 2020, after 82 years of service, having travelled an estimated 3 million miles in their working lives. Small wonder that their luxury, comfort and reliability might have become a little wanting by then. At this point, post-pandemic, the line was upgraded and newer trains, also requisitioned from the London Underground, made their appearance on the Island Line. These weren't the deep-level rolling stock of before; they were sub-surface trains that previously ran, in a little more comfort, on the District Line. But they were – *are* – still ex-Tube trains.

They are Tube trains that make all the same clanks, squeaks and whines that they once did on the lines of London. The same 'Mind the gap' warnings. The same sideways-facing seats.

But, nearly half a century after I first rode the line, the strange sensation remains: to be on a Tube train when the view out of both windows is that of the sea, of container ships, of hovercrafts. It still feels wrong.

The train pulls away down this 110-year-old curving pier and, half a mile later, arrives at Ryde Esplanade, our first station stop. Some people get off here for buses to parts of the island not served by the train. Several who walked here from the pier head, with suitcases in tow, opt to now get on board.

This decommissioned Tube train has only one opportunity to revert to its natural subterranean environment – when we disappear into the tunnel under Ryde, reappearing shortly before the town's third station, St John's Road.

I never sit down when I'm riding the Tube, so I elect to do similar here. It's only 28 minutes from the end of the pier to the end of the line in Shanklin anyway. And standing gives me a better view of the island as it slips past the window.

It has to be said, though, that it's not the most scenic of lines, especially for someone who in recent times has been geared up for the postcard vistas offered by trains to destinations like Wick and Whitby. The Island Line doesn't hog the coast like the Cambrian Line. There are no views that you scrabble to capture on your phone's camera. Much of the line is shrouded in greenery, enclosed by tree and bush. It's a line of function rather than a destination in itself, carrying commuters at the start and end of the day, and delivering daytrippers during the hours in between.

I glance up at the adverts above the seats. In the carriage's District Line days, these would have been singing the virtues of long-running West End shows or forthcoming exhibitions at the Tate. Now they nudge passengers towards the delights of Portsmouth's Naval Dockyard or Dinosaur Isle interactive museum.

Standing up also allows me to wander through the train to people-watch (and people-hear). This is another difference to the train's past life on the Underground. There's no deafening, stony silence throughout the carriage, no suspicion when someone starts talking to the person sat next to them.

Unsurprisingly, most conversation is on the polite and superficial side. Whether people have visited the island before. Which attractions they hope to take in today or over the course of the next week. And how much they paid for their hotel. The latter is a subject that causes one particular daytripper to do a comedy double-take, so extortionate is the nightly rate of a particular middling hotel. 'That's Ventnor for you,' a local man chips in. The daytripper is astonished by the price of three nights' accommodation. 'That's not much less than my monthly mortgage payment,' she notes, secretly rather relieved she'll be on a ferry home in a few hours' time, without the experience of an Isle of Wight hotelier clearing out her bank account.

The station that's sometimes the Island Line's seventh station is Smallbrook Junction, where trains only stop on days when the steam railway, which starts its journey to Wootton, five and a half miles from here, is running. Today is one of those days. 'Alight here for the steam railway' says a sign. That's actually all you can alight for. Smallbrook Junction is unique; the only station on the country's entire network that you can't enter or leave on foot. There is no entrance, there is no exit. You can only arrive by train to catch a train on the other line. That is the only option. A teenager on roller skates glides up and down the platform, dead ends in either direction.

After the station of Brading, we roll into Sandown, but those trees obscure most of the view of what appears, through the gaps in the greenery, to be an attractive-looking town. Past its Victorian station, though, it's just pretty anonymous Seventies and Eighties housing. There isn't, possibly thankfully, a view of the town's National Poo Museum, which is located in a former public convenience inside a Victorian fort high above the bay. Its advertising carries an amusing tagline: 'Britain's #2 museum'.

Lake is the penultimate station, where a solitary man, with an uncanny similarity to former England footballer Stuart Pearce, gets on. The guard has a small window in which to sell him a ticket. Lake station is just three minutes from Shanklin station.

The pair clearly know each other.

'What are you doing in Shanklin, John?'

'Better pubs.'

'Couldn't you have just walked?'

'And eat into my precious drinking time? I don't think so.' He's handed his ticket. 'Worth £1.60 of anyone's money…'

Waiting for me outside the station is Sammantha Cave. Sammantha is heavily involved in Shanklin's civic life; not only does she volunteer at the Shanklin Theatre, she also gives talks and walking tours of the town, imparting stories about its colourful past that would otherwise go untold and unheard. It might be a story about the hotel that not only had an alligator in the pool but a parrot that would call last orders in the bar. Or it might be the tale of how the son of Kaiser Wilhelm II, taking a break in Shanklin in 1914, had to make a swift and discreet exit from both town and country on the eve of war being declared.

It being lunchtime, we head for the garden of the Carlton Hotel, up on the cliff above the bay, for tea and sandwiches. It's here that Sammantha explains how her love for Shanklin began back in the 1960s as a young girl, when her family travelled from their home in Maidenhead to stay with her friend Miriam's family for a week in the summer holidays.

'We came to visit them when I was seven. I'm sure back then you drove onto the ferry over two planks of wood and then your car would be placed on a turntable inside the ferry and they'd push your car around so you were facing the right way to drive back off.

'We'd go to Blackgang Chine and, our favourite, Brading Wax Museum, which sadly is no longer there. I loved it. It had all these gruesome scenes.' All those traditional, timeless beach-based activities were happily pursued too.

'I thought the idea that my friend Miriam could go to the beach every day in summer was fantastic. On that first visit, I said to my dad, "I want to move here." He said, "There's no jobs." But that dream never went away. It's really hard to know what the appeal of the island is. I've spoken to other people who live here who aren't born and bred, and they say they fell in love with it in the same way. I think the island aspect – and coming here on a boat – had plenty to do with it.'

After that first trip, Sammantha's family became frequent visitors to the island, always staying in Shanklin – sometimes staying in summer, sometimes at Easter, sometimes in the October half-term.

'In those days, it was as dead as a dodo in October. You'd come down to the front and nobody would be about and nothing would be open. Absolutely nothing. It was like a ghost town.' In time, though, the tourist season on the island would stretch and expand. 'At Easter, nothing much used to happen, but over the years, you'd see places opening then and more tourists coming over. Things were really changing.' No more was the island's tourism industry exclusively focused on the six weeks of the school summer holidays.

Each time her family came to Shanklin, Sammantha would feel the pangs of those end-of-holiday blues when it was time to head back to the mainland. Since she moved here in adulthood, that's not a concern any more. 'I don't have to go home. I live here now!'

Who are the people who leave the mainland for island life? Is it mainly retirees?

'Yes, but not always. I have met some who perhaps started a business here, maybe a B&B or a hotel, but the bulk of them are of retirement age.'

And who holidays here these days, in what is still a fairly traditional Victorian seaside resort?

'It's hard to know as I'm not a hotelier or anything. A lot of the bread-and-butter of some of the hotels are coach trips for the older contingent. They come out of high season – in June or September. It's different in summer. I see all these SUVs with roof boxes. People tend to drive much older cars on the island, so they're quite noticeable. You start to see all these cars with 2023 or 2024 number plates. There's also more posh camping and chalets these days. There's definitely a growth in that side of it. Walkers and cyclists too.

'But the great thing about the island in the six weeks of the summer holiday is that it's still not packed out like everywhere else is. You can get a space in the car park. You can get on the beach.'

In its heyday in Victorian and Edwardian times, Shanklin would have been comparatively rammed; its trains packed, its hotels fully booked, its beach crowded. But the decline in numbers doesn't mean the death-knell is being sounded. Far from it.

'People say, "It's not like it used to be." No, it's not. But who wants the beach packed to the rafters? I definitely don't feel that the island is on the down. There are lots of little festivals and lots of innovations. Stuff's definitely happening. As a resort, I'd say Shanklin's doing all right. It's keeping its head above water, for sure. It's more of a year-round thing now as well. There will always be people down on the front and cafés will be open.'

We leave the hotel's tea garden to walk Shanklin's streets and dig into Sammantha's passion for the town's history. She's a natural guide, an evangelist about the town's past. 'I've always absolutely loved history.' She's on the committee of the local history society and is their current treasurer. 'I quite like a spreadsheet. It's only "money out" and "money in". But I've got a petty cash tin...'

For the next hour or so, Sammantha leads me on an unhurried, serpentine route around the town, both below and above the cliffs. We take in the thatched Crab Inn on the high street of the Old Village, where the American poet Henry Wadsworth

Longfellow once stayed. He described Shanklin as 'one of the quaintest and loveliest places in the kingdom'. Another poet, John Keats, once lodged at nearby Eglantine Cottage just off the high street.

Down on the esplanade, we pause for thought outside the Waterfront Inn. Back in Victorian times, this was known as Norfolk House and once, for a period of 18 months, Charles Darwin was resident here. It's firmly believed that he wrote at least part of *On the Origin of Species* in his rooms here. As with Ralph Vaughan Williams in Sheringham, the sea air seems to have helped liberate the mind. Charles Dickens also knew and appreciated Shanklin; he set a scene in *Our Mutual Friend* here.

Sammantha and I also take a stroll in Rylstone Gardens, an attractive and leafy park, and a known hideout for red squirrels. They're keeping themselves to themselves this afternoon, perhaps having a collective siesta ahead of tonight's performance by the Shanklin and Sandown Military Band at the gardens' bandstand. There could well be a few picnics to raid if the weather holds.

Our last destination is the Shanklin Theatre, where Sammantha volunteers a couple of times a week, either in the bar or behind the counter of the sweet shop. It's a further extension of her civic pride, and that of her fellow local residents too. Despite the theatre's busy schedule of events – the next month has 18 shows and concerts over its 30 days – it's largely manned by volunteers.

And the theatre isn't carrying all the cultural burden of the town. Sammantha tells me that planning permission has gone in around the corner for a new performing arts centre to take occupation of an old library.

'The island's on the up,' she concludes. 'It's reinventing itself. And it's doing so from the ground upwards, rather than people coming in and imposing it.' Her smile shows how content this makes her. She's still in love with the town she fell for at the age of seven.

I then head off solo, off to the wooded gorge that is Shanklin Chine. On those childhood daytrips of yesteryear, this would always be a place to fire my young imagination, a secret world of twisting paths and hidden corners, one made even more intriguing by it being frequented by smugglers back in the day.

As I wander down the chine, accompanied by the gentle tinkle of its waterfalls, I learn about its contribution to the Allied war effort in World War II. At that time, it was out of bounds to the public, with Royal Marine commandos taking possession of the gorge and using it as an assault course to fine-tune their preparation for sorties to the French mainland.

Even more significantly, the chine was used as a route for PLUTO, otherwise known as the Pipeline Under The Ocean, the secret underwater pipeline that stretched right under the English Channel, pumping fuel to storage tanks on the French coast to aid Operation Overlord – aka D-Day – in 1944. It liberated the Allies from a reliance on oil tankers that would have been susceptible – sitting targets, in fact – for German attacks either from the air or by submarines.

Sixty-five yards of pipeline still exist in the chine, part of the link that sent the fuel, with the help of gravity, to a pair of pumphouses down on the esplanade. Once I'm out of the chine's exit at the bottom of the gorge, I seek out evidence of these pumphouses. One is now an annexe to the Shanklin Beach Hotel, behind which it hid during wartime. The pumphouses' concealment was a stroke of genius, one that turned adversity into an advantage.

As Sir Donald Banks, director-general of the Petroleum Warfare Department during the war, noted, Shanklin had been visited by 'enemy low-flying planes which, in skimming in over the water under the radar beams, had devastated the picturesque row of Victorian hotels and villas that stood under the cliffs. Amongst these ruins, we built our pumphouses.' These pumphouses were ingeniously obscured from the German bombers' view. They were built behind those buildings still standing on the seafront, but above each of them, an iron-mesh platform was constructed. On top of this platform, rubble was placed, making it appear to German eyes in the skies that it was merely a bombsite, the location of a successful previous raid. Even if they knew an undersea pipeline existed, the crucial pumphouses were completely concealed from them.

Earlier on, Sammantha mentioned one particular member of the Luftwaffe who made himself well acquainted with the layout of the Isle of Wight during the war. Leopold Wenger was 21 years old when he made his first raid on nearby Ventnor in August 1942. Along with his appetite for bombing the island and taking civilian lives, Wenger also developed a parallel interest in photography and, from his cockpit, would cheerfully take photographs of the targets he was about to bomb. Even as he was coming in low, just about to despatch his bombs and unleash hell, Wenger would also be operating his camera, effectively taking the most ghoulish mementos imaginable. He would then send the photos to his parents.

In January 1943, Wenger was part of a 'tip-and-run' raid on Shanklin that targeted both a Catholic church and the local fire service headquarters, which was based in a requisitioned hotel. The attack claimed 23 lives, almost equally split between fire service personnel and civilians. 'This time it was Shanklin's turn to get it,' he wrote to his parents.

Six weeks later, Wenger returned to wreak more havoc and bloodshed on Shanklin, an attack that took the lives of another 12 citizens. Once again, he described the exercise in a callous manner; he'd given the town 'a good beating'.

I carry on along the seafront where, in 1987, the weather gave Shanklin a good beating. The town's pier bore the brunt. Having been constructed in 1890, it was three years shy of its centenary when that October's infamous hurricane ripped the structure to shreds, snapping it into thousands of pieces. The pier's theatre made an abrupt acquaintance with the seabed. Those parts of it left standing were demolished in 1993, but the pier was never rebuilt. Today, on that spot, people are forced to remember it in its heyday. Those too young to do so have to use their imagination.

It's time to head back to the station, which I need to do at a pace in order to make my ferry connection. The quickest way to get up the hill back into the town centre is to take Shanklin's long-running elevator, its equivalent of Ebbw Vale's funicular railway. For the price of a pound, it'll deliver you from the esplanade to the cliff top in a matter of seconds.

A problem is that, on the way to the station, there's a fine-looking, and hard-to-resist, bookshop. My relationship with book-shops is the same that iron filings have with magnets. Instant attraction. And Babushka Books looks like a doozy. I spend too much time lingering and loitering on its two floors; part of this is spent chuckling at the sub-genres that hand-written signs have created in the shop's poetry section: 'Poems You Already Have', 'Irrelevant Poetry', 'Depressing Poems', 'Boring and Dead'. Upstairs, a shelf of books is corralled together under a new genre: 'Weird Shit'.

I buy a copy of Truman Capote's *The Duke in His Domain*, his fascinating study of the young Marlon Brando, a slim volume that will only take me an hour to read on my journey back, once the sun's set and the view out of the window has been engulfed in an inky black. As I leave the shop, I have to step around a mother and her young son who are looking at the kids' books. 'Benjamin,' she says in a clipped, starchy voice, 'I think this book would move you.' Eight-year-old Benjamin doesn't appear to know what that means. 'Have they got any comics here, Mum?'

I can hear the train is at the platform as I walk-jog to the station, but soon see the guard puffing on a vape in the car park, so slow my pace a little. This time I elect not to stand but to take one of the sideways seats, but quickly wish I hadn't when I hear the machine-gun laugh of a fellow passenger a couple of seats away. The carriage is quite empty and it would be too obvious, too unsubtle, if I moved as quickly as I'd sat down, so I absorb the rat-a-tat guffaw that sprays forward every ten seconds or so, shortly after something not even moderately amusing has been said. Thankfully, the laugh and its owner get off at Brading, three stops in. In their place, two new passengers get on and make a much more welcome noise: a conversation about which high-street chain sells the best flapjacks. (Holland & Barrett are adjudged to be the winner, narrowly beating the Co-op.)

Further along my row of sideways-facing seats, opposite a man who looks too similar to Curiosity Killed The Cat's singer Ben Volpeliere-Pierrot not to be a relative of his, a pair of teenage lads are deep in conversation. Presumably at the midpoint of their A-level studies, they're discussing universities, in particular the thorny issue of student finance.

'I could always choose Portsmouth and live at home rent-free,' says the dark-haired one. 'My mum and dad say that would be fine. I think they'd like that. But it would still be the best part of thirty quid on the ferry every day and that's about the same as I'd be paying in rent in halls anyway. And doing the commute every day would be a ball-ache. My dad did it every day for work for twenty years and hated it. So I might as well get properly away. Time for some big-city living.'

'I'd like to live in London at some point in my life,' says the one in glasses, 'just for the experience. Just for a year or two. Do you reckon you'll come back here after uni?'

The dark-haired lad wears a slightly pained expression.

'I don't know. Would there be jobs?'

'The island needs architects as much as anywhere else.'

'And doctors, like you. I don't know. Wouldn't it feel a bit like admitting defeat or something? There's a big wide world out there...'

There's a pause in their conversation, so I ask them the best thing about growing up on the island.

'It feels very safe,' says the future doctor. 'Maybe too safe. People from outside always say life here is a decade or two behind the mainland. I don't know if it is as I've always lived here, but we definitely feel a little separate from the rest of the country because of the water. Well, I know I do.'

I'm reminded of another Mark Steel comment from that Radio 4 programme of his. With the irony again ratchetted up, he described the island as 'a splendid area, known for its modern outlook and youthful population, a place racing along at such a pace that it's already got to 1954'.

'Even if the island is at a slower pace than the mainland,' says the other student, 'we're not exactly far away. We're not miles and miles out to sea. It's twenty minutes on the ferry, so gigs in Ports-mouth are easy enough to get to. That's where we're off to tonight.'

'When we do go off to uni,' says the doctor, 'I'm sure it will feel like we're properly coming home at the end of term. At least I hope it will. The island is part of who we are and I don't want to lose that from being elsewhere.'

'Don't be worrying about that yet,' says his mate. 'We've got to pass our exams first. We might be stuck here forever if not...'

Further down the carriage, there's a grizzly kid who might just want to be stuck here forever. She's part of a family surrounded by a collection of ridiculously colourful suitcases. It's the end of their holiday, which their youngest member seems particularly upset about. 'But why...' she says, one slow word coming out at a time between big sobs, 'do... we... have... to... go... home?'

I'm reminded of the pre-teen Sammantha on board the ferry back in the 1960s, her heart growing sadder at the end of her latest holiday in Shanklin, the mainland looming larger by the minute.

When the train arrives at Ryde Pier Head, the tide is out as far as the station, that half-mile from the shore. There's a notice on the wall of the station; it turns out I've been a little fortunate in the timing of my reacquaintance with the island and its trains. In a fortnight's time, the entire Island Line will be closed for a month while 'a large programme of vital maintenance takes place'.

I had wondered why the guard on our train was in such a jovial mood. Perhaps he gets to have a month off on full pay while the line's out of action. Perhaps.

Beyond that closure, the notice also explains that Ryde Pier Head station will be out of use until next spring while engineers continue to repair and preserve the pier. Knowing that eight months' work is urgently needed on the rail pier makes the old

Victorian structure feel a little ricketier beneath my feet. The ferry suddenly feels more like solid ground. It can't arrive quick enough.

On the horizon, cross-Channel ferries gleam white in the evening sunshine. An incoming hovercraft has no difficulty with the low tide, segueing effortlessly, and impressively, from sea to sand without losing any of its speed.

Our ferry docks a few minutes later. It must be on at least its twentieth shuttle across the Solent today. Commuters, back from the mainland, march off the boat. Ready for dinner, ready for TV.

A steady stream of passengers get on board, mostly daytrippers but also the odd longer-staying party, such as the grizzly girl's family. Her tears seem to have subsided. For now, at least. That'll be the restorative power of a packet of Fruit Pastilles.

Among the daytrippers are a healthily tanned couple in their early twenties who've spent the day riding their bikes around the island's lanes. In shorts and T-shirts, their only luggage is their wallets and phones.

'Had a couple of pints at lunchtime,' says the man. 'That was a mistake. My legs afterwards…'

'We didn't learn our lesson from the last time we were here,' explains the woman. 'Then we visited a gin distillery.' A shake of the head is the punchline.

The train leaves the station for Shanklin and our ferry leaves the pier for the mainland. With each mile, the masts of Portsmouth's naval dockyard and the tower blocks of Gosport get closer and closer.

Back to life. Back to reality. Back to one last great train journey, to the final one of my final destinations, right down to the very bottom of the end of the line…

— 16 —

THE TRAIN IN THE NIGHT

London Paddington–Penzance

In the closing hours of the evening, on six evenings a week, a kind of magic descends on Paddington station. For a couple of hours, while tipsy passengers stumble towards the last trains to Bristol and Swansea, Hereford and Oxford, the train at Platform 1 stands unrushed, unhurried. It's getting its nightly care and attention, being prepped for its long haul across the country, through the shires, through the dark.

For this is the king of trains, the most regal of services to leave west London tonight. This is the Koskador Ruyer an Nos. For non-Cornish speakers, it's the Night Riviera Sleeper, the overnight train due into Penzance at breakfast-time tomorrow.

Its prepping is a well-honed nightly drill. Fresh sheets have been put on the bunks in each cabin, while the fridges of the lounge car are being replenished with refreshment both light and heavy.

When I was in Shanklin, in a charity shop I picked up a copy of the weekly periodical *Railway Wonders of the World* from 1935, inside which was the second part of a feature on the night trains of Europe. It painted an impossibly glamorous portrait of the kind of people riding sleeping cars to equally glamorous destinations like Cannes, San Remo and Istanbul. 'The passengers may consist of Royalties and crooks, artists and millionaires, diplomats and spies, scientists and generals, old ladies and film stars, infants in arms and death-defying octogenarians, all thrown together within the narrow space of a railway carriage.'

Judging by the clientele heading along the platform to whichever sleeping car they've been allocated, I don't think we've got too many diplomats or film stars in our midst for tonight's journey to the foot of Cornwall. We could well, of course, have a spy or two among our number; it's their job to go undetected, after all.

There may well be a millionaire, too. The prime suspects would be the American couple whose faces look a little concerned about the accommodation. Perhaps they're familiar with the more generous dimensions of high-ranking hotel suites and luxury cruise-liners. Both generous of girth, the couple are struggling with tonight's diminutive quarters.

'We can't both be standing up at the same time,' says the wife, her voice wafting out into the carriage's narrow corridor. 'And do you think that top bunk can hold your weight?' (Of course, if they *were* millionaires, I daresay they would have plumped for a cabin each. Or a helicopter.)

Another retirement-age couple are being waved off by their daughter and son-in-law – or son and daughter-in-law. The younger couple's Irish wolfhound is unsentimental about the parting. He's too busy giving Platform 1's bronze statue of Paddington Bear a series of quizzical looks, tipping his head from one side to the other in puzzlement.

That *Railway Wonders of the World* feature also talked about the required character of a night train's stewards, as well as the logistical demands placed on them, ensuring that their exacting passengers are catered for with the fullest range of repast and refreshment. 'There is no official record of the special dinner parties given in the company's cars,' explains the magazine's correspondent, nor 'of the bottles of Champagne consumed at some of these parties'.

If there is any Champagne on board tonight, it looks likely to remain unopened. This evening's intake doesn't appear to include too many hell-raisers. At the moment, an orderly queue is beginning to form as they look to cash in their vouchers for a complimentary cup of hot chocolate to take back to their berths.

I decide to start in slightly more glamorous fashion and order a gin and tonic, looking forward to spending a large proportion of the coming hours holding court here in the lounge car, chatting the night away with that cast of diplomats, crooks and film stars.

Then I discover there's a problem.

Neil the steward informs me that, as the owner of a ticket for the seated carriages upfront and not one of the cabins behind, the lounge car is out of bounds to me. I'm not permitted to place a buttock on its swivel chairs and sofas, to breathe even a lungful of its rarefied air.

Indeed, the bar area is partitioned by the kind of swinging door otherwise found in a Western saloon. This is the point that must not be breached by those without a cabin ticket. We can still order drinks at our end of the bar, but must take them back to our seats, unable to carouse into the wee small hours with the great and the good of cabin class. It's a two-tier system, a travel apartheid.

Not that the standard in the seated carriages is exactly shabby; it's superior to the first-class accommodation of many train companies. And the carriage is exceedingly quiet. There are no more than a dozen of us, so there's plenty of room should we wish to let the journey slip by by stretching out and sleeping through it.

One of the passengers in the cheap(er) seats is heading to St Austell for a wedding tomorrow. His suit hangs from the luggage rack across the aisle. For him, taking the Night Riviera isn't a special treat. It makes good financial sense.

'The ticket price is pretty much the same as a daytime ticket, but this way I save on the cost of a hotel tonight. Plus, I didn't have to take time off work to travel down this afternoon. And I'll be there first thing, fresh as a daisy.'

He pops open a can of Stella.

'Perhaps.'

Catching the sleeper service also makes practical sense to the pair of lads bound for the Boardmasters festival in Newquay. 'I had to do a lunchtime shift at the pub I work at,' one of them explains, 'so we wouldn't have been able to leave until this afternoon anyway, which would have meant arriving at dusk at the earliest. Finding a spot and putting a tent up in the dark is no fun. It'll be easier in the morning.'

Neil's voice comes over the PA.

'Becky,' he calls out. 'Come on down. We have a berth available for you.' A no-show means a vacancy, so Becky is being upgraded from her seat here in standard class to a bunk in a cabin. For the price of an additional £115, that is. This is no altruistic gesture. Regardless of the extra outlay for her golden ticket, she skips off towards the lounge car and beyond.

We leave bang on time, 15 minutes before midnight, inching our way into the west London night. The carriage is quiet. The only sound is that of two teenage girls talking softly to each other. But their discreet volume appears to be too much for the woman sat a couple of rows behind them. Despite wearing an enormous pair of ear defenders, she ups and leaves for the other standard-class carriage, bumping her suitcase into several seats as she departs.

At Reading, Neil is back on the PA, more effervescent than anyone should be at this hour. There's been another no-show.

'James, going to Truro? James, going to Truro? Do you still want a berth? Please come to the buffet.'

James, who's been keeping himself awake by playing backgammon on his phone, is straight up out of his seat, the lure of clean bedsheets too strong to resist, despite the additional cost. Our number keeps dwindling.

Once we head out of Reading, I make a return visit to the lounge car, this time sticking to the end of the bar where I'm permitted to be. Ahead of me, Neil is serving a young German in sunglasses and with a blond top-knot.

'I need alcohol.'

'OK, we've got plenty of that. What do you want?'

'Strong...'

Neil works this through-the-night shift three or four times a week, although these are never scheduled in a single consecutive run. Two nights on and one night off is the usual scheme of things.

'I'm in a permanent state of trying to catch up on sleep,' he admits. 'It's a bit like having constant jet lag. I shouldn't be on tonight, but there's no one else to do the shift. No one wants to do Thursdays or Fridays. But then I'll be off until Monday.'

I return to my seat with my drink, cupping my hand to the window, trying to get a glimpse of the night as it speeds past. Surprisingly, the lights in our carriage haven't been turned down lower now we're past 1 a.m. We're the last service of the day into the West Country. The rails are ours and ours alone, a single trail of lights among the black.

While tonight's eight-hour journey would suggest a leisurely glide on a route that's normally covered in three hours less, we're absolutely barrelling along, this train in the night, a blur across Berkshire, Wiltshire and Somerset. The orange streetlights of unnamed towns zip past the window. The stark white lights of each station too. We reach Taunton three-quarters of an hour before our scheduled departure from there. The train just sits in the empty station.

During this layover, a squat man with a mohican in his fifties takes the opportunity to stretch his legs on the platform – and, more importantly, have a great many long and satisfying pulls on his vape. The sole rail employee here at Taunton picks up a few items of rubbish that tonight's gentle breeze is blowing down the platform. He's presumably on duty to welcome both the service from Paddington and the corresponding sleeper up from Penzance. Quite often the two cross over here in the county town of Somerset, trains that meet in the night.

It's been almost 10 years since I last travelled on a night train. Then it was for a travel feature for the *Guardian*, taking the over-nighter from Berlin to Paris in the company of my then 10-year-old son. The highlight for him wasn't the romance of overnight travel in our own compartment. It was the breakfast-in-a-box delivered to our door at dawn. He ate long-life pastries and drank UHT milk on the top bunk while watching the green fields of France wake up outside the window.

Other through-the-night trains I've ridden were taken more out of necessity than out of romance. The distances involved dictated the hour of travel. For instance, you ride through the night between Chicago and New Orleans because the journey takes more than 19 hours. Then your subsequent passage west from New Orleans to Los Angeles takes in two overnighters, as that's how long the Sunset Limited service takes to cover the 2,000 miles. It's a similar deal when travelling between Minneapolis and Seattle.

The romance of a night train might dull a little on journeys of those lengths, but there is undoubtedly something most alluring about crossing the Mississippi at three in the morning, the moon-light turning the ink-black water to silver. Or, when you wake, on that ride to Seattle, to a dawn vista of the snow-capped Rockies.

At precisely 3.35 a.m., bang on schedule, we slide out of Taunton station and its bright lights, and continue heading south-west. Back into the last hour of full darkness. Back to black. The platforms at Exeter St David's – less than half an hour down the line – are similarly ghostly and vacant. But we don't linger any longer than needs be. No time for a quick vape here.

We remain in darkness for the next stretch, which is a great shame as it's here that the track rides the shoreline through coastal towns like Dawlish and Teignmouth, just above the high-water mark (and sometimes, in the foulest weather, just below). The line then traces the banks of the River Teign towards Newton Abbot. It's here – above the lights of a supermarket, inside which its shelf-stackers are two-thirds of the way through their nightshift – that the first patches of pale blue appear to the east. Morning is on its way. A quarter of an hour later, the first crack of orange arrives, backlighting a handful of wispy dark clouds. The sun is ready to chase us west.

Valleys and villages are revealed by the unfolding dawn. It's not the only light. A car wash has been unnecessarily illuminated through the night. A tanker's twin beams pass under a viaduct. The lights of back bedrooms are switched on, synchronised with the early alarm, the early shift. The West Country is waking up.

A phone alarm goes off in our carriage too, five minutes before we're due into Plymouth, an insurance policy against the phone's owner missing their stop, outstaying their welcome. The rest of the train's sleepers sleep on.

They don't know what they're missing; the stretch from Plym-outh across the Cornish landscape is arguably the best of the whole journey. This is when the show outside the window truly begins.

First off, there's the crossing of the River Tamar, the traditional boundary between the southern parts of Devon and Cornwall. This is done via the single-track Royal Albert Bridge, Isambard Kingdom Brunel's magnificent lenticular bridge, which opened just four months before the great man died. (Famously, of course, Brunel didn't live to see whether his Clifton Suspension Bridge actually worked, whether the theory of science and engineering matched up to the practicality of use. With 4 million vehicles a year crossing it these days, he'd surely be delighted by its longevity.)

The Tamar at this point is more than a thousand feet wide and the span of the bridge, high up over neat lines of countless yachts, makes for the grandest of all entrances into Cornwall. It's this line's Glenfinnan Viaduct moment, even if, unlike on the Highland Line, it's not heralded by an announcement over the PA – nor by the playing of tinny classical music.

The line then largely follows the western bank of the Tamar for a stretch before cutting back inland, riding a number of viaducts over both numerous rivers and steep, sharp valleys, the drops of which are often softened by copses of spruce at the bottom.

A few passengers get off at Liskeard. A few more at Bodmin Parkway. At both, Neil the steward is back on the PA. 'I must remind you that this is an old-fashioned train. You'll need to pull down the window, stick your arm out and undo the handle yourself...' The thump of those older-style doors closing, rather than the beep-beep-beep and the near-silent swoosh of more modern rolling stock, is a reassuring reminder of times past.

Neil continues to sound remarkably chipper. Perhaps he's been chugging artisan coffee all night, getting high on his own supply.

'Good morning!' he cries as we leave Lostwithiel. 'The buffet is still open. And our licensed bar if you're interested...' The German with the top-knot strides back through our carriage in Neil's direction.

At Par, the Boardmasters boys haul their rucksacks onto their backs and head off for the bus replacement service to Newquay. After making only a single stop between Paddington and Taunton, the stations now come thick and fast. Visitors for the Lost Gardens of Heligan are invited to alight at St Austell, but a cheerily optimistic sign on the platform also begs for attention. 'While you're here, please visit the town centre. Thanks for your support!'

We arrive at Truro – Cornwall's only city and the county seat – riding into town high above its rooftops, level with its cathedral's distinctive three spires. Here, a couple of out-of-term university students also leave our company, crossing the platform to where the Falmouth train is waiting. There are only three of us left in the carriage now, although that state of affairs lasts just a few seconds. Now that the clock has struck seven, a smattering of Truro's commuters step on board, bound for jobs in Redruth or Camborne or Penzance.

Redruth, the station closest to The Lizard, the most southerly point on the British mainland, reminds me that I'm almost at the end of all these ends of all these lines. Toto, we're not in Wick now.

Before we reach Penzance, the train skips across for the briefest encounter with the north Cornwall coast at Hayle, where there is no hail but there is drizzle. The county isn't gleaming this morning and the sky wears a jacket of cloud. Tractors undertaking early-morning hay-cutting duties carry on regardless.

Two minutes beyond Hayle comes St Erth, where art-loving passengers for St Ives need to change. A man who's spent the entire journey curled up on the floor under a seat suddenly wakes up in a panic and, in something approaching a frenzy, gathers two massive rucksacks and commands someone to hold the door open so that the train can't leave with him still on board. The lack of automatic doors is to his advantage. He tumbles onto the platform relieved – if also somewhat dazed and confused.

We cut across to the southern coast now, where St Michael's Mount – the steep, castle-topped tidal island – looms into view. The train runs along the shoreline, parallel to the South-West Coastal Path. It's not yet eight in the morning, and it's far from glorious weather, but there are plenty of early walkers heading towards the island.

Five minutes before 8 a.m., we slide into Penzance station. It doesn't have the glory of our Paddington point of departure, but it's not Stranraer's cattle shed either. We're a minute later than scheduled. After more than eight hours' travel, this can be excused. And it can be firmly blamed on Floor-Sleeping Rucksack Man's disorganised antics at St Erth.

The cabin-dwellers unfold themselves from their cramped quarters. Some look fully rested, others less so. That American couple appear decidedly shell-shocked. No one seems happier than a full-bearded adventurer type who is being enthusiastically greeted by a party of mother, wife, children and waggy dog. One of the tags on his luggage says KTM. This is the airport code for Kathmandu. While the last eight hours of travel have definitely represented some kind of adventure for most of us, this last leg has been a walk in the park for him, a short hop, a comparative sprint. I can't help thinking that he would have made good company in the lounge car over a couple of drinks, had I not been barred.

Not everyone has arrived at their journey's end. A quartet of Chinese tourists have onward travel on their mind – namely, making the connection with the next ferry to the Scilly Isles, the archipelago 28 miles off the Cornish coast. Outside the bus station, a group of local bus drivers are forming a picket line in support of improved working conditions. It's not the feistiest, nor the most furious, picket line in history. Two of the strikers are only too willing to break off from their protest to point the Chinese tourists in the direction of the ferry's jetty.

After eight hours cooped up in a train carriage, my legs are appreciating being used again and so, rather than heading straight into the town centre this early in the morning, I decide to stretch them further by heading out along the coastal path in the direction of Newlyn, a mile or so to the west. The drizzle has stopped.

In a basin across the road from Penzance's harbour, a gaggle of middle-aged women have taken to the water, a possibly illicit early-hours dip to get the blood flowing for the day ahead. 'Come on in!' one of them yells to a family of four walking past. 'It's lovely! And it's free, unlike the lido…'

The lido is the Jubilee Pool, a handsome triangle of art deco splendour just up the road. The UK's largest saltwater pool, it's been the playground of Penzance's swimmers for nearly 90 years. Even at this early hour, it's starting to get busy – despite the earlier swimmer's warning of its admission fee. What she failed to mention was that the lido also boasts both a geothermal pool and sauna.

While I saunter towards Newlyn, I'm overtaken by a pair of walkers who clearly mean business, matching each other stride for stride at quite some pace. And their speed isn't compromised by their supersized backpacks, to which groundsheets and sleeping bags are attached.

'Slow down,' I venture. 'You're making the rest of us look bad.'

One of the men, either Dutch or Flemish, stops to explain that they're hoping to be pitched up in Land's End by dinner time. 'We have a schedule,' he says, 'but bad service at the café back there means we're running late. Have a nice day.'

No one else is in a hurry. Relaxed contentment is all I see. The contentment of sea swimmers. The contentment of teen and sub-teen skateboarders in the skate park. The contentment of grandparents pushing buggies containing their grandkids.

Newlyn isn't tourist-cute like Port Isaac or St Ives. Its harbour is very much a working affair, home to dozens and dozens of trawlers and smaller fishing vessels. Indeed, it claims to be England's largest fishing port. I think back to the start of my journey, to Wick and its silent, moribund quaysides, to its industrial heyday that's consigned to the history books. Here in Newlyn, trawlers constantly come and go, and there are yellow-welly-booted fishermen everywhere. The contrast couldn't be any clearer.

This isn't to say that Newlyn – with all its working bustle, with the sharp stench of fish lingering in the air – holds no appeal to the casual visitor. There are bistros and galleries too, suggesting a balance between industry and tourism, between locals and visitors. Day visitors, at least. Those lingering somewhat longer aren't necessarily welcomed so warmly.

For instance, take the work of the Newlyn-born and raised (and still resident) filmmaker Mark Jenkin. Best-known for his low-budget film *Enys Men*, which won much critical acclaim and a couple of awards across the world, Jenkin's previous film, the monochrome and claustrophobic *Bait*, sharply drew the tension between Cornwall's locals and its second-homers, offering a brutal perspective on competing worldviews.

The film's main character, Martin, has been a fisherman all his working life, but that existence has been endangered by his brother's requisitioning of the family boat to offer tourist excursions instead, leaving Martin to scrabble together an existence. The family home has been sold off to incomers too, who are busy prepping it with fishing-themed nick-nacks for Airbnb customers. It's a raw piece of work in which Martin experiences something of an existential crisis, questioning his very identity and that of his home village.

This tension was a theme that had been brewing in Jenkin's work for many a summer. At the time of the solar eclipse of 1999, when Cornwall had been invaded to even more of a degree than usual, he considered making a film called *The Holiday Park*. He explained to the *Guardian* it would be 'like an Ealing comedy where the locals rise up against mass tourism, ending with the military carpet-bombing the whole of Cornwall, wiping it out and starting again'.

That film was never made, but that tension was the theme which underwrote *Bait*, lauded by Mark Kermode at the time as 'one of the defining British films of the year, perhaps the decade' and earning Jenkin a BAFTA.

That tension isn't dissolving any time soon; if anything, it's intensifying. There have been calls for tighter regulation of the local housing market, to make it more difficult to change the status of a house or flat from a permanently occupied home to a holiday let.

There have also been murmurs about the introduction of a tourist tax, a levy placed on rental accommodation which would be ringfenced to be reinvested in the county's infrastructure. The traffic on Cornwall's roads, for instance, more than doubles come August. The bill for road repairs, though, has to be met squarely by its permanent residents.

After a hot chocolate and a transcendental slice of Bakewell tart at one of Newlyn's galleries, I head back towards Penzance, back along the coastal path, back past the fun-seekers at the skate park and the lido. The town doesn't suffer from, or is suffocated by, the summer influx in quite the same way that the more picture-postcard destinations on the north Cornwall coast are. There the streets seem permanently clogged by traffic both pedestrian and vehicular, while queues form at every tea room, every chippy, every pasty shop, regardless of the hour.

Accordingly, there are no queues at any of Penzance's tea rooms, chippies or pasty shops, the latter of which are plentiful. The town is buzzy and bustling without being remotely overwhelming. Wandering among its cafés, galleries and independent shops is a fine way to spend a couple of hours. Indeed, an entire afternoon could be lost in the End of the World Bookshop, such is its judiciously curated selection of titles. (Yes, it was a case of iron filings and magnets again.)

I mosey up and down the two main shopping streets, both of which have curious names: Causewayhead and Market Jew Street, the latter being derived from 'marghas iou', or 'Thursday market' in Cornish. This moseying certainly comes without the frustrations that doing something similar in St Ives or Padstow would invariably provoke. The Down from London brigade seem yet to be taken by Penzance's charms. I hear as many North American accents as I do London voices.

By the middle of the afternoon, the bus drivers' picket line has drifted apart. In its place, one concerned citizen is telling a policewoman about a possible traveller encampment that's setting itself up in the main harbour car park. 'They've taken up about a dozen spaces and are sitting out in garden chairs. It doesn't look like they're budging any time soon. You can't miss them. Just look for the caravans.'

By now, the sky has jettisoned that jacket of cloud and so, still with an hour or two until my train, I set off along the coastal path in the opposite direction, eastwards towards St Michael's Mount. But my eyes are bigger than my legs and, after a mile or so, I opt to step down onto the beach instead. I find a huge boulder of quartz, one of many added to the sea defences to protect the adjacent railway line, and one that's flat enough for me to lie back on and soak up some rays.

After a (deliberately) sleepless night on the sleeper, I fall straight into a light snooze in the sunshine, and into a dream involving having a cream tea with Richard Osman. Minutes later – I'm not sure how many; it could have been 5, it could have been 50 – I come to, woken by the crunch of pebbles and the hack of a tobacco-induced cough.

'Sorry, didn't mean to disturb you. You were well away.'

Before me stands a man of around 60, short and with a day or two of silver stubble on his chin.

'No, that's fine. There was a danger I might miss my train anyway.'

'Don't blame you soaking up some rays. Gorgeous day, now. But you shouldn't be in a rush to leave here. Why would you?'

Unbidden, and in a tangy West Yorkshire accent, he proceeds to tell me the story of how he ended up here, here at almost the furthest tip of Cornwall.

'I'm from Huddersfield originally, but I outgrew it. I moved across to Leeds for a few years, but just couldn't settle there. So I then went to Manchester.'

He shakes his head.

'Too many dodgy episodes there. Nothing too terrible, but nothing particularly legal.'

His calm, sage-like manner is enhanced by his pausing to retrieve a roll-up from a small tin. He lights it gently and watches the first exhale of smoke float upwards. Only then does he continue.

'Then to Birmingham. Similar story. Then on to Bristol, working my way down the country. Then I came down here to work one summer and that was it. It felt so right here. It turned out I wasn't a city boy all along. I just needed space to settle somewhere. And less people.

'And this, of course…' He extends an arm towards the wide sea and the big sky. 'It's better than any booze, any medication.

'I haven't left the county once since in the six years I've been here. Stayed in Cornwall all that time. I do odds and ends. It's not what you'd call a career. Some electrical work, a bit of painting and decorating. Whatever really. But it's not *what* you do, but *where* you do it. That's the key. That's what makes you content. And I am content.

'He helps too, of course.'

He?

'Yeah, it's me and him.'

I'm hearing 'him' with a capital H. I'm hearing this because of the man's evangelical tone. Here on the beach, am I the target of a religious recruitment drive?

'Him?' I volunteer nervously.

'Yeah, he's a great boy.'

If a Jack Russell can gallop, then a Jack Russell is galloping towards us.

'This is Pinkie. He helped save me. And this place did too. I was running out of road. There's not much beyond here other than the sea. Got me just in time, Penzance did. Yeah, running out of road.'

I don't want to delve further. Our conversation has largely been a monologue so far and I'm happy just to listen. I'm a tired man. He can volunteer more information if he wants. And if he doesn't, his message, his worldview, is still clear. We sit in silence – but not awkwardly so – appreciating the sun and the sky and the day and the life.

I'm also appreciating all those journeys, all those trains, all those final destinations. Football fans in Wick. Curlers in Stranraer. Goths in Whitby. Park runners in Buxton. Vikings in Sheringham. Comedians in Chesham. They were who was waiting for me at the end of the line.

But now it's over. The sage almost ran out of road and I've run out of rail. I bid him and Pinkie farewell and head back over the boulders, up and onto the coastal path and towards the station. The last train sits at the platform waiting, waiting to take me away from the end of the line to my properly final destination.

Home.

ARRIVALS

Big thanks to each and all of those who took me under the skin of their home turf and explained at length about their town's history and culture and character and appeal, particularly Liz Barrett, Keith Brymer-Jones, Sammantha Cave, Daryl Eastlea, Tina Gharavi, Helen Gillilan, Marj Hogarth, Alex Horne, Fiona Macdonald, Sine MacKellaig Davis, Louisa McPhie and Robert Summers. Delighted you were all on board.

Thanks to Ian McMillan for his kind words, Andy/Birmingham81 for his vintage car knowledge, and Nigel Blackwell for both his permission to reproduce his lyrics and the keenly delivered culinary advice.

Thanks to everyone at Mudlark for their enthusiasm, professionalism and expertise, especially publisher Joel Simons, who commissioned the book, and editor Sarah Hammond, who made sure it departed on time. Thanks also to Lexi Bickell, Kara Nielsen and Gaurika Kumar, along with Gary Redford for his tremendous cover illustration.

Thanks to my longstanding/long-suffering agent Kevin Pocklington at The North Literary Agency, the guard to my driver.

And, the final destination for my gratitude is, as ever, at home, where Jess, Finn and Ned kept things on the rails while I was heading off, train tickets burning a hole in my pocket. Always much, much love.